# THE SUPREME COURT
## AND THE NATIONAL WILL

THE COMMITTEE OF JUDGES OF THE FIRST
THEODORE ROOSEVELT MEMORIAL
AWARD

DR. HAROLD WILLIS DODDS,
*President, Princeton University*

DR. HAROLD GLENN MOULTON,
*President, The Brookings Institution,
Washington, D. C.*

DR. HENRY SEIDEL CANBY,
*Vice-President and Chairman,
The Saturday Review of Literature*

PROFESSOR ROSCOE POUND,
*Dean Emeritus, Harvard University Law School*

THEODORE ROOSEVELT, JR.,
*Ex-governor-general of the Philippine Islands,
ex-governor of Puerto Rico*

# THE SUPREME COURT
## AND
# THE NATIONAL WILL

By

## DEAN ALFANGE

MEMBER OF THE NEW YORK BAR

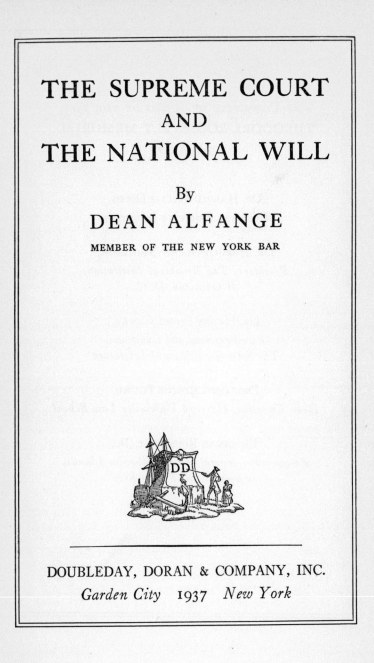

DOUBLEDAY, DORAN & COMPANY, INC.

*Garden City* 1937 *New York*

PRINTED AT THE *Country Life Press*, GARDEN CITY, N. Y., U. S. A.

This book was awarded the first
THEODORE ROOSEVELT MEMORIAL AWARD

# Preface

WHEN in the late spring of 1935 the Supreme Court began what looked like a systematic decapitation of the New Deal, it also started for millions of Americans a process of re-education in the fundamentals of their government. As one of the many who were thus jolted into revising accepted or conventional views, I experienced conflicting emotions. A lawyer by profession, and convinced of the utility of the judicial function as a stabilizer of social relations, I was naturally reluctant to join the hue and cry against the Supreme Court; the more so because, due to my training, I had come to look upon its interpretation of the Constitution by judicial review as the most distinctive—and possibly the least dispensable—feature of the American system of government. On the other hand, as a believer in popular government, and in the urgency and beneficence of many of President Roosevelt's policies, I was disquieted by the fact that judicial review could operate in such a manner as to impede the democratic process; and I felt anxious about the social consequences of such obstruction at a time of national emergency. It was this conflict of loyalties and the resultant perturbation that led me to re-examine the relationship of the executive and legislative branches to the judicial with a view to reaching for and by myself a more satisfactory understanding of how the American system functions. This re-examination, whose point of departure is indicated by its title, has been pursued intermittently since June 1935 during the intervals of leisure in a busy professional life; and it is now completed at a time when the conclusions it has reached concerning the relationship of the Supreme Court to the national will are about to undergo a further test during the new phase in the Court's history ushered in by the electoral verdict of 1936.

The following pages, then, present a modest essay in interpretation—an attempt to determine the relation of the historic decisions of the Supreme Court to their economic, social and political background. To this end I have reanalyzed what seem to me the relevant decisions and dissenting opinions under each of the great substantive powers conferred on Congress by the Constitution. And, especially, I have tried to interpret them in the light of the national will manifested at the time the decisions were made. Thus, this study is not a polemic for or against the Supreme Court and its offspring, judicial review; nor is it a polemic for or against the social philosophy of the New Deal. It is purely expository—designed to determine the historic place of the Supreme Court and judicial review in the traditional American system.

The frequent quotations from the opinions of the Supreme Court and the elaborate discussion of some of them will, I hope, show that there is nothing recondite or mysterious about legal language and reasoning; and that many important decisions in the field of constitutional law are not very different from congressional arguments for or against a given legislative enactment, except that they are usually more learned and, at their best, better reasoned. The implications of this similarity will be developed in the following chapters.

Much of the subject matter of the book will appear elementary to those trained in constitutional law and history. I offer no apology for this because the work is intended primarily for nonprofessional readers—those who seek some explanation and understanding of the relation of judicial review to the processes of democratic government and whose early knowledge of the underlying fundamentals may have become blurred with the passage of time. For this reason, the first two chapters deal briefly with the origins and nature of the American system and are intended as a background for the more interpretative chapters that follow.

For the historical background of the judicial decisions discussed in this volume, I have gone to the works of the great scholars in the field of constitutional history, especially of Professor Andrew C. McLaughlin, Mr. Charles Warren, Dr. Charles A. Beard and Professor Edward S. Corwin. To them I am indebted. I am especially indebted to my friend, Professor Nicholas S. Kaltchas, of Sarah Lawrence College, for reading the manuscript and for his valuable contribution in suggestions as to the relevance of materials and in historical criticism. I also thank my friend, Mr. N. C. Culolias, of the Massachusetts Bar, who read the chapters as I wrote them and with whom I enjoyed much profitable discussion. Acknowledgment is also due to my secretary, Miss Mary Malone, for indispensable assistance in supervising the detail incident to the preparation of the manuscript.

DEAN ALFANGE

*New York City,*
*January 4, 1937.*

# Postscript

---

THIS MANUSCRIPT was completed before President Roosevelt's proposal for the reorganization of the federal judiciary precipitated the latest constitutional crisis. It was not my original intention, and it is outside the province of this book, to propose or sponsor any specific plan of judicial reform. I hope, however, that this exposition of the relationship of Supreme Court decisions to the ever-changing national will will help the reader to understand the function of judicial review and to form a judgment on the current constitutional issues.

DEAN ALFANGE

*March 30, 1937.*

# Contents

# THE SUPREME COURT
## AND THE NATIONAL WILL

# CHAPTER I

# The Origins of the Constitution

THE CONSTITUTION OF THE UNITED STATES was born of an economic crisis. No sooner was independence achieved than economic insecurity began to threaten the newly born United States. The need, already felt by George Washington in 1780, of a "system" to replace the "expedients" and "temporary devices" by which the colonies had muddled through the war was felt even more urgently as they faced its aftermath of stagnant trade, an empty treasury, stifled confidence, and a latent class conflict.

The influential leaders of the nation discerned the close interrelationship of these ills and attributed them to the inadequacy of the government established since 1781 by the Articles of Confederation. Under the Articles, "the national government consisted of a legislature of one house in which the states had an equal voting power. There was no executive department and no general judiciary. The central government had no power to regulate commerce or to tax directly; and in the absence of these powers, all branches of the government were rendered helpless."[1]

[ 1 ]

This absence of centralized control resulted in impotence in every field of economic activity. Congress could take no measures to promote trade among the states, nor could it deal effectively with foreign nations on matters pertaining to commercial intercourse. It had no power to cope with the commercial rivalries of the states and to create a unified national economy. Jealously guarding their economic interests, the thirteen states had put into effect thirteen state tariffs and as many different state laws regulating commerce. Barges and trading vessels arriving in New York from New London or Hoboken were subject to the same treatment as foreign ships in docking and in clearing. Duties were levied on imports from one state into another not only without regard to uniformity but often with intentional discrimination. This intense protectionism of the states impaired confidence, clogged the flow of trade, and erected a formidable barrier to economic solidarity and national unity.

The disability of Congress to wield the taxing power resulted in financial delinquency towards foreign and domestic creditors. Congress earnestly attempted to raise funds for meeting interest charges of over ten million dollars on the domestic debt and more than two million dollars on the foreign debt, but its efforts were continually blocked by selfish opposition from the states. France and Holland, our principal foreign creditors who helped finance the war against Great Britain, were obliged not only to grant a temporary moratorium on maturing interest installments but also to sanction the overdrawing of our accounts. American credit had fallen to such depths that in 1784 John

[ 2 ]

Adams, acting as envoy of the United States, was unable to procure a three-hundred-thousand-dollar loan from Holland and was compelled to resort to the professional moneylenders of Amsterdam, who exacted an exorbitant rate of interest.

Yet despite these defaults, the maintenance of the credit of the United States abroad was not the most serious concern of the new government; for the shrewd finance ministers and bankers of Europe showed themselves at this time more confident concerning the future of the new nation than the American people themselves. The fiscal helplessness of the national government and its dependence on the states made it difficult to meet even the current costs of government and resulted in serious domestic repercussions and mutinous uprisings. Successive outbreaks of lawlessness reflected a tendency on the part of the common man to interpret the revolutionary slogans of liberty and equality with a disconcerting literalness that was fraught with menace for the vested rights of property. "The people who are the insurgents," wrote General Knox to Washington in 1786 apropos of Shays' Rebellion, "have never paid any, or but very little, taxes—but they see the weakness of government. They feel at once their own poverty, compared with the opulent, and their own force, and they are determined to make use of the latter, in order to remedy the former. Their creed is 'That the property of the United States has been protected from the confiscations of Britain by the joint exertions of all, and therefore ought to be the common property of all.' . . . In a word, they are determined to annihilate all debts public and private and have

[3]

agrarian laws, which are easily effected by means of unfunded paper money which shall be a tender in all cases whatever. . . . This dreadful situation has alarmed every man of principle and property in New England."[2]

The men "of principle and property" had good cause to be alarmed; for they must have recognized that they were confronted with the conflict, which appears sooner or later in the course of most revolutionary movements, between those who supplied the inspiration and leadership of the Revolution and the mass following which enabled it to attain its goal. "To a great extent," says Professor R. L. Schuyler, "the Revolution had been guided by the conservative classes, the planter aristocracy of the South, merchants and lawyers in New England and the middle states, men of education and property. But ideas of equality, expressed in the Declaration of Independence, aroused in the poorer classes envy of their more prosperous neighbors, while the emphasis placed upon liberty tended to relax respect for government. Office holders, legislators and judges were suspected of tyrannical designs and conspiracy against the 'people.' . . . It is not difficult to understand how many an ardent 'patriot' viewed the payment of debt as something to be avoided and how respect for property rights declined. Of these facts, paper money agitation and tender laws furnish abundant proof. Creditors, speculators, merchants, money lenders, courts and lawyers were objects of popular suspicion."[3]

It is clear from this analysis that the loose system established by the Articles of Confederation was more advantageous to the debtor than to the creditor classes.

With a Congress deprived of exclusive jurisdiction in any field, without a central executive, a national treasury or a federal judiciary, "money could not be secured to pay the holders of public securities, either their interest or principal . . .; the state legislatures were substantially without restrictions or judicial control; private rights in property were continually attacked by stay laws, legal tender laws, and a whole range of measures framed in behalf of debtors."[4] It was in order to remedy these conditions that the wealthy and creditor classes demanded a New Deal—the replacement of what was, in effect, a league of thirteen sovereign states by a closely knit federal state in which "Congress should have complete sovereignty in all that relates to war, peace, trade and finance"[5] and a federal executive and judiciary should exercise commensurate authority in their respective fields.

Thus, unlike the New Deal of 1933, which was mainly directed against the power of concentrated wealth, the New Deal which culminated in the Constitution aimed to provide greater security for property by transferring certain vital powers from the states to a national government so constructed as to make it less directly amenable to popular control. The New Dealers of that day envisaged a national government with power to tax, to regulate commerce, to protect contracts, to preserve property, to maintain the public credit, and with exclusive prerogative over the coinage of money.

The leaders who initiated this movement were among the most practical and sober-minded citizens of the country, and, for the most part, men of substantial means. They knew the abundant resources of the North American continent and appreciated the vast opportunities inherent in their development. They also knew that England and other European powers turned covetous eyes upon the Western Hemisphere, and they understood the far-reaching economic and political consequences of the continued weakness of the American government. Washington himself had given careful study to the problem of developing communications with the western and northwestern territories; and in 1785 he became president of a company to extend transportation by the Potomac and James rivers. To carry out this work he induced Virginia and Maryland to appoint commissioners to work out a plan to regulate commerce along this common waterway. The joint commission met and immediately invited Pennsylvania to join the plan. In their final report the commissioners recommended that their respective states adopt uniform rules for the imposition of import duties, the regulation of commerce, and the establishment of a standard currency. Inspired by this turn of events, James Madison on January 21, 1786, induced the legislature of Virginia to adopt the following resolution:

RESOLVED, that Edmond Randolph, James Madison, Jun., Walter Jones, St. George Tucker, Meriwether Smith, David Ross, William Ronald, and George Mason, Esquires, be appointed commissioners, who, or any five of whom, shall meet such commissioners as may be appointed by the other States in the Union, at a time and place to be agreed on, to take into consideration the trade of the United States; to examine the relative situation and trade of the said States; to consider how far a uniform system in their commercial regulations may be necessary to their common interest and their permanent harmony; and to report to the several States such an act relative to this great object as, when unanimously ratified by them, will enable the United States in Congress assembled effectually to provide for the same; that the said commissioners shall immediately transmit to the several States copies of the preceding resolution, with a circular letter requesting their concurrence therein, and proposing a time and place for the meeting aforesaid.[6]

In response to the call issued thereupon by the governor of Virginia, five states sent representatives to what may be called the first national Chamber of Commerce in the history of the United States. Though this meeting, which was held in Annapolis in September 1786, was unable to act upon the resolution of the Virginia Legislature because of the abstention of the majority of the states, it marked, nevertheless, a turning point in American history; for it issued an invitation to all the states to send delegates to a convention in Philadelphia in May 1787 to consider amendments to the Articles of Confederation; and by this action it spurred Congress to pass the following decisive resolution on February 21, 1787:

That in the opinion of Congress, it is expedient that on the second Monday in May next, a convention of delegates who shall have been appointed by the several states, be held in Philadelphia, for the sole and express purpose of revising the Articles of Confederation, and reporting to Congress and the several legislatures such alterations and provisions therein, as shall, when agreed to in Congress, and confirmed by the states, render the federal constitution adequate to the exigencies of government and the preservation of the Union.[7]

It would seem then that the Constitution of the United States did not originate in, nor was it designed to subserve, a lofty political ideology. It was rather the offspring of economic necessity and the instinct of self-preservation. Unlike the revolutionary movement of the seventies, which was propelled to its inevitable culmination by the pressure of the masses, the movement for the transformation of the confederation of states into a federal union was initiated by the propertied classes. Having rid themselves of subserviency to the oligarchic British Parliament, they were even more determined not to submit to urban democracy and frontier populism. They, therefore, addressed themselves to the task of building an institutional framework designed to safeguard their economic security, to facilitate the exploitation of the matchless material resources of the North American continent, and at the same time to provide the curb of law and order for a nation of rugged individualists about to embark upon a frenzied pursuit of happiness.

CHAPTER II

# The Nature of the American System

THE commercial, manufacturing and creditor interests, and the professional and educated classes generally, which initiated the movement for a New Deal, were overwhelmingly represented in the Constitutional Convention.[1] It was, therefore, easy for that relatively homogeneous gathering to agree on the need of creating a more efficient political system by conferring on the central government those powers which were recognized as essential to economic security, stability and expansion; and it was not until the Constitution was submitted to the states for ratification that the line of cleavage was sharply drawn between the economic interests which favored the Constitution and those—mainly the agrarian and debtor classes—that opposed it.

Yet despite the relative one-sidedness of the convention and the general agreement to create a strong central government, a divergence of views developed among the delegates with regard to the nature of the new government. This disagreement was determined less by class interest than by state loyalty, motivated

[ 9 ]

largely by the smaller states' fear of drastic innovation which might jeopardize their existence.[2]

Under the Articles of Confederation, which were, in effect, a compact of states, each state was completely sovereign and the central government could neither enforce its edicts against the states nor reach the individual citizens of each by legal process. The delegates of the smaller states, whose views were represented by the New Jersey plan, proposed to enlarge the powers of Congress by merely amending the Articles of Confederation and thus to retain the main attributes of the existing system—namely, the confederate principle: state sovereignty and its corollary, equality of representation regardless of size. But the representatives of the more populous states, whose views were embodied in the Virginia plan, wanted more radical change. They demanded a national government whose legislature would represent the people rather than the several states and whose laws would impinge immediately on all citizens. The Virginia plan won an initial victory when its third resolution calling for "a *national* Government . . . consisting of a *supreme* Legislative, Executive and Judiciary" was adopted, with six states voting in the affirmative, New York divided, and only one, Connecticut, in the negative.[3] And this victory was confirmed when, after a long debate, the New Jersey plan was rejected by seven states against three, with one, Maryland, divided.[4]

Thus the convention decided to frame a new constitution creating a federal state much more closely knit than the league of states established by the Articles of Confederation but still very far from the complete cen-

tralization of a unitary state. This compromise was succinctly described by Madison, the philosopher of the
Constitution, in a letter to Washington: "Conceiving
that an individual independence of the states is utterly
irreconcilable with their aggregate sovereignty, and
that a consolidation of the whole into one simple republic would be as inexpedient as it is unattainable, I
have sought for middle ground, which may at once support a new supremacy of the national authority, and
not exclude the local authorities wherever they can be
subordinately useful."[5]

The logic of this newly devised federal state and,
incidentally, the essentially economic motivation of
politics were expounded in masterly fashion in the *Federalist* by Hamilton and Madison. The latter began his
systematic exposition of the basic principles of the Constitution by claiming that the most important advantage of a "well-constructed union" is "its tendency to
break and control the violence of faction." He defined
faction as "a number of citizens, whether amounting
to a majority or minority of the whole, who are united
and actuated by some common impulse of passion, or
of interest, adverse to the rights of other citizens, or
to the permanent and aggregate interests of the community"; and, brilliantly anticipating Karl Marx, he
singled out the economic factor as the most important
determinant of political alignments. "The most common and durable source of factions," he wrote in a
memorable and oft-quoted passage, "has been the various and unequal distribution of property. Those who
hold and those who are without property have ever
formed distinct interests in society. Those who are

creditors and those who are debtors fall under a like discrimination. A landed interest, a manufacturing interest, a mercantile interest, a moneyed interest, with many lesser interests, grow up of necessity in civilized nations, and divide them into different classes actuated by different sentiments and views. . . ."

But while he deplored the mischievousness of factions, he deprecated the removal of their causes because that would involve either the destruction of liberty, which is as essential to faction as air is to fire, or the endowment of every citizen with "the same opinions, the same passions, and the same interests." In other words, he rejected the Communist ideal of a classless society and the present-day Communist and Fascist remedies of dictatorship, regimentation of opinion, and the totalitarian state. He recognized that, because "the principal task of modern legislation" is the "regulation", rather than the liquidation, of conflicting interests, the "operations of the government" are inevitably tainted with "the spirit of party and faction"; and he, therefore, expressed a decided preference for the second method of "curing the mischiefs of faction"—namely, that of "controlling its effects."

Such control is easy enough when a faction represents a minority, since, under a system of popular government, it can be deprived of power by the ordinary democratic process. But "when a majority is included in a faction, the form of popular government . . . enables it to sacrifice to its ruling passion or interest both the public good and the rights of other citizens." Hence, the framers of the Constitution undertook to devise a political system which would safeguard the rights, and particularly the property rights, of individuals and minorities against the depredations of equalitarian democracy and at the same time "preserve the spirit and the form of popular government."

How did the Constitution accomplish this dual purpose? In the first place, because the size of the country precluded a "pure democracy"—that is to say, direct government by all the citizens—it set up a "republic" in which the government is delegated "to a small number of citizens elected by the rest." Second, it divided the functions of government between the states, which retained the powers pertaining to "local and particular interests", and a new authority, national in scope, to which were delegated powers affecting "the great and aggregate interests." The line of demarcation between state and federal jurisdiction was drawn on the assumption that the narrower the sphere of governmental activity, the more amenable it is to the control of factions—an assumption which the domination of municipalities and states by political machines and the late Huey Long's dictatorship in Louisiana would seem to bear out. "The smaller the society, the fewer probably will be the distinct parties and interests composing it; the fewer the distinct parties and interests, the more frequently will a majority be found of the same party; and the smaller the number of individuals composing a majority, and the smaller the compass within which they are placed, the more easily will they concert and execute their plans of oppression. Extend the sphere and you take in a greater variety of parties and interests; you make it less probable that a majority of the whole will have a common motive to invade the rights of other citizens."[6] On this theory, which betrays fear of predatory democratic majorities, the matters of vital concern to the propertied classes were removed from the jurisdiction of popularly controlled state legislatures, and the following powers were delegated to the Congress of the United States:

> To lay and collect taxes, duties, imposts and excises, to pay the debts and provide for the common defence and general welfare of the United States.
> To borrow money on the credit of the United States.
> To regulate commerce with foreign nations and among the several states.
> To establish uniform laws on the subject of bankruptcies.
> To coin money, regulate the value thereof, and fix the standard of weights and measures.
> To secure for inventors the exclusive right to their respective discoveries.
> To make all laws which shall be necessary for carrying into execution the foregoing powers.

To the same end and in order to prevent the states from encroaching upon the above-enumerated exclusive powers of the federal government in the realm of taxation, commerce, money and credit, the Constitution specifically *denied* to the states the power:

> To coin money.
> To emit bills of credit.
> To make anything but gold and silver coin a tender in payment of debts.
> To pass any law impairing the obligation of contracts.
> To lay any imposts or duties on imports or exports.
> To lay any duty of tonnage.[7]

But the safeguards offered by federalism against democratic dictatorship were not deemed sufficient. The same concern for the rights of individuals and minorities against the tyranny of popular majorities which motivated the division of sovereignty between the states and the federal government dictated also an analogous division of authority among the various branches of the latter.[8] This further separation of powers was strengthened by the fact that the main agencies of government were so ingeniously constructed by the Constitution that they differed in their origin, the source of their power, and the duration of their tenure.[9] "The circumstances," wrote Hamilton, "which will be likely to have the greatest influence in the matter" [of preventing the domination of "some favorite class of men"] "will be the dissimilar modes of constituting the several component parts of the government. The House of Representatives being to be elected immediately by the people, the Senate by the state legislatures, the President by electors chosen for that purpose by the people, there would be little probability of a common interest to cement these different branches in a predilection for any particular class of electors."[10]

Thus the Constitution divided "the power surrendered by the people between two distinct governments" and then "subdivided . . . the portion allotted to each among distinct and separate departments." By this combination of federalism with the separation of powers, what was aptly called "the compound republic of America" offered "a double security"[11] to the private rights of individuals. Nor was this all. As an additional safeguard against the dangers of direct democracy, the Constitution was declared "the supreme law of the land" and its enforcement was entrusted to a federal judiciary, which derived its power from sources other than those of the executive and the bicameral legislature. On this third main department of the government devolved the defense of the "double security" to private rights embedded in the Constitution. It has become the function of the courts to guard the line of demarcation between the states and the federal government as well as among the several branches of the latter; and, after the addition of a third security—the Bill of Rights contained in the first ten amendments—to prevent the enactment of any state or federal laws violating the guarantees contained therein. The development of the constitutional law of the United States has been determined, as we shall see, by the manner in which the federal judiciary has performed this function.

Though the federal principle was accepted as the foundation of the new governmental structure, the smaller states exerted themselves to mitigate the consequences of federalism by making it difficult for the larger states to dominate the national government. The most important provisions of the Constitution represent compromises which resulted from this effort. While the principle of proportional representation was adopted for the House of Representatives, the smaller states secured equal representation in the Senate. But this concession was wrung only after it had been agreed that all bills for raising and appropriating money must originate in the Lower House and that the

Senators must vote as individuals and not as an ambassadorial team representing a sovereign state and following instructions of its government.

When the completed Constitution was signed on September 17, 1787, it was transmitted to the Continental Congress with the recommendation that it be submitted to conventions elected by the people of each state for approval or rejection. But as soon as the finished work of the Philadelphia Convention became available to the public, its essentially antiagrarian and antidemocratic character was realized and there developed throughout the states an avalanche of popular opposition. Though the struggle against ratification was inspired by a variety of motives, economic interests played the most important part in the case of small farmers and the debtor class generally, and of such entrenched groups as Governor De Witt Clinton's faction in New York, who saw their ascendancy menaced by the intrusion of a national government. But whatever its motives, opposition to the Constitution was expressed in political terms: distrust of a new experiment fraught with incalculable possibilities, fear that the national government would impair the freedom of the individual citizen and the self-government of the states —that it would, in short, be prejudicial to liberty. The leader of this movement was, fittingly enough, the respected patriot, Patrick Henry. It was charged that under the Constitution the President with his broad powers would become a tyrannical despot; that he would fall under the influence of European powers; that states' rights would vanish; that the larger states would crush the smaller ones; that the Congress would consist of the wealthy and the well-born; that the hard-won liberties of the common man would perish, and that other untold calamities would befall the people. The militant approval of the Constitution by the commercial and propertied classes, its failure to provide a Bill of Rights, and the lukewarmness of some of the framers over their finished work lent additional cogency to the arguments of the opposition.

The battle for ratification may be described as a clash of the spirit of 1776 with the spirit of 1787. The most sincere of the opponents of the Constitution were the radical thinkers and leaders who had launched the movement for independence and whose conception of democracy was not incompatible with liberty. These men were, above all, suspicious and fearful of government. Believing with Jefferson that the best government is one that governs the least, they preferred self-government to the compulsion of a remote and uncontrollable authority. Having but recently been delivered from what they regarded as monarchical absolutism, they viewed with misgivings the attempt at centralization which had been made in Philadelphia; the more so because they felt that the federal government had been equipped with extensive powers in order to serve the interests of the propertied and creditor classes, and because they feared that the extensive powers conferred upon the federal government spelled less liberty for the individual citizen and would ultimately make for the extinction of the states and a "consolidated" government.

After a protracted debate, during which there developed a public interest in politics comparable to that produced by the depression and the New Deal of the early 1930s, the Constitution was finally ratified—but only after the ratifying states had proposed over one hundred reservations to the original document. These reservations became the First Ten Amendments to the Constitution and are commonly known as the Bill of Rights. They reflect and epitomize the motives of opposition to the Constitution, since the first nine are designed to safeguard the liberties of the individual and the tenth provides that "the powers not delegated to the United States by the Constitution, nor prohibited by it to the states, are reserved to the states respectively, or to the people." The constructive statesmanship of Washington, Hamilton, Madison and Jay contributed materially to ratification, but, even with their powerful support, defeat was averted by the narrowest of margins in the pivotal states of New York, Virginia and Massachusetts. It is probable that had the people of the United States enjoyed the privilege of universal suffrage at that time, the Constitution would have been rejected by a vote of landslide proportions.

The sharp cleavage of public opinion which divided the states over the question of accepting or rejecting the Constitution was the genesis of our two major political parties. While the adoption of the Constitution brought about the desired social and economic security, the issue of national power versus states' rights has remained with the American people to this day. During the initial phase of our constitutional development, Hamilton and Marshall advocated loose construction of the Constitution as a means of expanding the sphere of action of the federal government and creating a strong national authority. Jefferson, on the other hand, while a strict-constructionist and a zealous defender of states' rights in theory, was compelled as President to exercise extensive powers which were not explicitly granted by the Constitution. And Madison, with greater consistency, strove to maintain "the balance between the states and the national government" and opposed the encroachments of national power because they threatened "to convert a limited into an unlimited government."[12] Since then the attitude of the major parties on the constitutional issue has been determined less by their traditional allegiances than by the political needs of the moment, which in turn were largely dictated by economic necessities. Thus, while many prominent Democrats continue to cling to this Jeffersonian and Madisonian faith, the Democratic party under Franklin D. Roosevelt finds itself compelled to invoke the Hamiltonian doctrines of national power; for only by asserting national power to the utmost extent permitted under our system of constitutional limitations can it hope to sustain the new and broad legislative departures of the New Deal.

# CHAPTER III

# Expansion of the Constitution

---

## ORIGINS OF JUDICIAL REVIEW

THE CONSTITUTION, then, was an instrument of government designed to meet the needs of the young nation which emerged from the victorious War of Independence. It organized national power in order to deal with national problems. But the system it created, though a radical innovation, was far from a complete break with the past. It was built on the existing realities of state autonomy and individual liberty. And in order to safeguard these against the dreaded encroachments of the new leviathan, the Constitution established a national government of strictly limited powers. It distributed sovereignty between the federal government and the states by delegating certain enumerated powers to the former and reserving all remaining powers to the latter; it divided the federal powers among the Legislative, the Executive and the Judicial branches, which it sought to make independent of one another; and it prohibited both federal and state governments from passing laws which violated fundamental personal rights.

This means that under the American system a constitutional sanction must be found for all governmental action, state or federal. When Congress is about to pass a law, the question is, or should be, asked: "Is there a federal power under the Constitution which warrants the proposed legislation?" Conversely, when a state legislature is about to enact, the question is, or should be, posed: "Is a federal power encroached upon by the proposed legislation?" In the former case the existence of a federal power must be shown; in the latter, the absence of a federal power must be established. And in both cases the fundamental individual rights guaranteed by the Constitution must not be violated.

While the powers of the federal government are defined and enumerated, the powers of the states are undefined and unenumerated and comprehend all prerogatives of sovereignty with the exception of those delegated to the federal government or specifically denied to the states by the Constitution. Almost the entire domain of the common law is comprehended within the residual powers of the states. They include the whole field of criminal jurisprudence, torts, domestic relations, corporations, and, in general, the laws dealing with contractual obligations and the disposition of property. To the states, too, belongs the field of social welfare legislation—the protection of public health, safety and morals, and the regulation of all businesses within their boundaries which are affected with a public interest.

At first sight, this strict delimitation of the sphere of government in general, and of the jurisdiction of the federal government in particular, would seem to constitute an insuperable obstacle to social progress insofar as social progress depends on governmental action; for these curbs on the state are imposed by a written Constitution which, being the supreme law, wields, in effect, the power of veto over ordinary legislation and is protected against change by the very nature of the political system it created.

Because this system is founded on the principles of federalism and the separation of powers, its most distinctive characteristic is the *diffusion* of sovereignty— the absence of any one body or agency in which supreme authority, including power to change the Constitution, is located. This is the exact opposite of the unitary system prevalent in England, where Parliament is sovereign; which means that it has "the right to make or unmake any law whatever; and, further, that no person or body is recognized by the law of England as having the right to override or set aside the legislation of Parliament."[1] The essence of parliamentary sovereignty is that it does not differentiate between the law-making and the constitution-making process, and that it endows ordinary legislation and constitutional enactment with equal sanction. Hence, strictly speaking, there is no English Constitution. As the foremost English commentator on the American Commonwealth has pointed out, whereas the American Constitution is a single document which, including the amendments, may be read in twenty-three minutes, "the Constitution of England is contained in hundreds of volumes of statutes and reported cases."[2] Such basic parts of the English Constitution as the Habeas Corpus Act, the Bill of Rights and the Act of Settlement were passed by Parliament like any other statute; and such fundamental matters as the extension of the franchise, the duration of Parliament, the relations of Church and State, the legal status of trade unions, have been and are regulated by legislative enactment. Even the "King occupies the throne under a Parliamentary title; his claim to reign depends upon and is the result of a statute."³ Moreover, it was by another statute, the Parliament Act of 1911, passed by the Commons, reluctantly ratified by the Lords, and approved by the King, that a drastic redistribution of power was effected within Parliament itself through the emasculation of the veto power of the House of Lords.

Now an analogous change in the American Constitution—namely, a redistribution of power between the Senate and the House of Representatives—would require, of course, a constitutional amendment. And the complexity of the amending process reflects the basic trait of the American system—the diffusion of sovereignty, as against its concentration in Parliament under the English system—and the consequent absence of any one body having the right to exercise the constituent power. According to Article V, amendments may be initiated either by resolution adopted by two thirds of both Houses of Congress or by a convention called by Congress on application of the legislatures of two thirds of the states. In either case they become effective as part of the Constitution "when ratified by the Legislatures of three fourths of the several States, or by Conventions in three fourths thereof, as the one or the other Mode of Ratification may be proposed by the Congress."

It has been estimated that since the adoption of the

Constitution over three thousand proposed amendments have been suggested to Congress from various sources. Yet only twenty-one out of the twenty-seven which Congress has seen fit to propose to the states have been ratified. From 1804, when the Twelfth Amendment prescribed in detail the method of electing the President, until the passage of the income-tax amendment in 1913, "no amendment had been added to the Constitution except the three that were born out of the sanguinary travail of the Civil War."⁴ It is indeed surprising that since the adoption of the Bill of Rights in 1791 only eleven additional amendments have gone into effect despite the fact that during the intervening years the face of America has been completely transformed as a result of territorial expansion and settlement, increasing urbanization, and all the cumulative achievements of science and technology.

Had the Constitution depended for its development only on formal amendments, the contention would be warranted that its framers drew up a rigid, almost a static instrument for the governance of the most dynamic society of modern times. Such a charge, however, cannot be justifiably made. It is true that the American Constitution is both written and "rigid"; that it emanates "from an authority superior to that of the legislature" and that, therefore, it cannot be "bent or twisted by the action of the legislature, but stands stiff and solid, opposing a stubborn resistance to any majority who may desire to transgress or evade its provisions."⁵ It is also true that revision by formal amendment has been surprisingly infrequent. But this is not entirely due to the cumbersomeness and complexity of the amending process; for, as the repeal of the Eighteenth Amendment has shown, that process can be greatly accelerated by strong popular sentiment. As a matter of fact, despite the relative infrequency of formal revision, the Constitution has proved an exceptionally flexible instrument of government due to a continuous process of amendment by political usage and judicial interpretation.

In the first place, the exigencies of politics have built up a body of customs or conventions which have modified, supplemented or even contravened the letter of the Constitution. For example, as has often been pointed out, since the rise of political parties the method of electing the President has not followed constitutional prescriptions. Whereas the Constitution provides that the President shall be chosen by electors meeting in their respective states, in practice the electors have become mere abstractions, and the voters' choice is confined only to those candidates who have been nominated by party conventions. Similarly, it is a caucus of the majority party in the House of Representatives rather than the entire House that selects the Speaker. Again the non-reeligibility of a President for a third term, though nowhere decreed by the Constitution, has become so deep-rooted a tradition that its violation is inconceivable even by the most ambitious or powerful of Presidents.[6]

Even the separation of the three branches of the federal government has been radically modified by usage. Writing shortly after the Civil War, Walter Bagehot, the English publicist, exulted in the superiority of the "cabinet government" of England over the "presidential system" of America, and pointed to Lincoln's and Johnson's difficulties with Congress to support his contention that "the division of the legislative and the executive in presidential governments" conduces to the weakness of both.[7] It is doubtful whether he would have persisted in this view if he had lived through the administrations of Theodore and Franklin D. Roosevelt and the first term of Woodrow Wilson. For though the Constitution vests the legislative power in Congress, these forceful Presidents, particularly when they commanded a majority in both Houses, exercised as much legislative initiative as an English prime minister. That the major measures of Franklin D. Roosevelt's first administration have either been dictated or inspired by the White House is undeniable. Nonetheless, the contention of the "Jeffersonian Democrats" and the Republicans that the President has violated the Constitution by usurping the functions of Congress loses its force when we reflect that Congress and the country, especially in an emergency, have tended more and more to look to the Chief Executive for legislative initiative; and that, by what has now become a convention of the Constitution, even those of Mr. Roosevelt's predecessors who have allowed Congress a freer hand have been judged by the country on the strength of their legislative record rather than by the strictly executive aspects of their administrations. In short, without any formal amendment or statutory enactment, the presidential system, which is grounded in the principle of the separation of powers, has been evolving toward that "close union", if not "the nearly complete fusion of the executive and legislative powers", which Bagehot regarded with pardonable complacency as "the efficient secret of the English Constitution."[8]

Moreover, the American Constitution has not developed only by means of formal amendments, or the accretions and modifications wrought by usage. More potent than either of these processes has been the method of amendment by judicial interpretation which is peculiar to the American system and implicit in the Constitution itself. The negative aspect of this method is the power of the courts to declare statutes void on grounds of unconstitutionality. Yet despite the importance it rapidly assumed, the question of judicial review was barely touched upon by the Philadelphia Convention, and this power, which has often been hotly contested and is today perhaps the most explosive issue before the American people, is nowhere expressly granted in the Constitution. It rests upon the second paragraph of Article VI, which reads:

> This Constitution, and the Laws of the United States which shall be made in Pursuance thereof; and all Treaties made, or which shall be made, under the Authority of the United States, shall be the supreme Law of the Land; and the Judges in every State shall be bound thereby; anything in the Constitution or Laws of any State to the contrary notwithstanding.

That this article would provide the leverage for dislodging legislation which, in the opinion of the Court, conflicted with the Constitution was intimated by Hamilton in the *Federalist*. "The complete independence of the courts of justice," he wrote, "is peculiarly essential in a limited Constitution . . . which contains

[ 28 ]

certain specified exceptions to the legislative authority
. . . Limitations of this kind can be preserved in practice no other way than through the medium of courts
of justice, whose duty it must be to declare all acts contrary to the manifest tenor of the Constitution void.
Without this, all the reservations of particular rights
or privileges would amount to nothing." To the contention that judicial review "would imply a superiority
of the judiciary to the legislative power", he replied:
"There is no position which depends on clearer principles than that every act of a delegated authority, contrary to the tenor of the commission under which it is
exercised, is void. No legislative act, therefore, contrary to the Constitution can be valid. To deny this is
to affirm that the deputy is greater than his principal;
that the servant is above his master; that the representatives of the people are superior to the people themselves; that men acting by virtue of powers, may do
not only what their powers do not authorize, but what
they forbid." He envisaged the courts as "an inter-
mediate body between the people and the legislature, in
order, among other things, to keep the latter within
the limits assigned to their authority."[9]

So far as the laws enacted by state legislatures are
concerned, there can be no demur from Hamilton's
argument. The provision of Article VI that judges in
every state shall be bound by the Constitution, "anything in the Constitution or laws of any state to the
contrary notwithstanding," clearly established the
supremacy of the federal Constitution over those of
the respective states. And since the power to negative
state legislation on grounds of unconstitutionality was

wisely denied to Congress,[10] it was implicitly vested in the courts, state and federal. The exercise of this power by the federal courts in the last instance is imperative under our dual government, for if the state legislatures were to encroach upon federal power or violate fundamental individual liberties, the Constitution would be nullified and the fabric of national government would collapse. "I do not think," said the late Justice Holmes, "that the United States would come to an end if we (the Supreme Court) lost our power to declare an Act of Congress void. I do think the Union would be imperiled if we could not make that declaration as to the laws of the several states."[11] While those to whom judicial review is an article of faith might take exception to the first part of this statement, only a fanatical upholder of the defunct doctrine of state sovereignty would disagree with the second.

The implications of Article VI, however, are not as clear with regard to the right of the federal courts to invalidate congressional legislation, unless we read into the words "in pursuance thereof" the meaning that only those laws which are in accord with the Constitution "shall be the supreme law of the land." This was plainly the view of Hamilton. "A constitution," he wrote, "is, in fact, and must be regarded by the judges, as a fundamental law. It, therefore, belongs to them to ascertain its meaning as well as the meaning of any particular act proceeding from the legislative body. If there should happen to be an irreconcilable variance between the two, that which has the superior obligation and validity ought, of course, to be preferred; or, in other words, the Constitution ought to be preferred to the statute, the intention of the people to the intention of their agents."[12] This argument is based on the hardly tenable and rather mystical proposition that the members of the Philadelphia Convention represented "the people" for all time; and that "the intention of the people" which they wrote into the Constitution in 1787 reflects more accurately the will of the American voters in 1936 than do their "agents" in Congress. Those who do not believe that the general will was miraculously incarnated in the Constitution and thus placed, as it were, in "cold storage" for posterity assert that whenever the Court invalidates a law passed by Congress, it nullifies an act of an equal and co-ordinate branch of the national government which, as the immediate representative of the people, is empowered to declare the public policy of the United States. "It is always a serious thing," as Judge Hand has said, "to declare an act of Congress unconstitutional."[13]

This far-reaching power by which a Court, or even a single judge,[14] may veto an act of Congress and stem the tide of popular will without accounting to any constituency was masterfully ingrafted upon our constitutional system by the eminent Chief Justice John Marshall through a series of decisions beginning with the famous case of *Marbury* v. *Madison*[15] decided in 1803. This case arose under the Judiciary Act of 1789 by which Congress authorized the Supreme Court to issue writs of mandamus to persons holding office under the authority of the United States. William Marbury, who had been appointed justice of the peace by President Adams, but whose commission had not been delivered during Adams' incumbency and was withheld by Madison, Jefferson's secretary of state, invoked the new law and petitioned the Supreme Court for a mandamus to Madison to deliver the commission. Under Article III, Section 2, Paragraph 2 of the Constitution, the original jurisdiction[16] of the Supreme Court was limited to "cases affecting ambassadors, all other public ministers and consuls, and those in which a state shall be party." The question before the Court, then, was whether Congress could authorize the Supreme Court to issue writs of mandamus and thus extend its original jurisdiction beyond the limits set by the Constitution. Marshall decided that it could not, and by his opinion, which went beyond the necessities of the case, he formulated the doctrine of judicial review. "The Constitution," he said, "is either a superior paramount law, unchangeable by ordinary means, or it is on a level with ordinary legislative acts, and, like other acts, is alterable when the legislature shall please to alter it. . . . If the latter part be true, then written constitutions are absurd attempts on the part of the people to limit a power in its own nature illimitable. Certainly all those who have framed written constitutions contemplate them as forming the fundamental and paramount law of the nation, and, consequently, the theory of every such government must be that an act of the legislature, repugnant to the Constitution, is void."

But why should the courts concern themselves with this question? Because "it is emphatically the province and duty of the judicial department to say what the law is. . . . If two laws conflict with each other, the courts must decide on the operation of each. So . . . if both the law and the Constitution apply to a particular case, so that the court must either decide that case conformably to the law, disregarding the Constitution; or conformably to the Constitution, disregarding the law", it must choose the latter course, since "the Constitution is superior to any ordinary act of the legislature." If the courts were to follow the opposite course, if they were to "close their eyes on the Constitution and see only the law", they would "subvert the very foundation of . . ." and reduce to nothing "what we have deemed the greatest improvement on political institutions, a written constitution."[17] By this reasoning, which does not differ substantially from Hamilton's argument in the *Federalist,* Marshall set aside a section of the Judiciary Act and thereby affirmed as an inherent power of the courts under a written constitution their right to void laws passed by Congress. It was characteristic of the great chief justice's essential political-mindedness that he combined the assumption of this far-reaching power by the Supreme Court with a self-denying gesture—the invalidation of a law which proposed to widen the Court's jurisdiction.

The priority of a written constitution, however, is a rather formal argument which might in the long run have proved too weak to sustain the doctrine of judicial review of federal legislation. The consolidation of this doctrine may be explained by reference to the issues raised by the Kentucky and Virginia Resolutions, which were drawn up respectively by Jefferson and Madison and passed by the legislatures of the two states toward the close of 1798.[18] These resolutions were an emphatic protest against the Alien and Sedition Acts by which, it was claimed, Congress had not only violated the constitutional guarantees of individual liberty but in order to do so had usurped powers which had never been delegated to it and hence rightfully belonged to the states. In making this protest, Jefferson and, less emphatically, Madison advanced the doctrine that the states were the judges of whether the federal government had exceeded the powers granted to it by the Constitution. The Virginia Resolution declared that "in case of a deliberate, palpable and dangerous exercise of other powers not granted by the said compact [the Constitution], the States, who are parties thereto, have the right and are in duty bound to interpose for arresting the progress of the evil, and for maintaining within their respective limits the authorities, rights and liberties appertaining to them." And the Kentucky Resolution stated more intransigently that "to this compact each state acceded as a state, and is an integral party, its co-states forming, as to itself, the other party; that the government created by this compact was not made the exclusive and final judge of the extent of the powers delegated to itself; since that would have made its discretion, and not the Constitution, the measure of its powers; but that as in all other cases of compact among parties having no common Judge, each party has an equal right to judge for itself, as well of infractions as of the mode and measure of redress."[19]

The issue raised by these resolutions was subsequently sharpened by Calhoun's advocacy of "nullification" into a dilemma which struck at the very foundations of the Union. Clearly, if the decision as to the constitutionality of federal laws were left to the states, the consequence would be, as Calhoun contended, state sovereignty; and since the concomitant of state sovereignty is the right to secede, the Union could only be preserved by federal coercion and civil war. If, on the other hand, the federal government were to be "the exclusive and final judge of the extent of the powers delegated to itself", it would cease to be a government of limited powers, would eventually become omnipotent with respect both to the states and to the individual citizen, and the concept of limited government, basic to the American system, would be destroyed. The obvious escape from these perilous alternatives would seem to be to refute the assertion of the Kentucky Resolution about the absence of a "common judge" by making the Supreme Court the judge of constitutionality; the more so because, by its origins and composition, it is the most independent organ of the federal system, the creature of the Constitution and not of the national government, and because in standing guard over "the supreme law of the land" it performs an eminently judicial function.

It is because judicial review has established itself as a historical necessity imposed by the inner logic of the American system that it has survived the violent controversies over usurpation and is the most firmly rooted, as well as the most characteristic, of the conventions of the Constitution. The logic of its development has been summarized by Chief Justice Hughes in the following terms: "If there was to be a written constitution defining, and thus limiting, federal powers, and these definitions were to have the force of constitutional or supreme law, it would be essential that

[ 35 ]

the tribunal which interpreted and applied Federal law should recognize and apply the limits of both Federal and State authority, and as that [the national] government acted upon the individual citizen, he was deemed to be entitled to invoke its limitations. Thus, in the most natural way, as the result of the creation of Federal law under a written constitution conferring limited powers, the Supreme Court of the United States came into being with its unique function."[20]

This does not mean that the judicial veto of federal legislation has been acquiesced in without protest, especially when it has been used to nullify or hold in abeyance measures dictated by widespread popular sentiment and calculated to promote the national good. There has been a periodic revival of opposition to judicial review, and various plans have been suggested for curbing the powers of the Supreme Court, such as requiring a majority of seven judges for the invalidation of federal laws, authorizing Congress to override a judicial veto by more than a majority of both Houses, increasing the membership of the Court or placing legislation designed to promote the "economic welfare" beyond the reach of the judicial veto.[21] The motive of this opposition is the conviction that when the Supreme Court declares an act of Congress unconstitutional it nullifies an act of national sovereignty, and, to the extent that this nullification affects public policy, the function of the Court ceases to be judicial and becomes essentially legislative. This was the burden of Abraham Lincoln's complaint when, in the course of his first inaugural address, he commented as follows on the Dred Scott decision:[22]

[ 36 ]

At the same time, the candid citizen must confess that if the policy of the Government, upon vital questions affecting the whole people, is to be irrevocably fixed by the Supreme Court, the instant they are made in ordinary litigation between parties in personal actions, the people will have ceased to be their own rulers, having to that extent resigned their government into the hands of that eminent tribunal.[23]

The claim to fix the policy of the government "upon vital questions affecting the whole people" was advanced by Mr. Justice Sutherland when, in delivering the majority opinion in the *Adkins Case,*[24] he defined the function of the Supreme Court in the following terms:

The liberty of the individual . . . is not absolute. It must frequently yield to the common good, and the line beyond which the power of interference may not be pressed is neither definite nor unalterable, but may be made to move within limits not well defined, with changing need and circumstance. Any attempt to fix a rigid boundary would be unwise as well as futile. But nevertheless, there are limits to the power, and when these have been passed, it becomes the plain duty of the courts, in the proper exercise of their authority, to so declare.[25]

Now while in many cases it is relatively easy to determine at what point governmental interference with the liberty of the individual becomes unconstitutional, in many others such determination involves judgment not only on whether Congress has the power to enact a certain law, but on its desirability and wisdom as well. It is in such cases that the Court functions, in effect, as a third branch of the legislature and judicial review becomes the means to judicial supremacy. Nor is there

[ 37 ]

much warrant for believing that judges, when they thus intrude into the legislative field, are guided by more objective canons than ordinary legislators. Indeed, between the letter of the Constitution and the provisions of a given statute there is an enormous gap which must be filled with judicial interpretation; and judicial interpretation cannot but be influenced by the intellectual bent and the emotional bias of the judges. And so it comes about that, when the state attempts to interfere with economic enterprise, eminent justices become embattled defenders of laissez faire and their decisions tend, in the words of Justice Holmes, to incorporate in the Constitution "Mr. Herbert Spencer's *Social Statics*" by stretching the "due process of law" clause far beyond its procedural meaning.

When the Court, under the guise of standing guard over the Constitution, assumes legislative functions, the people whose will is thwarted may well ask: "Who will guard our guardians?" The custodians of the Constitution, answers Mr. Justice Stone, must stand guard over themselves. In a memorable dissenting opinion he urged a more self-denying attitude upon his brethren in the following terms:

> The power of courts to declare a statute unconstitutional is subject to two guiding principles of decision which ought never to be absent from judicial consciousness. One is that courts are concerned only with the power to enact statutes, not with their wisdom. The other is that while unconstitutional exercise of power by the executive and legislative branches of the government is subject to judicial restraint, the only check upon our own exercise of power is our own sense of self-restraint. For the removal of unwise laws from

the statute books appeal lies not to the courts but to the ballot and to the processes of democratic government.[26]

This warning is needed at a time when the judicial veto is being exercised more freely than at any other period of our history. More than half a century elapsed after *Marbury* v. *Madison* before a second Act of Congress was declared unconstitutional, though during that time scores of state statutes fell under the judicial ax. And though the rate has increased progressively since the Civil War, it was not until the administration of Franklin D. Roosevelt that an almost permanent opposition developed between the President and Congress on the one hand, and a majority of the highest federal tribunal on the other. With the exception of the National Industrial Recovery Act,[27] the major measures of the New Deal that were adversely reviewed by the Supreme Court, such as the Railway Retirement Act,[28] the Agricultural Adjustment Act,[29] and the Bituminous Coal Conservation Act,[30] were struck down by majorities of one or two, a process unpleasantly reminiscent of the *liberum veto* in eighteenth-century Poland whereby the opposition of a single member could frustrate the will of the national Diet.

Yet despite the emasculation of the New Deal by judicial veto, judicial review and the Constitution did not figure prominently among the issues of the presidential campaign of 1936. President Roosevelt, after his "horse-and-buggy" criticism of the NRA decision, ignored the issue, and a "clarifying amendment" was envisaged by the Democratic platform only in case the President's objectives could not be achieved through legislation within the Constitution.[31] As for the Republicans, they, too, were content not to press the matter. Their enthusiasm for the Court as the watchdog of the Constitution and the defender of the states against federal encroachment became a decided political liability after the invalidation of the New York Minimum Wage Law by a five-to-four decision had apparently set up a barrier to all government interference with economic enterprise.

This deliberate avoidance of the constitutional issue by the two major parties[32] has been, of course, dictated by political expediency. But political expediency, in this instance, reflects the almost mystical faith of the American people in the Supreme Court as the guardian of the Constitution. Nor is this faith entirely unfounded. For, while watching over the Constitution, the Supreme Court has not consistently obstructed the national will. It has often delayed, but not permanently impeded, progress. As the subsequent chapters will show, it has, with but few exceptions, adjusted itself in the long run to the dominant currents of public sentiment during successive periods of American history. Even the oft-cited Dred Scott decision, though it accelerated the political realignment which eventually reversed it on the battlefield, was handed down at a time when the country was governed by a Democratic President and Congress; hence it was not contrary to the political will of the party in power and it merely ratified the repeal of the Missouri Compromise by the Kansas-Nebraska Bill of 1854. At the same time it must be admitted that the Court has not infrequently lagged behind popular sentiment on momentous issues; but whenever it disregarded the popular will on vital questions affecting the whole nation, it either modified or reversed its position subsequently, or, less frequently, it acquiesced in its reversal by the people through the process of constitutional amendment.[33]

Judicial review has a positive as well as a negative aspect. It not only contracts national power by nullifying acts of Congress which have gone beyond the letter of the Constitution; it also expands national power by stretching the letter of the Constitution in order to broaden the ambit of federal legislation. Thus a Constitution framed in the late eighteenth century, when the Industrial Revolution had barely begun, has adjusted itself by the subtle process of judicial interpretation to the needs of a society which has been immeasurably expanded and radically transformed by the ever-quickening pace of science and technology. Because this transformation created problems which were not specifically provided for in the Constitution, the courts were obliged to read into it a large number of implied powers—that is to say, powers which they considered essential to the exercise of those functions which had been expressly delegated to the national government.

National power has thus expanded through the development by the courts of implied federal powers—i.e., powers that could be derived by reasonable implication from such explicit grants as the taxing power, the power to regulate interstate commerce, and the power to coin money. By this process an effort has been made to attain those desirable objectives of government which are within the legal power of the states but beyond their capacity, and within the capacity of Congress but beyond its explicitly defined legal power.

But notwithstanding the accretions brought about by the development of implied powers, there still remains a large field of social and economic activity which the national government, apparently, has no power to regulate. For example, social welfare legislation has been assumed to be one of the powers reserved to the states. But in view of the fact that the social consequences of industrialism, especially since the débâcle of 1929 has made social welfare a matter of national concern upon which the several states are unable to exercise effective control, what agency shall give direction to these forces? Obviously, the national government. But if the national government cannot act because it lacks the legal power, and the action of the state governments lacks efficacy, a vital field of economic activity escapes effective regulation. Thus, the situation was bad enough even without the recent five-to-four decision[34] which, by invalidating the New York Minimum Wage Law on the ground that it violated the "due process" clause, created a no man's land in the field of sovereignty where neither the state nor the federal government has legal power to act.

Moreover, the courts have not been prone to concede to the federal government the inherent power[35] to act upon matters affecting the national good in the absence of a constitutional warrant, expressed or implied, even though the states are admittedly unable to act upon such matters. The late Chief Justice Taft, speaking for the Court in *Bailey* v. *Drexel Furniture Co.*,[36] said:

[ 42 ]

It is the high duty and function of this Court in cases regularly brought to its bar to decline to recognize or enforce seeming laws of Congress, dealing with subjects not intrusted to Congress, but left or committed by the Supreme Law of the land to the control of the states. We cannot avoid the duty, even though it require us to refuse to give effect to legislation designed to promote the highest good. The good sought in unconstitutional legislation is an insidious feature, because it leads citizens and legislators of good purpose to promote it, without thought of the serious breach it will make in the ark of our covenant, or the harm which will come from breaking down recognized standards.

In the maintenance of local self-government on the one hand, and the national power, on the other, our country has been able to endure and prosper for near a century and a half.

Theodore Roosevelt, while President, had assailed this type of legal reasoning. In his effort to obtain judicial sanction for his Antitrust Crusade, which met legal snarls through constitutional limitations imposed by states' rights, he urged that the national government should possess the inherent power to act where the object involved was beyond the power of the states to manage. He clearly set forth his views in a speech delivered at Harrisburg, Pa., on October 4, 1906, where he said: "I cannot do better than base my theory of governmental action upon the words and deeds of one of Pennsylvania's greatest sons, Justice James Wilson. He developed even before Marshall the doctrine (absolutely essential not merely to the efficiency but to the existence of this nation) that an inherent power rested in the nation, outside of the enumerated powers conferred upon it by the Constitution, in all cases where the object involved was beyond the power of the several States and was a power ordinarily exercised by sovereign nations. In a remarkable letter in which he advocated setting forth in orderly and clear fashion the powers of the National Government, he laid down the proposition that it should be made clear that there were neither vacancies nor interferences between the limits of state and national jurisdictions, and that both jurisdictions together composed only one uniform and comprehensive system of government and laws; that is, whenever the States cannot act, because the need to be met is not one merely of single locality, then the National Government, representing all the people, should have complete power to act. . . . Certain judicial decisions have done just what Wilson feared: they have, as a matter of fact, left vacancies, left blanks between the limits of actual National jurisdiction over the control of the great business corporations. . . . The legislative or judicial actions and decisions of which I complain, be it remembered, do not really leave to the States power to deal with corporate wealth in business. Actual experience has shown that the States are wholly powerless to deal with this subject; and any action or decision that deprives the nation of the power to deal with it, simply results in leaving the corporations absolutely free to work without any effective supervision whatever; and such a course is fraught with untold danger to the future of our whole system of government, and, indeed, to our whole civilization."[37]

The end sought by Theodore Roosevelt was the effective prosecution of monopolies under the Sherman Antitrust Act, and the theory of constitutional interpretation he expounded was a means to that end. The Supreme Court has not accepted the doctrine of *inherent powers,* presumably because of the fear that its application would disintegrate states' rights and hence our dual form of government. Had the doctrine been accepted, it is doubtful whether the National Industrial Recovery Act, the Agricultural Adjustment Act, the Railway Retirement Act, and the Bituminous Coal Conservation Act would have been declared unconstitutional. At the same time, Roosevelt's advocacy of the expanding national sovereignty under the doctrine of *inherent powers* made a profound impression which was not without its effect upon the courts. Although the Supreme Court did not adopt the Rooseveltian conception of constitutional interpretation, it did give substantial effect to the desired end by another means—the enlargement of the scope of the interstate commerce clause. Of this, more will be said later. Suffice it to say that the political will was not completely ignored.

That the Supreme Court should heed the national will as expressed through Congress has been the insistent plea of some of our greatest jurists. "It must be remembered," said Justice Holmes, "that legislators are the ultimate guardians of the liberties and welfare of the people in quite as great a degree as the courts."[38] And Mr. Justice Stone, citing this maxim with approval, concluded his dissent in the AAA case with the following admonition to his brethren:

Courts are not the only agency of government that must be assumed to have capacity to govern. Congress and the courts both unhappily may falter or be mistaken in the performance of their constitutional duty. But interpretation of our great charter of government which proceeds on any assumption that the responsibility for the preservation of our institutions is the exclusive concern of any one of the three branches of government, or that it alone can save them from destruction is far more likely, in the long run, "to obliterate the constituent members" of "an indestructible union of indestructible states" than the frank recognition that language, even of a constitution, may mean what it says: That the power to tax and spend includes the power to relieve a nation-wide economic mal-adjustment by conditional gifts of money.

The basic problem of government—the reconciliation of liberty with authority, of individual freedom with social organization—presents itself more acutely today than probably at any other period of history. It has, in fact, assumed more and more the form of a dilemma so urgent and inescapable that large sections of humanity have given up liberty in exchange for the modicum of security to be derived from the effective regimentation of society by authoritarian government. Democracy is thus challenged to prove that freedom and organization, the two needs of human beings living in society, are not incompatible and mutually exclusive. The American system, with its federalism, separation of powers, written constitution and doctrine of judicial review, provides a most effective institutional equipment for meeting this challenge; and of this equipment the Supreme Court is the most crucial part. The exercise of its unique function of judicial review tends, on the negative side, to safeguard individual liberty against governmental encroachment, and, on the positive side, to foster organization by expanding the letter of the Constitution to meet the needs of a dynamic society. Because the Supreme Court, acting in both capacities, is the strongest bulwark of limited government, it is imperative that it should continue, as in the past, to check, revise—in short, to act as a corrective to but never permanently to obstruct the national will.

## CHAPTER IV

## National Power and States' Rights

---

DURING THE FIRST YEAR of Franklin D. Roosevelt's administration, when all classes anxiously focused their gaze on the national capital and breathlessly waited for the government's next move, little was heard about constitutional powers and limitations. The nation was so intent upon the end—the fight against the economic paralysis that had afflicted it since 1929—that it did not feel much concern about the means. It was only after it had staggered up from the slough of the depression that those who thought that they were adversely affected by Mr. Roosevelt's measures of recovery and reform began to examine more critically their constitutional implications. Encouraged by a series of momentous judicial decisions, the President's critics accused him of undermining both the separation of powers and federalism, the twin pillars of the American system, by arrogating to himself powers vested in Congress and by pushing the federal government into the domain reserved by the Constitution to the states.

The first of these charges has been heard in the past

[ 48 ]

whenever a forceful personality or an eminent national figure occupied the White House. States' rights, on the other hand, a constitutional concept and a political battle cry as old as the nation, has served different interests at different periods of American history, depending upon the ever-changing economic and social conditions. It was, as we have seen, very much in the thought of the framers of the Constitution; it epitomized the differences between the first political parties; and it was probably the determining factor in the elevation of the arch-Federalist John Marshall to the chief-justiceship[1] following the defeat of the Federalists but before the induction into the presidency of Jefferson, the leader of the states' rights party.

When Marshall assumed office at the dawn of the nineteenth century, the Union was still a new world struggling to be born. The states and their governments were a living reality, while the federal government was something new, alien and shadowy, a blueprint of aspirations and possibilities rather than a going concern. Its functions were few, simple and impersonal. It did not engage in many activities which could bring it into close contact with individual citizens. There were no income taxes, no Farm Boards, no federal regulation of business, and the power over interstate commerce was limited mainly to the supervision of coastwise and foreign shipping. Furthermore, to the early American the idea of centralization was synonymous with tyranny; something to be avoided, not sought. If relief or favor was forthcoming, he looked not to the federal government but to his state. The state was the means to his economic security and the protector of his special rights. Moreover, rivalries among the states had created a keen sense of local pride and a hierarchy of loyalty in which, oft-times, duty to the state took precedence over duty to the nation. The Virginia and Kentucky Resolutions revealed an ominous tendency to invoke the doctrine of state sovereignty against unpalatable measures of the national government. On the other hand, the opposition of the New England states to Jefferson's embargo and to the War of 1812 showed that state and sectional loyalty could assert itself in the North with equal vehemence; and that the various sections of the country had not yet developed sufficient community of interests and feelings to serve as a foundation for a national foreign policy. In short, despite the Constitution, more than ten years of Federalist rule, and the economic and fiscal policies of Alexander Hamilton, the centripetal forces that make for nationalism were not yet strong enough to overcome the inertia of particularism. Hence, the basic constitutional problem at the beginning of the nineteenth century was quite different from that of the fourth decade of the twentieth. Today, as a result of the cumulative impact of the nation-making forces upon our political institutions, the task of judicial statesmanship is to salvage the remnant of states' rights from the encroachments of national power. Marshall, on the other hand, conceived his mission to be the building of national power and the concomitant curtailment of the authority of the states.

Consistently with the brutal frankness which characterized the politics of the time, no attempt was made to conceal the partisan purpose of Marshall's appointment. It was the parting gift of John Adams, the defeated Federalist President, to his states' rights successor; and it was designed to retain Federalist control of the Judiciary and thus to mitigate the effects of what Jefferson called "the revolution of 1800"—namely, his election to the presidency. Marshall's nomination was confirmed by the Senate on January 27, 1801; and when on March 4 of the same year the chief justice administered the oath of office to his fellow Virginian and arch-opponent, the stage seemed set not only for an epic clash of personalities but for a protracted conflict of the executive with the judicial branch of the federal government. Superficially, these expectations were not disappointed. Jefferson inaugurated his first term with a systematic offensive against the federal judiciary, the citadel of Federalist power. He removed the new district judges appointed by Adams immediately before his retirement; and he instituted impeachment proceedings against Judge Pickering and Supreme Court Justice Samuel Chase, whose partisan zeal was excessive even by contemporary standards, which did not yet include the nonpartisanship of the federal Bench as a firmly established convention. He greeted the epochmaking decision in *Marbury* v. *Madison* with the lament that it gave to the one branch of the government which is "unelected by and independent of the nation" the exclusive right "to prescribe rules for the government of the others"; and that it made the Constitution "a mere thing of wax in the hands of the judiciary which they may twist and shape into any form they please."[2] The conflict reached a climax during the trial of Aaron Burr, when Jefferson's efforts to prove and punish conspiracy against the integrity of the nation were thwarted by the chief justice.

Yet the constitutional differences of the President and the chief justice—strict construction and states' rights versus broad construction and national power—did not figure prominently in this fierce partisan struggle. Indeed, throughout the proceedings which led to Burr's indictment and during the trial itself, the rôles of the two protagonists seemed to have been reversed. For it was Marshall who, by the strictest possible construction of the constitutional definition of treason, was chiefly instrumental in securing a qualified acquittal which was extremely distasteful to Jefferson.[3] The chief justice's handling of this case was admittedly influenced by partisan motives. At the same time, though a broad-constructionist and an exponent of national power—i.e., of the authority of the state—he was performing an eminently judicial function when he extended to an accused person the maximum of protection under the Constitution. Jefferson, on the other hand, though a strict-constructionist and a liberal—i.e., a defender of the individual against the state—was compelled, as Chief Executive, to protect the nation against the treasonable activities of an ambitious politician.[4]

That the exigencies of high office forced Jefferson to jettison the doctrines of strict construction and states' rights has been pointed out often enough. But it has not been, perhaps, as strongly emphasized that in so doing he promoted by political action the same end that Marshall was pursuing by judicial means—namely, the expansion of national power through liberal interpretation of the Constitution. By purchasing Louisiana, despite grave misgivings about the absence of constitutional sanction, he not only dealt a blow to the doctrine of strict construction but, by adding half a continent to the national domain, he provided the territorial prerequisite for the development of American nationalism. In order to compel the belligerents of the Napoleonic War to respect American neutral rights, he asked and secured congressional consent to a complete embargo on international trade. Thus, by stretching to the utmost the federal government's power to "regulate commerce with foreign nations", the statesman who had all along advocated strict construction of the Constitution and deprecated governmental interference resorted to a measure so drastic that its enforcement would necessitate the abandonment of "customary and essential safeguards for personal property and liberty and the right of individual redress in courts of law."[5]

The expansion of national power continued under Jefferson's successors. During the War of 1812 Madison successfully asserted the constitutional powers of Congress and the Chief Executive in wartime against the strict-constructionist and states' rights opposition of the New England states. And though he had advanced the most telling constitutional arguments against Hamilton's economic and fiscal policies, he reversed his position so far as to advocate internal improvements under federal auspices and sign the bill creating the second Bank of the United States. It has been cogently argued that this reversal of Jefferson and the Jeffersonians on the constitutional issue was one "of means not ends"; that it was designed in the main to serve the agricultural interest which constituted the major part of Jefferson's following and had been the object of his constant solicitude.[6] But the fact that the very sections and classes which had at first distrusted a strong central government were becoming habituated to the uses of national power would seem to show that the forces making for nationalism were on the march. Indeed, under Madison, Monroe and John Quincy Adams, Jeffersonianism, though still nominally in power, had become increasingly indistinguishable from Federalism; and the Jeffersonian principles of states' rights and agrarianism regained their pristine vigor only by becoming reincarnated as the weapon and symbol of new forces—the secession movement of the Southern planters championed by John Calhoun and the frontier democracy of Andrew Jackson.

It can be safely asserted, then, that the anxiety of the Federalists about the consequences of the "revolution of 1800", however justified from the strictly partisan viewpoint, turned out to be quite groundless with respect to the fate of the Constitution. Despite Jefferson's antecedents and theoretical convictions, the powers of the federal government expanded during his administration and those of his successors. Far from attempting to apply the states' rights doctrines of the Virginia and Kentucky Resolutions, Jefferson and Madison combated them when they were invoked by the preponderantly Federalist New England states against their embargo and war policies. In short, though the Federalist party was defeated, the inexorable logic of stubborn facts compelled the victors to uphold its constitutional principles. The fact that the maintenance of these principles was also the aim of Marshall's historic decisions goes to show that underneath the stormy surface of partisan politics the main trends of political and judicial statecraft flowed in the same direction.

Yet this essential concordance (which, it must be admitted, is more evident in retrospect than it was to the protagonists or their contemporaries) does not detract from Marshall's achievement. He was a passionate partisan, but for once passionate partisanship was made to serve the national interest. He saw in the "revolution of 1800" the menace of retrogression to the anarchy and impotence of the "critical period" from which the young Republic had been rescued by the Constitution and ten years of Federalist rule; and he, therefore, set out deliberately to checkmate what seemed at the time the triumphant popular will. From the statesman who was the foremost spokesman of that will he was separated not only by personal and partisan differences but also by a basically divergent political philosophy. While recognizing that the needs of a growing nation must be served by a national government, Jefferson was deeply disturbed by the thought that the strengthening of the national government would result in the impairment of individual liberty and the decline of democracy and local self-government. Under the compulsion of events and forces beyond his control, he invoked national power but felt grave misgivings about the consequences of its growth. Marshall, on the other hand, regarded a strong central government as a blessing; something to be fostered as an indispensable prerequisite to national development rather than deplored as its undesirable but inescapable concomitant. He, therefore, addressed himself to the task of formulating the judicial philosophy of national power and fashioning the Constitution into an effective instrument for its expansion.

This grandiose conception of his functions determined his method. He was not concerned merely with the immediate object of the case under litigation but, even more keenly, with the effect of the decision, and the precedent established thereby, on the destinies of a growing nation. His point of departure was the premise that if the American people were to achieve the promise of American life, they must be welded into a united and powerful nation; and the Constitution must, therefore, be made adaptable to what he termed an undefined and expanding future. He thus reversed the usual historical sequence between law and politics. He expounded the law of the Constitution in such a manner as to make it a progressive rather than a conservative force; not a bulwark of the status quo created by the political will of the past, but a path-blazer anticipating and, to a great extent, molding the political will of the future.

This view of the Constitution as a dynamic instrument of government was epitomized by Marshall in the following paragraph of his famous decision in *McCulloch* v. *Maryland:*[7]

> This provision is made in a constitution intended to endure for ages to come, and, consequently, to be adapted to the various crises of human affairs. To have prescribed the means by which government should in all future times execute its powers would have been to change entirely the character of the instrument and to give it the properties of a legal code.

[ 56 ]

It would have been an unwise attempt to provide by immutable rules for exigencies, which, if foreseen at all, must have been seen dimly and can best be provided for as they occur.

In *Martin* v. *Hunter*,[8] the Supreme Court, after re-echoing the nationalism of Marshall, reaffirmed, in the following words, the inherent adaptability of the Constitution to new and ever-changing conditions:

The instrument was not intended to provide merely for the exigencies of a few years, but was to endure through a long lapse of ages, the events of which were locked up in the inscrutable purposes of Providence. It could not be foreseen that new changes and modifications of power might be indispensable to effectuate the general objects of the charter; the restrictions and specifications which, at the present, might seem salutary, might, in the end, prove the overthrow of the system itself. Hence its powers are expressed in general terms, leaving to the legislature, from time to time, to adopt its own means to effectuate legitimate objects, and to mould and model the exercise of its powers, as its own wisdom and the public interests should require.

Having established this conception of the Constitution, Marshall proceeded to mold it into an instrument of national power. In *Cohens* v. *Virginia*[9] he affirmed the right of the Supreme Court to review decisions of state courts, and he derived this right from what he regarded as the true nature of the Union. He attacked the prevailing notion that the Union was but a compact of states, and he proclaimed in cogent terms the doctrine of the supremacy of the people. Taking his text from Article VI, which declares that the "Con-

[ 57 ]

stitution and the laws of the United States which shall
be made in pursuance thereof . . . shall be the
supreme law of the land . . .", he said:

> This is the authoritative language of the American people,
> and, if the gentleman please, of the American States. . . .
> The people made the Constitution and the people can un-
> make it. . . . But this supreme and irresistible power to
> make or unmake resides only in the whole body of the
> people; not in any sub-division of them. The attempt of any
> of the parts (the States) to exercise it, is usurpation, and
> ought to be repelled by those to whom the people have dele-
> gated the power of repelling it. . . .

He broadened the ambit of national power and at
the same time delivered another telling blow at states'
rights by his decision in *McCulloch* v. *Maryland,* which
invalidated an act of the Maryland legislature imposing a tax on the note issues of a branch of the Bank of
the United States doing business in Baltimore. In this
historic opinion Marshall formulated the doctrine of
implied powers in order to derive from it the right
of Congress to create a bank. "Let the end," he said,
"be legitimate, let it be within the scope of the Constitution; and all means which are . . . plainly adapted
to that end, which are not prohibited, but consist with
the letter and spirit of the Constitution, are constitutional." After thus expanding the power of the federal
government, he proceeded to restrict the authority of
the states. He argued that to allow the State of Maryland to impose a tax on a federal institution would be
tantamount to extending the sovereignty of a state "to
those means which are employed by Congress to carry

into execution powers conferred on that body by the
people of the United States." And since "the power to
tax involves the power to destroy", he declared the
Maryland law unconstitutional on the ground that the
use of the taxing power might enable a state to "defeat and render useless the power to create" which is
vested in Congress, and thus to thwart the will of the
entire people.[10]

In the famous *Dartmouth College Case* he invoked
the constitutional prohibition of state laws "impairing
the obligation of contracts" (Article I, section 10) in
order to invalidate an act of the legislature of New
Hampshire which drastically amended the college's
charter of incorporation.[11] Thus, by applying the constitutional concept of contract to charters of corporations, he placed them under the aegis of the Constitution and hence beyond the power of state legislatures.

These and several other important decisions[12] (a)
established the right of the Supreme Court to review
both state and federal legislation as well as decisions
of state courts, (b) expanded the jurisdiction of the
federal government by the broadest possible interpretation of the powers vested in it and by invoking the
doctrine of implied powers, (c) limited the residual
authority of the states, and (d) placed business enterprise and property rights generally beyond the reach
of government regulation and interference by spread-
ing over them a mantle of inviolability provided by a
very broad construction of the "contract" clause. Considered in their totality, they served magnificently "the
two fixed conceptions which dominated Marshall
throughout his long career on the bench: the

sovereignty of the federal state and the sanctity of private property."[13]

Marshall's decisions not only aroused the ire of the champions of states' rights but even provoked the trenchant censure of the more moderate Madison. The thinker who had so magistrally expounded the principles of federalism[14] could not but view with alarm Marshall's increasingly intransigent nationalism; and he repeatedly expressed the fear that the conception of the United States as a government of "sovereign powers" would eventually destroy "the balance between the states and the national government"[15] which, in the words of De Tocqueville, created a union "as happy and as free as a small people, and as glorious and strong as a great nation."[16] Thanks to his strong personality, great prestige and the compelling logic of his decisions, the chief justice was able to withstand this criticism so long as his decisions did not run counter to the general trend of national development. Toward the close of his life, however, the emergence of powerful sectional interests which enjoyed determined political sponsorship foreshadowed a reversal of the trend of judicial statesmanship—i.e., the end of the war of attrition on states' rights and of the corresponding expansion of national power. Once again economic forces expressed themselves in political aspirations and alignments; and this new political will in turn exerted a decisive influence on constitutional development.

Eli Whitney's cotton gin, which was patented in 1794, had made American cotton a universally demanded commodity. "Unaided by machinery, a slave could extract the seeds from about one pound of raw cotton in a whole day; but with Whitney's first crude instrument, a slave could clean fifty pounds and when the invention was improved and harnessed to steam, a thousand pounds a day."[17] The result was low prices, an expanding market, increasing production, and the rise in the Southern states of a new wealth and a new privileged class. "When George Washington was inaugurated President only two million pounds of cotton were produced annually in the United States; by 1860 the output had risen a thousand-fold—to more than two billion pounds. When Jefferson Davis took his place at the head of the Southern Confederacy, nearly two-thirds of all the slaves in America were engaged in cultivating that crop alone."[18] The newborn prosperity of this Cotton Kingdom which stretched from North Carolina to Louisiana depended primarily on the constitutional sanction of ownership and traffic in colored slavery. Hence, the maintenance of slavery and the opening up of new areas to the cultivation of cotton and to slave economy became the paramount concern of the ruling class of Southern planters. The defense of slavery, combined with their opposition to the protective tariff,[19] which raised the prices of the commodities they bought while it lowered the purchasing power of their foreign customers, created a sectional solidarity of economic interests which found expression in the political and constitutional philosophy of John C. Calhoun.

This philosophy was, in the last analysis, a brilliant attempt to consolidate the political supremacy (in order to safeguard the economic interests) of the South against the much more rapidly advancing industrial

North and the ever-expanding agricultural West.[20] Its fundamental aim was, therefore, so to interpret the Constitution as to establish "some restriction or limitation" calculated to "effectually prevent any one interest, or combination of interests, from obtaining the exclusive control of the government."[21] In other words, Calhoun's anxiety about the menace of "interests" did not differ materially from Madison's concern over the dangers of "factions." Both statesmen were anxious to protect minorities against the tyranny of democratic majorities. But whereas Madison sought such protection in the double security provided by federalism and the separation of powers, Calhoun twisted the compact theory of the Constitution into the theory of the "concurrent majority"—i.e., the consent of "each interest or portion of the community, which may be injuriously affected by the action of the government."[22] The consequence of this doctrine would be either the bestowal upon a minority—i.e., the state "injuriously affected"— of a veto power over a measure of the national government, or nullification of that measure by the non-concurring state and its secession from the Union. Ultimately, however, Calhoun's theory would prove ruinous to state sovereignty itself, in whose behalf it was originally conceived; for it could also be invoked by minorities within a given state and thus lead to a plural, in fact, a pulverized, sovereignty which would spell anarchy.

It is, therefore, not to be wondered at that Calhoun's political philosophy aroused passionate opposition in all other sections of the country. Daniel Webster reformulated the nationalist doctrines of Hamilton and

Marshall in order to proclaim the demands of the industrial and commercial North. The industrialism of New England, New York and Pennsylvania depended upon wage labor and domestic markets; hence, upon the restriction of slavery and the erection of high tariff walls. Caught between the conflicting interests of North and South was the ever-expanding agricultural West over whose future hung the fateful question whether it was to be "slave or free." It came into its own politically in 1828 when it elected to the presidency the backwoodsman Andrew Jackson, who, though a Democrat, a states' rights champion and an ally of the South against the interests dominant in the North, drew the line at state sovereignty and detested Calhoun and his nullificationism. Less of a frontiersman than Jackson, another Westerner, Henry Clay of Kentucky, strove to mitigate sectional antagonisms and to create an "American system" of interdependent national economy through the generous use of the constitutional and fiscal powers of the national government.

Such was in broad outline the state of the Union when Marshall died in 1835. He had labored to establish impregnably the supremacy of the national government, to protect property rights and to remove the obstacles which might beset the path of business enterprise. When he was elevated to the chief-justiceship at the turn of the century, these principles which were the legacy of Hamilton seemed threatened by the triumph of Jefferson. At the time of his death they were challenged again by a more radical version of both aspects of Jeffersonianism—Jacksonian democracy and the separatism of John Calhoun. In other words, there was a wide divergence between the Supreme Court, in which, despite several appointments made by Jackson, Marshall's influence was still dominant, and the popular will, which had emerged victorious from the election of 1828 and 1832. Hence, the passing of the venerable chief justice made it possible to complete the reorientation of judicial statesmanship and to bring the Court into harmony with the prevailing political temper of the nation.

President Jackson, as was expected, appointed, to succeed Marshall, Roger Brooke Taney of Maryland, a devoted states' rights adherent.[23] Though the appointment was a foregone conclusion, it intensified the consternation of the Whig party (as the Hamiltonian Federalists now called themselves) and its supporting press. "Our Constitution is in imminent danger"; "the crisis involves the existence of our institutions"; "the Constitution must be saved"—these and other dire warnings, which have since been periodically re-echoed whenever the status quo was rudely disturbed, were sounded by Whig politicians and newspapers throughout the country.[24] Though the aspersions of the Whigs on the new chief justice's ability and character were unwarranted, their forebodings concerning the course of the Supreme Court under his leadership were not entirely groundless. When Justice Story, Marshall's disciple, and Daniel Webster expressed the fear that the Supreme Court was *"gone"*,[25] what they meant was that the trend of judicial statesmanship under Taney would be quite different from what it had been during the incumbency of his great predecessor. This forecast was fulfilled. From the accession of Taney to the out-

break of the Civil War, the Court, almost entirely re-
constructed by the political authority,[26] gave judicial
recognition to the political will which was in turn determined by the economic and social forces that were in
the ascendant during that period. It was, in other
words, a preponderantly Democratic Court, because
the Democrats were in almost continuous control of
the presidency and Congress; and while it did not follow slavishly the dictates of Democratic Presidents or
the Democratic party, its decisions by and large were
patterned upon the principles of Jefferson and Madison,
rather than on those of Hamilton and Marshall.
States' rights was elevated to equal rank with national
power, and the Court ceased to be the consistent exponent of federal supremacy and became the mediator
between these "equal" spheres of sovereign authority.

This does not mean, however, that the Supreme
Court under Taney subscribed to the extreme doctrine
of state sovereignty propounded by Calhoun. The chief
justice was as strongly opposed to separatism as the
President who appointed him. But he was emphatically
a states' rights champion. While he did not wish to deprive the federal government of any of its powers, he
deprecated their expansion by judicial interpretation at
the expense of the states. He was, therefore, a strict-
constructionist; and he condemned the broad interpretation of such explicit prohibitions as the "contract"
clause because they whittled down the residual authority
of the states and impaired their power to interfere with
individual rights in order to promote the welfare of
the community. As a matter of fact, Taney was more
of a humanitarian than Marshall. Yet such is the

adequacy and the flexibility of the language of the Constitution that its text could be so interpreted by the two masters as to serve two diametrically opposite objectives with equal efficacy. Marshall's objective was national supremacy, the preservation of contracts and the protection of property; and he pursued the first of these objectives the more zealously because the greatest menace to the second and third inhered in the tendency of the state legislatures to interfere with vested rights. He, therefore, interpreted the Constitution *broadly* in order to give the central government power to fulfill its sovereign functions and, at the same time, to reduce to a minimum the power of the states over the liberty and property of the individual citizen. Taney's objective, on the other hand, was the widest possible latitude for local self-government and the elimination of national interference in matters of domestic concern. He, therefore, interpreted the powers of the federal government and the constitutional prohibitions on state action *narrowly* in order to give the states sufficient latitude to work out their economic and social problems; the more so because the consequent impairment of vested individual rights was a prerequisite to imperatively needed governmental regulation and social reform. "It was this change of emphasis," writes the most objective historian of the Supreme Court, "from individual property rights to the personal rights and welfare of the general community which characterized Chief Justice Taney's Court. And this change was but a recognition of the general change in the social and economic conditions and in the political atmosphere of that period, brought about by the adoption of universal manhood suffrage, by the revolution in methods of business and industry and in means of transportation, and by the expansion of the Nation and its activities."[27] Nothing shows more clearly that constitutional interpretation is a means to an end than the fact that, a century after Taney, Marshall's broad constructionism and exalted conception of national power are invoked because, owing to "the expansion of the nation and its activities", the social objectives pursued by Taney are beyond the capacity of the states to achieve and must, therefore, be dealt with on a national scale by the national government.

The contrast between the two chief justices' judicial philosophy (and the adaptability of the Constitution to changing economic conditions) may be best illustrated by a comparison of two famous decisions: the *Dartmouth College Case*[28] and the *Charles River Bridge Case,*[29] the former decided by Marshall in 1819 and the latter by Taney in 1837. Both cases involved the application of Section 10 of Article I of the Constitution, which prohibits the states from passing any "Law impairing the Obligation of Contracts."

The *Dartmouth College Case* involved the following facts: The British Crown in 1769 granted a charter incorporating twelve persons as "The Trustees of Dartmouth College" with power to establish an institution of learning in New Hampshire, govern its affairs, acquire property, and fill such vacancies as may occur in their own number. Under the charter the college was founded and funds acquired for its operation through private donations. In 1816 the legislature of New Hampshire, as successor to the Crown, passed a law to amend the charter by increasing the trustees to twenty-one and creating a Board of Overseers to inspect and control their acts. The trustees of Dartmouth refused to accept the amendment and brought suit. The Court held that the charter granted by the British Crown was a contract and that the act of the legislature *altering its terms* was an act impairing the obligation of contract and hence void.

In the *Charles River Bridge Case* the Massachusetts Legislature had granted a charter to the Charles River Bridge Company, authorizing it to erect a bridge between Boston and Charleston. The charter provided that the company would collect tolls for its own use for a period of seventy years, commencing 1786, and that thereafter the bridge should revert to the commonwealth as a free bridge. In 1828 the legislature granted a charter to the Warren Bridge Company, authorizing it to erect a new bridge adjacent to the Charles River Bridge. Under the terms of this charter the Warren Bridge was to be surrendered to the state as a free bridge as soon as the proprietors should be reimbursed from the tolls, but this period was not, in any event, to exceed six years. The charter of the Charles River Bridge was rendered virtually worthless by the subsequent charter to the Warren Bridge Company, and its proprietors, relying on the precedent of the *Dartmouth College Case,* brought suit on the ground that the authorization of the Warren Bridge impaired the obligation of contract between the commonwealth of Massachusetts and the Charles River Bridge Company. In the *Dartmouth College Case,* it should be noted, the New Hampshire Legislature did not seek to diminish the value of the property held under the charter but merely sought to supervise its management. In the instant case, however, the legislature by its act had actually destroyed the value of the property held under and by virtue of the charter. With all that, the Supreme Court, disregarding the precedent of the *Dartmouth College Case,* sustained the legislature and dismissed the complaint. By this decision the Court held, in effect, that private rights must yield to the rights of the community; in other words, the economic and social interests of a state must take precedence over the economic interests of the individual—a doctrine never sanctioned by Marshall. Chief Justice Taney, delivering the opinion of the Court, clearly reflected the new judicial perspective in the following words:

> But the object and end of all government is to promote the happiness and prosperity of the community by which it is established; and it can never be assumed that the government intended to diminish its power of accomplishing the end for which it was created. . . . A State ought never to be presumed to surrender this power, because, like the taxing power, the whole community have an interest in preserving it undiminished. . . . We cannot deal thus with the rights reserved to the states; and by legal intendments and mere technical reasoning, take away from them any portion of that power over their own internal police and improvement, which is so necessary to their well being and prosperity.

But more important than this new reaffirmation of states' rights was the obvious and far-reaching implication that constitutional guarantees must yield to economic necessities, albeit Taney had in mind the economic necessities of the several states as distinguished from those of the whole nation. In this regard, the chief justice said:

> If this Court should establish the principles now contended for, what is to become of the numerous railroads established on the same line of travel with turnpike companies; and which have rendered the franchises of the turnpike corporations of no value? . . . The millions of property which have been invested in railroads and canals, upon lines of travel which had been before occupied by turnpike corporations, will be put in jeopardy. We shall be thrown back to the improvements of the last Century, and obliged to stand still, until the claims of the old turnpike corporations shall be satisfied; and they shall consent to permit the states to avail themselves of the lights of modern science, and to partake of the benefit of those improvements which are now adding to the wealth and prosperity, and the convenience and comfort, of every other part of the civilized world. . . . The Court are not prepared to sanction principles which must lead to such results.[30]

Just as Marshall had invalidated state legislation in the interest of national power for a period of over thirty years, so Taney for nearly the same length of time upheld the acts of the states. It is arguable that his course preserved national unity during a period of intense sectional antagonism as much as Marshall's policy had promoted it during the preceding era; and it is, therefore, the more to be deplored that his decision in the *Dred Scott Case* at one stroke destroyed the achievement of his wise and realistic statesmanship. For just as there came a time when the constitutional theories of Marshall had to be superseded by those of

Taney, likewise, in due course the constitutional doctrines of Taney could no longer withstand the pressure of political events generated by new economic forces. In twenty years from the accession of Taney, Ohio, Illinois and the Middle West territory had become a prosperous commercial as well as an agricultural country with new and virile leaders of the type of Lincoln whose thinking and vision were unencumbered by the bias of intrenched sectional interest. This fact, coupled with the gradual growth of mechanical science, conduced to a natural alliance between the West and the industrial Northeast on the paramount economic, cultural and moral question of slavery. The Supreme Court, ignoring these realities and closing its eyes to historic precedent, believed it could settle this vital politico-economic question by judicial process and so decided in the fateful *Dred Scott Case* that Congress was without power to regulate slavery in the new territories of the United States. This decision was, in final analysis, an attempt to uphold judicially a social system which was being undermined, and hence doomed to extinction, by the inexorable march of economic forces. It was so daring a defiance of the trend of history—though not of the dominant political will of the moment—that it inevitably led to the Civil War, which rendered a definitive judgment on the long-standing suit of state sovereignty versus national power.

## CHAPTER V

# The Supreme Court versus The Political Will

D URING THE CIVIL WAR the government of the United States was to all intents and purposes a presidential dictatorship. Confronted by a situation without precedent, President Lincoln was compelled to exercise unprecedented powers, to break new ground, and to initiate policies of questionable constitutional validity. The most spectacular of these policies, the freeing of the slaves, would, under normal circumstances, have been held unconstitutional because it usurped the right of each state to deal with slavery within its boundaries and it violated the Fifth Amendment by depriving the slaveowners of their property without due process of law. But circumstances were not normal. The federal government was at war against armed secession, and the Emancipation Proclamation was a war measure, an edict by the Commander in Chief depriving slave-owning rebels of their property. Because it applied only to slaves in enemy territory—i.e., in states which were at war against the Union—it could only be enforced to

[ 72 ]

the extent that rebel territory was occupied by loyalist armies; and its ultimate effectiveness was contingent upon the final victory of the Union cause. That victory was won under Lincoln's presidential dictatorship; it was translated into political terms during President Johnson's administration, the first and more militant phase of the so-called Reconstruction Era, which was virtually a congressional dictatorship; and the results of these ten years of war and dictatorship registered their impact on the Constitution in the form of the Thirteenth, Fourteenth and Fifteenth amendments.

Now dictatorship under the American system is government without the restraints of federalism and the separation of powers. Was the Constitution then, which imposes and defines these restraints, in abeyance during the Civil War and the Reconstruction Era; and to what extent did the Supreme Court, the interpreter and custodian of the Constitution, fail to defend its permanent safeguards against the ephemeral embodiments of the political will—represented successively by President Lincoln and the radical Reconstructionist majority in Congress?

When we attempt to answer these questions we are at once struck with the fact that during the Civil War, and particularly after Chief Justice Taney's death in 1864, the Supreme Court was very different in composition and temper from the tribunal which had interpreted the law of the Constitution during the three preceding decades. Jackson had an opportunity to remake the Court when it became historically necessary that the Marshallian doctrines of national power and the immutability of contracts should be superseded by

[ 73 ]

the rival concept of states' rights and its democratic implications. Lincoln had the same opportunity when states' rights and the denial of national power, carried to the extremes of state sovereignty and secession, precipitated a civil war whose stake was the very existence of the nation. Within three years he was called upon to appoint four associate justices and a new chief justice to succeed Taney.[1]

While these appointments were not partisan in the strict sense,[2] the new members could not but be of one mind on the great issue of the day. Their conformity to the prevailing temper of the nation was not only demanded by the logic of the situation but was in accord with the views and the intentions of the President. Lincoln's attitude toward the Constitution and the Supreme Court was one of reverence tempered by a profound sense of his duty as the supreme leader of the embattled nation. He did not practice dictatorship lightheartedly, nor did he conjure up an emergency in order to play the Messiah and indulge his lust for power. But neither was he a pedantic legalist. The emergency was a grim reality; and he did not believe that in the gravest crisis since the founding of the Republic the Supreme Court should—or could—rise above the battle, or that it should interpose the Constitution as an obstruction to the defense of the nation that begot it. "Thoroughly imbued," he wrote in explanation of his policy, "with a reverence for the guaranteed rights of individuals, I was slow to adopt the strong measures which by degrees I have been forced to regard as being within the exceptions of the Constitution and as indispensable to the public safety. . . .

[ 74 ]

I concede that the class of arrests complained of can be constitutional only when in cases of rebellion or invasion the public safety may require them; and I insist that in such cases they are constitutional wherever the public safety does require them, as well as in places in which they may prevent the rebellion extending as in those where it may already be prevailing."[3] Holding these views, he did not hesitate to admit that he wanted a Supreme Court which would not impede his conduct of the war or attempt to whittle down its achievements by judicial veto. "We wish," he said in connection with the appointment of a successor to Taney, "for a Chief Justice who will sustain what has been done in regard to emancipation and the legal tenders. We cannot ask a man what he will do, and if we should, and he should answer us, we should despise him for it. Therefore, we must take a man whose opinions are known."[4] That his other judicial appointments were similarly motivated is a reasonable assumption.

Insofar as the Civil War period is concerned, Lincoln's expectations were not disappointed. The Supreme Court attuned itself to the temper of the nation throughout the war and did not seriously interfere with its conduct. Chief Justice Taney, it is true, in the *Merryman case*,[5] held that the suspension of *habeas corpus* in Maryland by the President was unconstitutional. But this opinion, which was handed down very early in the war, before the attitude of the North had crystallized into grim militancy, was the last gesture of judicial independence. The Supreme Court showed its determination to avoid conflict with the Executive in the darkest hour of the war by denying itself jurisdic-

[ 75 ]

tion in the *Vallandingham Case*,[6] which would have tested the Executive's right to substitute military justice for the judicial procedure prescribed by the Constitution. But when the war was over and military rule was no longer absolutely essential to public safety, the Court reversed itself unanimously in the *Milligan Case*[7] and declared the military commission established during the war in Indiana by order of the President to have been illegal. It is obvious that the attitude of the Judiciary in these three essentially similar cases reflected the changes in public sentiment and the dominant political will during those five years. Constitutional orthodoxy, represented by a chief justice notoriously hostile to national power, yielded during the war to political expediency, or to a sense of even higher public duty, but was reaffirmed when the war was over and the pressure—or the inner obligation—to conform to the political will was somewhat lightened.

For much the same reasons the Court upheld the arm of the federal government by its favorable decisions in the *Prize Cases,* which involved nothing less than the right of the Union to establish a blockade of the Confederate ports. Due to Lincoln's and Secretary Seward's insistence that the war was merely an insurrection, the rules of international law obtaining between belligerent sovereign states were obviously inapplicable to neutral trade with the Confederacy. The Supreme Court, however, brushing aside the distinction between ordinary war and insurrection, upheld the federal government's power to capture neutral vessels and to confiscate property belonging to rebels, even though they were legally deemed to be citizens of the United States.[8] It thus sustained the government in the exercise of a war power absolutely indispensable to victory and saved it from complications, fraught with dire consequences, with the neutrals. Similarly, it upheld the constitutionality of the national banking system and the emergency tax legislation enacted during the war.[9] Hence, it would not be unreasonable to assume that if the Court was, throughout Lincoln's administration, "absolutely free from the partisan criticism prevalent during the decade from 1850 to 1860",[10] this immunity was mainly due to the fact that in a time of national crisis it silenced its constitutional scruples and made itself not merely the judicial branch but the judicial tool of the national government.

While the Supreme Court did not bow as readily to the dominant political will of the Reconstruction Era, it resisted the congressional dictatorship much less resolutely than President Johnson. The most pressing political issue of the period resolved itself into a struggle for power between the President and Congress, growing out of a profound divergence of views on the policies to be adopted toward the ex-rebel states. President Johnson insisted that they should be allowed to set up their own governments and be readmitted to the Union as full-fledged members; and that such federal supervision as would be needed in the process should be exercised by the Executive. Congress, on the other hand—or, rather, the radical majority dominated by such leaders as Thaddeus Stevens, Lyman Trumbull and Charles Sumner—demanded that the secessionist states should be treated as "conquered belligerents" and subjected, on the initiative of Congress rather than the President, to a period of probation in the form of military government.

In view of the Supreme Court's decision in the *Milligan Case,* the Reconstruction Acts of March 1867, which embodied the policy of Congress and had been passed over the President's veto, seemed unlikely to survive judicial scrutiny. Yet the first attempt to test their constitutionality was frustrated by the Court's refusal to assume jurisdiction in the case.[11] The victims of Reconstruction returned to the charge shortly afterward when the state of Georgia filed a bill in equity, praying the Supreme Court to enjoin the secretary of war, Edwin M. Stanton, from carrying into execution the Reconstruction Acts on the ground that such execution would unconstitutionally annul the existing state government and unlawfully subject its citizens to military rule in time of peace.[12] The Court, however, ingeniously avoided the constitutional question involved and dismissed the suit on the ground that it called for a judgment upon a purely political question over which it alleged it could exercise no jurisdiction. Ignoring the fact that it had frequently decided political questions since *Marbury* v. *Madison,* the Court said, speaking through Justice Nelson:

> That these matters, both as stated in the body of the bill, and, in the prayers for relief, call for the judgment of the Court upon political questions, and, upon rights, not of persons or property, but of political character, will hardly be denied. For the rights for the protection of which our authority is invoked, are the rights of sovereignty, of politi-

cal jurisdiction, of government, of corporate existence as a State, with all its constitutional powers and privileges. No case of private property infringed, or in danger of actual or threatened infringement, is presented by the bill, for the judgment of the Court.

This decision did not end the anxiety of the Reconstructionists, for shortly after it was rendered there arose a new and more vital test of the constitutionality of these acts. The military commission in Mississippi, functioning by virtue of the Reconstruction Laws, had arrested a Southern editor, McCardle by name, and held him for military trial. McCardle, having failed in his effort to obtain a writ of *habeas corpus* from the Federal Circuit Court, appealed forthwith to the Supreme Court of the United States. On this appeal, the facts squared perfectly with the formula laid down by the Court in *Georgia* v. *Stanton,* for this time the Court was not asked to render judgment on a "political question", but on the personal rights of Mr. McCardle, who apparently had been deprived of his constitutional right of trial by jury. Naturally, the validity of McCardle's arrest and military trial depended upon the validity of the legislation impugned. The attorney general of the United States refused to argue the case for the government because, as he said to the Court, he had advised the President that the Reconstruction Acts were unconstitutional. The Court having assumed jurisdiction, despite its decision in *Stanton* v. *Georgia,* the case was argued by special counsel for the government; and while speculation was rife as to whether the justices would undertake to block a determined congressional policy supported by a determined public opinion, Congress intervened and averted a judicial collision with the popular will by passing a law over the President's veto which deprived the Supreme Court of its appellate jurisdiction in *habeas corpus* proceedings and prohibited the exercise of any such jurisdiction on appeals which had been or might be taken.[13] The Court bowed to this declaration of legislative authority and thus what might have become a *cause célèbre* went down in the records as a judicial abortion. In dismissing the suit, the chief justice sustained the power of Congress to modify the Court's appellate jurisdiction in the following terms:

> It is quite true . . . that the jurisdiction of this Court is not derived from Acts of Congress. It is, strictly speaking, conferred by the Constitution. But it is conferred "with such exceptions and under such regulations as Congress shall make" . . . We are not at liberty to inquire into the motives of the legislature. . . . It is quite clear, therefore, that this Court cannot proceed to pronounce judgment in this case, for it has no longer jurisdiction of the appeal; and judicial duty is not less fitly performed by declining ungranted jurisdiction than in exercising firmly that which the Constitution and the laws confer.[14]

Through these congressional maneuvers, and the Supreme Court's willingness to bend in order not to break, a legal test of the Reconstruction Acts was avoided until, their objective having been attained, such a test could no longer serve any useful purpose.

The militancy of the Reconstruction Congress, however, represented merely the most virulent aspect of the profound change which the outcome of the Civil War brought about in American politics. This change, which can be adequately described as the triumph of nationalism, was reflected in the course of judicial statecraft quite as clearly as the more obvious pressures of the radical majority in Congress. The victory of the North brought to an end the long debate concerning the origin of the Constitution and the nature of the Union. The compact theory and its corollaries—state sovereignty and the right of secession—lost their validity after the *de facto* decision, reached at Appomattox, that no state could withdraw from the Union. This historical fact received judicial recognition in Chief Justice Chase's opinion in *Texas* v. *White*,[15] which substantially reiterated Webster's doctrine of the indissolubility of the Union in its most uncompromising form. Said the chief justice:

> The Constitution, in all its provisions, looks to an indestructible Union, composed of indestructible states. When, therefore, Texas became one of the United States, she entered into an indissoluble relation. All the obligations of perpetual union, and all the guarantees of republican government in the Union, attached at once to the State. The act which consummated her admission into the Union was something more than a compact; it was the incorporation of a new member into the political body. And it was final. The union between Texas and the other States was as complete, as perpetual and as indissoluble as the union between the original States. There was no place for reconsideration, or revocation, except through revolution, or through the consent of the States. Considered, therefore, as a transaction under the Constitution, the ordinance of secession, adopted by the

[ 81 ]

Convention and ratified by a majority of the citizens of
Texas, and all the acts of her legislature intended to give
effect to that ordinance, were absolutely null.

While the economic and social forces that make for
nationalism were gathering momentum, the Supreme
Court was orienting itself to the new trend. The states'
police power, whose scope had been broadened during
Taney's chief-justiceship, was curtailed; the jurisdiction
of state courts was clipped and the taxing power of
the states was restricted. In short, Marshall's judicial
philosophy was being resuscitated in a new and ampler
setting.[16]

Yet when the validity of the Legal Tender Acts
passed during the Civil War was challenged, the Court
was confronted with a case which involved a difficult
choice between the dominant Marshallian doctrines:
broad construction of the Constitution for the benefit
of national power, and the sanctity of contracts. In
*Hepburn* v. *Griswold*[17] the Supreme Court was called
upon, for the first time in American history, to decide
whether the federal government possessed the power
to issue paper currency inconvertible into gold or silver
and to make such fiat money legal tender for the payment of debts. On this point the Constitution is silent.
It is noteworthy, however, that while it expressly denies
to the states the power to "make anything but gold and
silver coin a tender in payment of debts", no such prohibition is imposed upon the national government. The
question of vesting the latter with the power to issue
inconvertible paper money was discussed in the Constitutional Convention, but the framers apparently

preferred to leave the matter for future exigencies to decide and made no express provision. In the light of this background, the Court, in deciding the validity of the Legal Tender Acts, was afforded unusual judicial latitude.

The Court, after withholding judgment for over two years, handed down on February 7, 1870, a four-to-three decision invalidating the Legal Tender Acts so far as they applied to contracts made before their passage. The majority opinion was read by the chief justice, who, as secretary of the treasury, had approved the acts. It was thus, in a sense, an appeal from the governmental and political to the judicial temper, and from wartime to peacetime mentality.[18] It held that the right to issue inconvertible paper currency could not be properly deduced from the war powers, that the acts stretched the doctrine of "implied powers" beyond reasonable limits, and that they impaired the obligation of contracts.

Public anxiety, which had been intense during the long pendency of the case, was heightened after the decision, especially as it was realized that the chief justice's argument was equally applicable to debts contracted after the passage of the acts. The Court's action was heartily approved by the bankers and the creditor classes, whose interest it was to receive payments in specie and who naturally contended that the invalidation of the acts, by upholding the sanctity of contracts, would restore confidence in the dollar and contribute to business stability. Opposite these interests stood the agrarian classes, mortgagors, municipalities with heavy bonded indebtedness, and debtors in general, who were determined to preserve the obvious advantages of the greenback law and predicted that the decision would precipitate a drastic economic dislocation to the detriment of the productive majority of the nation. The vigorous support of this thesis by a majority of Congress and a large section of the Press placed the Supreme Court in the unenviable position of appearing to ignore and to resist the popular will. Because reconsideration of the issue had become politically imperative, it was assumed that the appointment of two additional justices by President Grant, immediately following the decision in *Hepburn* v. *Griswold,* was designed to "pack" the Court.[19] While this charge is not borne out by the evidence, the fact remains that the new associate justices, William Strong of Pennsylvania and Joseph P. Bradley of New Jersey, being strong exponents of national power, changed the complexion of the Court and made possible revision of its decision in accordance with the prevailing public sentiment.

With the Court thus reconstituted, the government moved for a rehearing on all questions involved under the Legal Tender Acts. The rehearing was directed by a vote of five-to-four, Justices Strong and Bradley voting with the previous minority of three to make the new majority of five. The entire issue having been reopened, the decision in the *Hepburn Case* was reversed in *Knox* v. *Lee,*[20] which sweepingly sustained the validity of legal tenders as applied to all transactions, whether entered into before or after the passage of the acts. The majority opinion frankly acknowledged, in the following significant passage, that the Court cannot disregard economic realities.

It would be difficult to overestimate the consequences which must follow our decision. They will affect the entire business of the Country and take hold of the possible continued existence of the Government. If it be held by this Court that Congress has no constitutional power, under any circumstances, or in any emergency, to make treasury notes a legal tender for the payment of all debts (a power confessedly possessed by every independent sovereignty other than the United States), the Government is without those means of self-preservation which, all must admit, may in certain contingencies, become indispensable, even if they were not when the Acts of Congress now called in question were enacted. It is also clear that if we hold the Acts invalid as applicable to debts incurred, or transactions which have taken place since their enactment, our decision must cause, throughout the Country, great business derangement, widespread distress, and the rankest injustice. . . . Men have bought and sold, borrowed and lent, and assumed every variety of obligations contemplating that payment might be made with such notes. Indeed, legal tender treasury notes have become the universal measure of values. If now, by our decision, it be established that these debts and obligations can be discharged only by gold coin; if contrary to the expectation of all parties to these contracts, legal tender notes are rendered unavailable, the Government has become an instrument of the grossest injustice; all debtors are loaded with an obligation it was never contemplated they should assume; a large percentage is added to every debt, and such must become the demand for gold to satisfy contracts, that ruinous sacrifices, general distress, and bankruptcy may be expected. These consequences are too obvious to admit of question.

This statement neatly disposes of the oft-repeated dictum that the Court ignores consequences and concerns itself solely with constitutional powers and limitations. Under normal conditions the judicial mind is —and should be—more objective than the political mind. But when judges are confronted with cases whose repercussions radiate far beyond the immediate litigants; when the path of absolute judicial objectivity leads to disastrously impolitic decisions; when, in short, the members of the Court are called upon to be legislators as well as judges, it is impossible—as it would be undesirable—for their verdict not to be influenced both by their personal views on the issues at stake and by concern for the consequences.

There has been no greater crisis in American history than the Civil War and the years of Reconstruction which followed it. The responsibility of meeting this crisis rested upon the political branches of the government, and the policies they pursued to this end were fully approved by the people. Constitutional guarantees and limitations were put to a severe strain, yet throughout the crisis the Court was powerless to stem the tide of a determined political will. On the whole, it followed the irresistible trend of the day, adapting the Constitution to an inevitable situation with a remarkable demonstration of its flexibility. On the few occasions when the Court resisted or vacillated, either Congress intervened to curtail its power, as in *Ex parte McCardle,* or it fell back into line of its own volition, as in *Knox* v. *Lee.*

This, after all, is as it should be. For the Supreme Court cannot conduct a war or meet a national crisis. Such emergencies demand emergency government. And when the Court attempts to impede the action of emergency government backed by strong popular support, it invariably precipitates another crisis, and in the ultimate result the Court's prestige is weakened and its power jeopardized. Mindful of this, the Court has been, as a rule, loath to come to grips with the political authority. For it knows that in case of conflict the political authority controls all the weapons that determine the decision. It makes and executes the laws; it controls the purse; it may increase or decrease the number of judges; it may curtail or modify the jurisdiction of the Court, and, finally, it may resort to the most potent of all weapons, the appeal to public support. When, therefore, Congress, the President and the people are united and determined upon a policy, judicial review cannot permanently frustrate it, and the popular will is bound ultimately to prevail.

On the other hand, when the worst of the emergency is over and the unanimity induced by common objectives and emotions is dissipated, the Supreme Court performs a most useful function by accelerating the return to constitutional government. The victory of the North killed state sovereignty. But before the end of the Reconstruction Era the Supreme Court showed, by its decision in the *Slaughterhouse Cases*,[21] that it was determined, despite the dominant nationalistic trend of the times, to save states' rights and to maintain the basic safeguards of the federal system.

CHAPTER VI

# Liberty, Property and Due Process of Law

THE DENIAL of the right of secession by the unanswerable argument of superior force put an end to the claim that the American states were full-fledged and independent sovereignties. Vindicated by victory, Marshall's and Webster's doctrine of nationalism was, as we have seen, explicitly recognized by the Supreme Court in *Texas* v. *White* and was proclaimed even more emphatically two years later in *Knox* v. *Lee*. "The Constitution of the United States," said Justice Bradley, "established a government, and not a league, compact or partnership. It was constituted by the people. It is called a government. . . . As a government it was invested with all the attributes of sovereignty. . . . The doctrine so long contended for, that the Federal Union was a mere compact of states, and that the states, if they chose, might annul or disregard the acts of the national legislature, or might secede from the Union at their pleasure, and that the general government had no power to coerce them into submission to the Constitution, should be regarded as definitely and forever overthrown. This has been finally effected by the na-

[ 88 ]

tional power, as it had often been before, by over-whelming argument." This was more than the opinion of a nationalist jurist. It was the verdict of history which denied the paradox that the parts were equally sovereign with the whole and affirmed the sovereignty —one, indivisible and supreme—of the American nation.

But the triumph of nationalism raised a new and grave issue. Just as before and during the Civil War the unity of the nation was threatened by the distortion of states' rights into the separatist doctrine of state sovereignty, so during the Reconstruction Era it was the peculiar character of American unity—its federalism—that was in jeopardy as a result of the defeat of separatism. Was the mighty surge of the forces that were unleashed by the victory of the Union cause to sweep away the constitutional barriers to national power? Was states' rights to be also submerged by the tidal wave that destroyed state sovereignty—its illegitimate offspring? Or would the Supreme Court reassert itself as the custodian of the Constitution, call a halt, and, by using states' rights as a rule of constitutional law, save the federal system from extinction?

There was no doubt as to where the majority of Congress stood on this issue. The laws passed over President Johnson's veto were primarily aimed, of course, at the rebel South. But whatever their immediate object —whether they were designed as punitive measures, as a cloak for the predatory schemes of carpetbagger politicians, or as a protection of the freedmen against their former masters—they tended to restrict the autonomy of the states and to expand correspondingly the federal government's authority over them. For while the Southern states were the immediate target of these laws, their underlying principles were applicable to all other states as well.

This was especially the case with the Civil Rights Bill of 1866, which made the federal government the guardian of rights inherent in state citizenship. It was equally true of the Fourteenth Amendment, which was primarily designed to give the principle of the Civil Rights Bill greater security and permanence by lodging it in the Constitution. The pith of the amendment lies in the second sentence of Section 1 : "No State shall make or enforce any law which shall abridge the privileges or immunities of citizens of the United States; nor shall any State deprive any person of life, liberty, or property, without due process of law, nor deny to any person within its jurisdiction the equal protection of the laws."[1]

The primary purpose of the Fourteenth Amendment was to place the newly enfranchised Negroes under the aegis of the federal government in order to prevent the states from replacing the positive disabilities of slavery with a new status of bondage based upon denial of the rights of citizenship. But in order to achieve this purpose, the amendment had to authorize the intrusion of the federal government into a large and hitherto jealously guarded part of the domain that had been reserved to the states. It is generally agreed that this extension of national power into a field that had been untouched even by Marshall was just as much the intent of the sponsors of the amendment as the protection of the colored freedmen. "They desired to

[ 90 ]

nationalize all civil rights; to make the Federal power supreme; and to bring the private life of every citizen directly under the eye of Congress."² Indeed, according to Senator Roscoe Conkling of New York, they took an even longer view of the possible uses of their handiwork. Remembering, no doubt, the expansion of the state police power under Taney and visualizing the tremendous upsurge of business enterprise which was to follow the Civil War, they conceived the amendment as a shield for corporations against state legislatures. Thus the elevation of the Negro to the status of citizenship was the occasion—and the excuse —for a fundamental change which placed not only civil rights but vested interests as well under the protection of the Constitution. This change is, in a sense, a gauge of the progress of American nationalism since the founding of the Republic. The first ten amendments, it will be remembered, were considered so vital that ratification of the Constitution by the original thirteen states was virtually conditioned upon their adoption. Now these first ten amendments—the so-called Bill of Rights—were restraints only upon the federal government. Their plain intent was to enjoin national power from encroaching upon the civil liberties of the people and the rights reserved to the several states. The intent of the Fourteenth Amendment was diametrically opposite. It sought to limit the states in the very same field of civil rights wherein the states had originally sought to limit the national government. "By the Constitution as it stood before the war," said Justice Swayne, "ample protection was given against oppression by the Union, but little was given against wrong and oppression by the states. That want was intended to be supplied by this Amendment."³

Nevertheless, the Supreme Court refused to view states' rights through the reducing lenses of the Fourteenth Amendment, despite the unmistakable intent of its framers. And this pronounced deviation of judicial statesmanship from the nationalism of the Civil War and Reconstruction marked both the passing of the crisis and the emergence of new and urgent problems, toward the settlement of which the constitutional concept of states' rights was to prove a serviceable instrument. Among the rights reserved to the states Chief Justice Taney had invoked and assiduously expanded the so-called police power. His aim was to establish constitutional warrant for legislation by the states designed to promote the social welfare of their citizens, even though such legislation encroached upon liberty and the vested rights of property. The Fourteenth Amendment, by conferring dual citizenship, was deliberately framed to overthrow the most historic—and the most destructive—of Taney's decisions. Was the constructive part of his work also to be thrown into the discard by a broad construction of the same amendment? At the time of its enactment it was expected by its sponsors that the Supreme Court would regard it as a mandate to restrict the unfettered use of the police power and to prevent the states from indulging in social reform at the expense of liberty and private property. But this expectation was not fulfilled. In the *Slaughterhouse Cases*,⁴ the first judicial test of the amendment, the Court subjected its "privileges and immunities" clause to the strictest possible construction in order to uphold the police power of the state of Louisiana. The majority opinion, delivered by Justice Miller, after establishing that the granting of a monopoly is well within the power of a state legislature, stressed the distinction between state and United States citizenship, insisted that the language of the Fourteenth Amendment prohibits state legislation which tends to abridge the privileges and immunities pertaining solely to *national* citizenship, contended that "the privileges and immunities relied on in the argument [of the plaintiffs] are those which belong to citizens of the States as such", and concluded that the Louisiana statute did not violate the Fourteenth Amendment because the latter was not intended "to bring within the power of Congress the entire domain of civil rights heretofore belonging exclusively to the States."

The state police power, having thus been rescued from the long arm of the "privileges and immunities" clause, was reaffirmed four years later by the Court's decision in *Munn* v. *Illinois,*[5] which applied equally strict construction to the "due process" clause. The litigation involved an Illinois statute enacted in 1871 for the regulation of grain elevators—the first noteworthy effort in the United States to fix monopoly prices by legislation. The legislature declared this business to be vested with a public interest and proceeded, on that theory, to fix the maximum rates which it could charge. The grain-elevator proprietors contended that the state legislature could exercise no such prerogative over their private property; that the imposition of arbitrary and unreasonable rates was tantamount to confiscation, and that they were, therefore, deprived of their prop-

[ 93 ]

erty without due process of law. The Court was confronted with three correlated questions: May the state legislature fix prices to be charged by a business in the nature of monopoly? If so, must these prices be reasonable, and, if they must be reasonable, who shall be the judge of reasonableness, the Legislature or the Court? The decision, which was handed down by Chief Justice Waite,[6] affirmed that "property does become clothed with a public interest when used in a manner to make it of public consequence, and affect the community at large", sustained the Illinois Legislature on the common-law principle that property clothed with a public interest may be controlled by the public for the common good, and held that "this statute simply extends the law so as to meet this new development of commercial progress." Having conceded to the legislatures the power over rates and prices, the Court asserted it could afford no protection against the possible abuse of such power. "For protection against abuses by legislatures," said the chief justice, "the people must resort to the polls, not to the courts." In brief, *Munn* v. *Illinois* established the doctrine that what constitutes a reasonable charge is not for the Court to decide, but solely for the legislature.[7] The principles laid down in *Munn* v. *Illinois*—broad construction of the state police power, the inapplicability of the "due process" clause to laws based on that power, and refusal to supplant the legislature's judgment concerning the wisdom of a given statute—were subsequently invoked by the Supreme Court in upholding sumptuary legislation enacted by the states.

In *Mugler* v. *Kansas*[8] the Court was asked to invalidate a Kansas prohibition statute which failed to compensate liquor manufacturers for the attendant depreciation in the value of their properties. The statute was upheld as a valid exercise of the police power, although it restrained the citizen's right to eat and drink at his own discretion, and it was conceded that large property values were destroyed by the prohibitory enactment. Justice Harlan, speaking for the Court, after remarking that the "power to determine such questions so as to bind all, must exist somewhere", and that "under our system that power is lodged with the legislative branch of the government", proceeded to limit the scope of judicial interpretation in the following terms:

> If, therefore, a state deems absolute prohibition . . . to be necessary to the peace and security of society, the courts cannot, without usurping legislative functions, override the will of the people as thus expressed by their chosen representatives. They have nothing to do with the mere policy or legislation . . . it is not for the courts, upon their views as to what is best and safest for the community, to disregard the legislative determination of that question. . . . This conclusion is unavoidable, unless the Fourteenth Amendment of the Constitution takes from the states of the Union those powers of police that were reserved at the time the original Constitution was adopted. But this Court has declared, upon full consideration, that the Fourteenth Amendment had no such effect. . . . A prohibition simply upon the use of property for purposes that are declared, by valid legislation, to be injurious to the health, morals or safety of the community, cannot in any just sense be deemed a taking or an appropriation of property for the public benefit.

All these decisions had one constitutional aim, however varied may have been their political, economic or social consequences. Whether the Court refused to interfere with a monopoly wrested from a corrupt state legislature, or allowed the Southern states wide legislative latitude with respect to the social status of their Negro population,[9] or granted the right of a state to regulate business enterprises clothed with a public interest, or extended the police power into the sumptuary field, it narrowed in every instance the scope of the Fourteenth Amendment and prevented it from being used to whittle down states' rights and to alter the character of the American system. The reaffirmation of Taney's doctrine and the holding "with a steady and an even hand the balance between State and Federal power"[10] seemed to the Court all the more imperative because the Marshallian position had been tremendously strengthened by the three post-Civil War amendments. The opinion might, therefore, be ventured that the motivation of the Court in these cases was as purely judicial as it is possible for any constitutional decision to be. But insofar as these decisions were influenced by the prevailing public sentiment, they reflected the subsidence of the passions of the Reconstruction period, the marked appeasement effected during the administration of President Hayes, and the determination of the bulk of the American people to liquidate the legacy of the past and to face the problems of a new era.

It was with one of the most pressing of these problems that the Court dealt in *Munn* v. *Illinois;* and its decision, precisely because it denied to vested interests the protection of the "due process" clause, may be said to have given effect to what was, at the time, a strong and clamorous popular will. Big business, during its early stages of expansion, was devoid of any sense of public duty. Avid for wealth and power, it was impervious to all appeals for fair play and increasingly contemptuous of political authority. Railroads, in particular, discriminated between shippers and localities and, by sanctioning unequal rates, special privileges and secret rebates, assumed the power to ruin at will any person or business depending on their facilities. This was a power not even to be assumed by government. Yet the privately owned common carriers, with a monopoly on the means of transportation and with their charters protected against repeal by the "contract" clause, possessed and exercised it with impunity. The reaction of their immediate victims found an outlet in the so-called Granger movement, which enabled the farmers of the predominantly agricultural states to capture the state legislatures and to enact regulatory legislation. The refusal of the Supreme Court, in *Munn v. Illinois,* to invalidate this legislation, while it was viewed with alarm by the investors in corporate securities, reflected a widespread determination not to allow irresponsible monopolies to exercise the powers of a supergovernment. "The Court feels the touch of public opinion," was Lord Bryce's conclusion from *Munn v. Illinois* and the other *Granger Cases.* These decisions, he pointed out, "evidently represent a different view of the sacredness of private rights and of the powers of a Legislature, from that entertained by Chief Justice Marshall and his contemporaries. They

[ 97 ]

reveal that current of opinion, which now runs strongly in America, against what are called monopolies and the powers of incorporated companies."[11]

But that current of opinion was soon changed by the cavalcade of economic forces. Great Civil War fortunes harnessed to the exploitation of the nation's resources produced a cyclopean movement which in time swept everything before it. Within scarcely two decades after *Munn* v. *Illinois* this movement received an acceleration that made it politically irresistible. It was the age of empire builders, and the destinies of the American people passed from legislators and politicians to industrial geniuses intent on demonstrating the validity of the law of natural selection. Availing themselves of the cumulative and many-sided advances of technology, and aided by the concessions of a generous government, these men, within a single generation, transformed the nation's bountiful resources into private fortunes of incalculable magnitude. Vast wealth begot vast power—power in the sovereign sense— power over political parties, over public opinion, over social trends and over education. Indeed, the Rockefellers and the Goulds, the Harrimans and the Hills had become the real source of government in the United States. Commenting on the impact of one of these imperial enterprises on American politics, Professor Beard says: "Public policies, lawmaking, and judicial reasoning become unintelligible except in relation to the interests of oil producers, shippers and refiners."[12] What was true of the oil producers was equally true of the railway magnates, the mining interests, the meat packers, the steel manufacturers and the financiers who were the sponsors of these industries.

With the legislators sharing the usufruct and politicians receiving their due emoluments; and with an ever larger public being drawn into the corporate organization of business enterprise, a decided change in public sentiment was inevitable. Just as planter aristocracy, based on slavery, was once extolled as a noble social order, so now industrialism based on laissez faire was hailed as the acme of economic and social evolution. This shift in the national psychology endowed private property with even greater sanctity than it enjoyed in the heyday of Marshall. There were, to be sure, on the political landscape large segments of dissent and protest whose size varied with the fluctuations of the business cycle. But thanks to the pervasiveness of finance capitalism and the suggestibility of its would-be beneficiaries, the captains of industry and finance could now mobilize against the successive outbreaks of agrarian populism even larger mass support of economic orthodoxy; while an incipient labor movement, whose violence was the measure of its impotence, was soon drawn into the nexus of capitalist enterprise and lulled into contentment by the promise of a "full dinner pail."

It was not long before this prevailing sentiment percolated to the Judiciary. Already in *Mugler* v. *Kansas,* though the Court sustained the state police power, it set limits to its exercise and, significantly enough, made itself the judge of those limits. "If," said the Court, ". . . a statute purporting to have been enacted to protect the public health, the public morals, or the public safety, has no real or substantial relation to those

[ 99 ]

objects, or is a palpable invasion of rights secured by the fundamental law, it is the duty of the Courts to so adjudge and thereby give effect to the Constitution." But it was in a case similar to *Munn* v. *Illinois* that the new trend of judicial opinion was decisively disclosed. By 1890 the transportation industry had experienced a phenomenal growth. Great trunk lines stretched across vast areas of the continent, and from any given point the Atlantic or the Pacific was accessible by rail. At that date the capital represented by railroads aggregated ten billion dollars, or one sixth of the then total national wealth. Newly developed municipalities borrowed to their limit to procure rail connections, and the people's savings poured into railroad securities at an unprecedented pace. America had become a railroad-minded nation, and this state of mind was reflected in a changed judicial attitude toward railroad rates and regulation. The shipper's interest was now relegated to second place as the Supreme Court became solicitous of the stockholders' investment. The railroads must earn a fair return on their invested capital; their property must not be confiscated through improper legislative exactions. But *Munn* v. *Illinois* had laid down the doctrine that "for protection against abuses by legislatures, the people must resort to the polls, not to the Courts." If the Court, then, was to be the protector of invested capital, *Munn* v. *Illinois* had to be reversed, and reversed it was, to all intents and purposes, in the famous *Minnesota Rate Case*.[13]

The Minnesota Legislature in 1887 created a commission with power to establish its own rates whenever, according to its findings, unequal or unreasonable rates were charged by the railroads. The findings of the commission were to be final and conclusive. The commission found that the rate on milk charged by the Chicago, Milwaukee and St. Paul Railroad was excessive and ordered a reduction. The railroad contended that the commission's rate was too low, hence confiscatory, and hence unconstitutional. The contention was sustained. By a divided Court the Minnesota statute was held unconstitutional as depriving the company of its property without due process of law under the Fourteenth Amendment. By this decision the Court repudiated its previous position that the reasonableness of rates was solely for the legislature to decide and ruled that reasonableness was a matter for ultimate judicial determination. This was emphasized in the dissenting opinion of Justice Bradley (concurred in by Justices Lamar and Gray), of which the following is a most illuminating passage:

> I cannot agree to the decision of the court in this case. It practically overrules *Munn* v. *Illinois*, and the several railroad cases that were decided at the same time. The governing principle of those cases was that the regulation and settlement of the fares of railroads and other public accommodations is a legislative prerogative, and not a judicial one. This is a principle which I regard as of great importance. . . . But it is said that all charges should be reasonable, and that none but reasonable charges can be exacted; and it is urged that what is a reasonable charge is a judicial question. On the contrary it is pre-eminently a legislative one, involving considerations of policy as well as of remuneration; and is usually determined by the legislature, by fixing a maximum of charges in the charter of the company, or afterwards, if its hands are not tied by contract. . . . By

the decision now made we declare, in effect, that the judiciary, and not the legislature, is the final arbiter in the regulation of fares and freights of railroads and the charges of other public accommodations. It is an assumption of authority on the part of the judiciary which, it seems to me, with all due deference to the judgment of my brethren, it has no right to make.

Thus the doctrine of *Munn* v. *Illinois* was overturned by the *Minnesota Rate Case,* and states' rights, which had until then weathered the attack of the Fourteenth Amendment, suffered a serious setback. The Supreme Court, having apparently caught up with the economic forces which were transforming the nation and the dominant political will that ministered to them, abandoned a constitutional concept which it had used as a check against the rampant nationalism of the Reconstruction Era. It was demonstrated once more that a principle of law can be put to varied uses and that constitutional interpretation cannot be disassociated from the economic and political realities of a given period of history.

By the doctrine laid down in the *Minnesota Rate Case* the Court gave substantive value to the "due process" clause. In the earlier cases under the Fourteenth Amendment "due process" was treated in its organic sense, as a term applicable to legal procedure.[14] It meant fair trial pursuant to the rules of the common law, or law administered in accordance with the sanctions of settled usage, or, according to Chancellor Kent, simply "judicial process." But now, with the shift in the Court's position, the meaning of "due process" is extended beyond mere judicial procedure. By the purport of the Minnesota decision all rate-fixing legislation which in the judgment of the Court is unreasonable becomes, by that token, a deprivation of property without due process of law. In other words, whenever the Court, by its own standard of thinking, concludes that established rates are too low to permit a fair return on "the fair value"[15] of the property, it will declare them confiscatory, or a taking of property without due process of law, even though the procedure, or process by which the rates were legislatively determined, was due and proper and in accordance with wise public policy. Thus, by judicial interpretation, "due process" was engrafted on the substantive law of the Constitution. Instead of being only the means of protecting persons from harsh or improper procedure, it became a muniment of property and a haven for the corporate enterprise. As Justice Matthews declared, due process "must be held to guarantee not particular forms of procedure, but the very substance of individual rights to life, liberty and property."[16] This was precisely the intention of Roscoe Conkling and those framers of the Fourteenth Amendment whose motives were primarily economic.

The consequences of this shift in the Court's position were felt immediately in the field of state control over economic enterprise. The police power, as construed by Taney and redefined in the *Slaughterhouse Cases* and *Munn* v. *Illinois,* had given the states wide scope for regulatory legislation and for economic and social reform. Hence, this power was repugnant to the tenets of laissez faire, and the judicial mind soon discovered that it was violative of liberty and property. Because state legislation was hostile to the rights of incorporated wealth, states' rights was pointed at as the enemy, just as in later years, when regulation was attempted on a federal scale, the encroachments of national power were viewed as a menace to states' rights. Though, for instance, it is demonstrably true that long hours in certain trades are especially injurious to the workers' health, state statutes regulating hours of labor in these trades were tested primarily by their effect on the property of the employers rather than, as heretofore, by their effect on the health of the employees. In *Lochner v. New York*[17] the Supreme Court, by a five-to-four decision, held that a New York statute limiting employment in bakeries to ten hours a day was an "unreasonable," "unnecessary," "arbitrary," "illegal" and "meddlesome interference with the rights of the individual."[18] "It must, of course, be conceded," said Justice Peckham, speaking for the Court, "that there is a limit to the valid exercise of the police power. . . . Otherwise the Fourteenth Amendment would have no efficacy and the legislatures of the States would have unbounded power, and it would be enough to say that any piece of legislation was enacted to conserve the morals, the health or the safety of the people; such legislation would be valid, no matter how absolutely without foundation the claim might be. The claim of the police power would be a mere pretext—become another and delusive name for the supreme sovereignty of the State to be exercised free from constitutional restraint."

Superficially, Justice Peckham did not reject Justice Harlan's principle (in *Mugler* v. *Kansas*) that "it is not for the courts, upon their views as to what is best and safest for the community, to disregard the legislative determination of that question." He protested that there was no question "of substituting the judgment of the Court for that of the legislature. If the act be within the power of the state, it is valid, although the judgment of the Court might be totally opposed to the enactment of such a law. But the question would still remain: Is it within the police power of the state? And that question must be answered by the Court." Again, this dictum was in apparent agreement with the significant limitation of the police power in *Mugler* v. *Kansas,* which reserved to the Court the right to "adjudge" whether "a statute purporting to have been enacted to protect the public health . . . is a palpable invasion of rights secured by the fundamental law."[19] But in order to adjudge whether the New York statute had exceeded the police power of the state, the majority opinion had to decide on the comparative healthfulness of work in bakeries; and it was after a lengthy disquisition on the subject that it reached the conclusion: "We do not believe in the soundness of the views which uphold this law. On the contrary we think that such a law as this, although passed in the assumed exercise of the police power, and as relating to the public health, or the health of the employees named, is not within that power, and is invalid." In other words, the Court could not decide the presumably constitutional question whether the statute was within the state police power without doing precisely what it had denied that it intended to do—substituting its own judgment for that of the legislature "as to what is best and safest for the community." It was by this assumption of legislative prerogative, despite its protestations to the contrary, that Justice Peckham's majority opinion invalidated the act as a "meddlesome" interference with the rights of the individual—"liberty of contract as well as of person"—which are protected by the Constitution.

How then is this conundrum to be resolved? Can the Supreme Court decide the fate of a given law on purely constitutional grounds, without substituting its opinion and will for those of the legislature? Is judicial review possible without judicial supremacy? The question was answered as well as it can be answered in the brief but pregnant dissenting opinion of Justice Holmes, which is herewith quoted extensively, with its most telling passages italicized:

> This case is decided upon an economic theory which a large part of the Country does not entertain. If it were a question whether I agreed with that theory, I should desire to study it further and long before making up my mind. *But I do not conceive that to be my duty, because I strongly believe that my agreement or disagreement has nothing to do with the right of a majority to embody their opinions in law.* It is settled by various decisions of this court that state constitutions and state laws may regulate life in many ways which we as legislators might think as injudicious or if you like as tyrannical as this, and which equally with this interfere with the liberty to contract. Sunday laws and usury laws are ancient examples. A more modern one is the prohibition of lotteries. The liberty of the citizen to do as he likes so long as he does not interfere with the liberty of others to do the same, which has been a shibboleth for some well known writers, is interfered with by school laws, by the Post Office, by every state or municipal institution which takes his money

for purposes thought desirable, whether he likes it or not. The Fourteenth Amendment does not enact Mr. Herbert Spencer's Social Statics. . . . But a Constitution is not intended to embody a particular economic theory, whether of paternalism and the organic relation of the citizen to the State or of *laissez faire*. It is made for people of fundamentally differing views, *and the accident of our finding certain opinions natural and familiar or novel and even shocking ought not to conclude our judgment upon the question whether statutes embodying them conflict with the Constitution of the United States.*

General propositions do not decide concrete cases. The decision will depend on a judgment or intuition more subtle than any particular major premise. But I think that the proposition just stated, if it is accepted, will carry us far toward the end. Every opinion tends to become a law. *I think that the word liberty in the Fourteenth Amendment is perverted when it is held to prevent the natural outcome of a dominant opinion, unless it can be said that a rational and fair man necessarily would admit that the statute proposed would infringe fundamental principles as they have been understood by the traditions of our people and our law.* It does not need research to show that no such sweeping condemnation can be passed upon the statute before us. A reasonable man might think it a proper measure on the score of health. Men whom I certainly would not pronounce unreasonable would uphold it as a first instalment of a general regulation of the hours of work. Whether in the latter aspect it would be open to the charge of inequality I think it unnecessary to discuss.

A comparison of the *Slaughterhouse Cases, Munn* v. *Illinois* and *Mugler* v. *Kansas* with the *Minnesota Rate Case* and the *Lochner Case* will serve to illustrate the mutability of the words "liberty" and "property." The earlier decisions on the "due process" clause of the Fourteenth Amendment, remarked Justice Holmes, "went no farther than an unpretentious assertion of the liberty to follow the ordinary callings. Later that innocuous generality was expanded into the dogma, Liberty of Contract."[20] The judicial reactions to legislative restrictions on liberty and property were largely determined by the economic environment in which the Court at the time functioned.[21] In 1888 it was not a violation of "due process" for the Pennsylvania Legislature to prohibit the manufacture, sale, or possession for sale of oleomargarine, and a statute to that effect was sustained.[22] In 1924, however, "due process" was held to be violated when the Nebraska Legislature prescribed the weights of loaves of bread, and a statute to that effect was declared repugnant to the Constitution.[23] While during the first two decades of the twentieth century the judicial trend was, on the whole, restrictive of legislative interference with liberty and property, the Court did not remain impervious to the fluctuations of public sentiment. Western progressivism, muckraking, the Bull-Moose movement, Woodrow Wilson's "New Freedom", the development of a peculiarly American pragmatic approach to sociology, and the growth of a more critical spirit in legal teaching left their impress not only on state and federal statute books and on the Constitution[24] but also, of necessity, on the decisions of the Supreme Court. Hence, the course of judicial statesmanship during this period was not uniform nor were its guiding principles very clear. Thus, despite *Lochner* v. *New York,* the Court three years later upheld an analogous exercise of the police power in an Oregon statute which fixed a maximum ten-hour day for women working in laundries and factories.[25] A much more comprehensive law than the one which had been invalidated by *Lochner* v. *New York*—another Oregon statute establishing a uniform ten-hour working day in mills and factories—was also upheld in 1917.[26] Nor did the Court allow "freedom of contract" to obstruct employers' liability legislation by New York and other states.[27] Yet in 1923 a law passed by Congress fixing minimum wages for women and children in the District of Columbia was invalidated despite the Court's affirmative decision on the Oregon statute, which, in the opinion of Chief Justice Taft, had overruled the *Lochner Case "sub silentio"!*[28]

The denial of the right of Congress to enact a minimum wage for women and children in the District of Columbia was not an isolated case. The trend of judicial decisions in the nineteen-twenties was, on the whole, conservative, and this judicial conservatism was not unrelated to the political standpatism which followed the exhaustion of progressivism and was encouraged by the illusory prosperity of the "New Era." The concept of liberty and property was thus inflated to about the same unwarranted level as the industrial securities it was intended to serve.

In defending liberty and property the Court showed a tendency to assume legislative functions, particularly in the field of price-fixing. Here, antithetical interpretations of constitutional law become patent in the Court's effort to shift from one position to another. *Munn* v. *Illinois* had already settled the proposition that the "due process" clause of the Fourteenth Amendment did not deprive a state of its inherent authority to regulate a business which is "clothed with a public interest." This meant that the legislature could fix prices for commodities, services or even labor so long as the business or property regulated was affected with a public interest or devoted to a public use. But the *Munn Case* went much further. It left the legislature free to determine when a business becomes affected with a public interest so as to require regulation for the public good. Not only did the Court concede to the legislature this power, but it removed all restrictions incident to its use. "Of the propriety of legislative interference within the scope of legislative power," said the Court, "the legislature is the exclusive judge." In a similar case[29] decided at the same time, where an Illinois statute fixing maximum railroad rates was sustained, Chief Justice Waite saliently remarked: "Our province is only to determine whether it could be done at all, and under any circumstances. If it could, the legislature must decide for itself, subject to no control from us, whether the common good requires that it should be done."

As time passed, however, the Court began to pare away the broad doctrines of legislative power laid down in *Munn* v. *Illinois*. First, it asserted the right of judicial review of *all* prices which it thought arbitrary or unreasonable.[30] This first step demolished the buttress erected by Chief Justice Waite when he said: "For protection against abuses by legislatures the people must resort to the polls, not to the courts." The second step was still more devastating; it challenged the power of legislatures to determine for themselves what businesses are affected with a public in-

terest. This second step, then, went to the source of
legislative power, and, in fact, usurped it, for the right
to determine what is "clothed with a public interest"
is of the essence of public policy. Without the power to
decide whether property is devoted to a public use or
affected with a public interest, there can be no regulation, no price-fixing. It was by degrees that the Supreme
Court reached this second step, but once the premise
was established, it had to be followed to its natural
conclusion and there meet the test of public opinion, a
test which all judicial doctrines must ultimately meet.

The case of *Tyson & Brother* v. *Banton*[31] may be
cited as the natural conclusion of this second step in the
demolition of legislative authority by the judicial process. The state of New York passed a law forbidding
the resale of any theater ticket at a price in excess of
fifty cents of the price printed on the face of such ticket.
The New York Legislature felt that the people were
mulcted by the ticket racketeers and that the traffic in
the resale of tickets had become so widespread as to be
affected with a public interest and, therefore, should be
regulated. As it was, a bare majority of the justices of
the Supreme Court failed to agree with the views of
the New York Legislature. They held that the price
of admission to theaters not being a matter "affected
with a public interest", the statute in question was an
unconstitutional interference with the ticket owners'
property rights in violation of the Fourteenth Amendment. By this decision the judicial pendulum swung to
the extreme right. The Court had asserted in unequivo-
cal language that it was in no way bound by the legislative declaration that a particular business is vested with

a public interest. In other words, the Court reserved the right to substitute its own judgment of public policy for that of the legislature. Four of the justices refused to accept the anomalous results of the *Tyson Case* and dissented vigorously. The personal dissent of Justice Holmes, however, deserves special note in view of its profound effect on subsequent decisions:

> Coming down to the case before us I think . . . that the notion that a business is clothed with a public interest and has been devoted to the public use is little more than a fiction intended to beautify what is disagreeable to the sufferers. The truth seems to me to be that, subject to compensation when compensation is due, the Legislature may forbid or restrict any business when it has a sufficient force of public opinion behind it. Lotteries were thought useful adjuncts of the State a century or so ago; now they are believed to be immoral and they have been stopped. Wine was thought good for men from the time of the Apostles until recent years. But when public opinion changed it did not need the Eighteenth Amendment, notwithstanding the Fourteenth, to enable a state to say that the business should end. *Mugler* v. *Kansas* 123, U.S. 623. What has happened to Lotteries and Wine might happen to theaters in some moral storm of the future, not because theaters were devoted to a public use, but because people had come to think that way. . . . I am far from saying that I think this particular law a wise and rational provision. That is not my affair. But if the people of the State of New York speaking by their authorized voice say that they want it, I see nothing in the Constitution of the United States to prevent their having their will.

The *Tyson Case* was decided in 1927. By this time the Supreme Court had pretty well defined the classes of business which, in its judgment, were affected with a public interest. Three years before the *Tyson Case* the Court had held that the manufacture of food and clothing and the production of fuel were not sufficiently vested with a public interest to justify compulsory arbitration of wages in these industries.[32] "It has never been supposed, since the adoption of the Constitution," said Chief Justice Taft, "that the business of the butcher, or the baker, the tailor, the wood chopper, the mining operator or the miner was clothed with such a public interest that the price of his product or his wages could be fixed by State regulation." In the same opinion the late chief justice remarked: "The public may suffer from high prices or strikes in many trades, but the expression 'clothed with a public interest', as applied to a business, means more than that the public welfare is affected by continuity or by the price at which a commodity is sold or a service rendered." About the only businesses, then, which could safely be classified as "affected with a public interest" were the railroads and other common carriers, electric power and gas companies, grain elevators and grist mills, innkeepers, and a very few others, such as insurance,[33] which, though not public at their inception, had gradually assumed that status by virtue of the indispensable nature of the services they rendered. The power of state legislatures to regulate rates, prices and wages was, therefore, limited to this comparatively small group of businesses, and even then such regulation had to be "within reason", according to judicial standards. By 1927 the laissez-faire conception of the state had received such complete judicial recognition that, for all practical purposes, industry and commerce, functioning within state boundaries, were placed beyond the pale of compulsory government regulation and, in the name of liberty and property, enjoyed almost unrestricted freedom of action.

The depression which began with the stock-market crash of October 1929, and was accentuated by the collapse of the currency and credit structure of several European countries in 1931, necessitated a reorientation of American economic and fiscal policy. It would be inaccurate to describe the policies which had prevailed during the nineteen-twenties as unmitigated laissez faire. The Hawley-Smoot tariff and the shipping subsidies, for example, represented considerable governmental interference with the free play of economic forces; but it was interference designed, in the main, to help, not to regulate and hinder, economic enterprise, on the theory that under the American system prosperity invariably tended to spread out and seep down to all classes of society and to all parts of the national economy.

But when the breakdown of the spurious prosperity of the twenties showed the woeful inadequacy of this theory, a readjustment of American economic and fiscal policies, under new political leadership, became imperative. The New Deal, though admittedly empirical and unsystematic, was actuated by one guiding principle—wholesale and pervasive governmental interference with all branches of private business in order to reactivate and thus to save the national economy. Whether it "primed the pump" through large-scale government spending, or reduced the private debt structure and took other measures to stop the downward spiral of deflation, or corrected crying abuses in the banking and credit system, or regulated agricultural and industrial production and working conditions, it was attempting to establish, at least for a trial period, a managed economy and to transfer back to government the powers which industry had acquired over the security of the people.

This reorientation of policy, to become effective under the American system, required a readjustment of constitutional values. For the past half century the Supreme Court, despite periodic and more or less important deviations, had nurtured the concepts of liberty and property in order to serve the prevailing economic system. This development, as we have seen, was a normal adjustment of law to environment; of constitutional concepts to the dominant economic realities. But the adaptation of the Constitution to a managed national economy would require new conceptions of liberty and property, quite different from those reflected in *Lochner* v. *New York* and in *Tyson* v. *Banton.*

The first indication of the Court's willingness to make this adaptation was revealed in the *Minnesota Moratorium Case.*[34] In April 1933 the Minnesota Legislature passed a law[35] which, in substance, declared a two-year moratorium on foreclosure of real-estate mortgages. The enormous shrinkage of land values had placed all mortgagors in jeopardy and the legislature acted on the score of emergency to protect their property from legal seizure. The statute provided that during the emergency declared to exist execution sales of real estate could be postponed and periods of redemption extended. By another provision of the Act, no action could be maintained for a deficiency judgment until the new period of grace prescribed by law had expired.

The Home Building & Loan Assoc., a mortgagee, sought to invalidate the legislation as being repugnant to the "due process" clause of the Fourteenth Amendment and to Section 10 of Article 1 of the federal Constitution, which prohibits states from passing any "law impairing the obligation of contracts." Actually, the moratorium did impair the obligation of existing mortgage contracts and so the mortgagee's contention was not ill founded. Notwithstanding this ostensible constitutional barrier, the Supreme Court upheld the law[36] in one of the most significant opinions of recent years. A close study of the majority opinion, which was delivered by Chief Justice Hughes, reveals the Court's labored effort to stretch the constitutional principle involved so as to give recognition to the demands of the heavily indebted farmers in the Middle West.

By going out of its way to sanction a statute which was designed to remedy an explosive situation, the Court performed a statesmanlike act. But the enduring value of the moratorium decision lies in the fact that it reaffirmed Marshall's organic interpretation of the Constitution. If the Constitution was made for an indefinable future and "intended to endure for ages to come", it must be rendered adaptable "to the various crises of human affairs."[37] It was this thought that ran between the lines of the chief justice's reasoning, which upheld the Minnesota statute. He translated the Marshallian doctrine into contemporary terms in the following classic passage:

> It is manifest from this review of our decisions that there
> has been a growing appreciation of public needs and of the
> necessity of finding ground for a rational compromise between individual rights and public welfare. The settlement
> and consequent contraction of the public domain, the pressure of a constantly increasing density of population, the
> interrelation of the activities of our people and the complexity of our economic interests, have inevitably led to an
> increased use of the organization of society in order to
> protect the very bases of individual opportunity. Where,
> in earlier days, it was thought that only the concerns of
> individuals or of classes were involved, and that those of the
> State itself were touched only remotely, it has later been
> found that the fundamental interests of the State are
> directly affected; and that the question is no longer merely
> that of one party to a contract as against another, but of
> the use of reasonable means to safeguard the economic
> structure upon which the good of all depends.

Having thus restated the need for constitutional growth, the chief justice proceeded to overcome by skillful argument the implications of the "contract" clause. The prohibition upon states of legislation impairing the obligation of contracts is not, he said, "an absolute one and is not to be read with literal exactness like a mathematical formula", but is general and "the process of construction is essential to fill in the details. . . . The economic interests of the State may justify the exercise of its continuing and dominant protective power, notwithstanding interference with

contracts. . . . The question is not whether the legislative action affects contracts incidentally, or directly
or indirectly, but whether the legislation is addressed
to a legitimate end and the measures taken are reason-
ble and appropriate to that end." In other words, subject to this criterion, sovereign authority is above individual rights and, therefore, no private contract can
stand in the way of a legitimate exercise of government
power.[38] For, after all, "the policy of protecting contracts against impairment presupposes the maintenance
of a government by virtue of which contractual relations are worthwhile,—a government which retains
adequate authority to secure the peace and good order
of society." Every contract, then, is subject to the future exercise of the power of the state to interfere
with its operation or enforcement where an urgent
public interest requires such interference. Such is the
clear import of the Court's language. "Not only are
existing laws read into contracts in order to fix obligations as between the parties, but the reservation of
essential attributes of sovereign power is also read into
contracts as a postulate of the legal order." Applying
this reasoning to the conditions which prompted the
passage of the Moratorium Law, the chief justice concluded: "And if state power exists to give temporary
relief from the enforcement of contracts in the presence
of disasters due to physical causes such as fire, flood or
earthquake, that power cannot be said to be non-existent
when the urgent public need demanding such relief is
produced by other and economic causes."

The Minnesota Moratorium decision reduced materially the protection afforded to private rights by the

"contract" clause of the federal Constitution. It placed the security of society above the security of vested rights. By toning down, on the one hand, the sanctity of private property and stressing, on the other, the paramount interest of the whole community, the Court gave recognition to a widely prevalent popular will during the first phase of recovery.[39]

Two months later the Supreme Court handed down an equally momentous opinion. It was in the *New York Milk Case*[40] (*Nebbia* v. *New York*) and involved the validity of a New York statute which authorized a Milk Control Board to regulate the price for milk.[41] The Board fixed the retail price at nine cents a quart. Nebbia, a grocer, sold two quarts of milk and a five-cent loaf of bread for eighteen cents. He was arrested and convicted on the ground that giving away a loaf of bread amounted to unlawful price-cutting. The conviction was challenged on the theory that the price-fixing statute violated the "due process" clause of the Fourteenth Amendment. Upon this contention and the foregoing facts, the Supreme Court rendered a decision which changed the whole trend of constitutional law as expounded during the last thirty years and particularly during the last fifteen.

Counsel for the convicted grocer confronted the Court with an impressive array of its own decisions, any one of which would warrant nullification of the New York law. They cited the Court's definite and repeated assertion that the production or sale of food is "not affected with a public interest" and cannot, therefore, be subjected to legislative price-fixing.[42] They pointed to a host of decisions which held the business of the grocer, the butcher, the baker and the dairyman to be essentially private and thus immune from legislative control.[43] They showed, citing chapter and verse, where the Court had clearly defined the class of businesses devoted to a public use, and used the Court's own language to prove that the business of dealing in food commodities did not come within that category.[44] They referred to the Court's frequent disapproval of price-fixing under pretext of exercising the police power.[45] They stressed the numerous decisions where the "due process" clause was successfully invoked to restrain encroachments upon individual liberty and private property in cases far less drastic than the one at bar.[46] They alluded to the well-known rule that extraordinary conditions do not suspend the operation of constitutional provisions.[47] And finally they alleged the absence of grave emergency which alone might justify regulation as a temporary measure.[48]

In the light of the above precedents the New York Milk Law was obviously doomed; yet the statute was upheld.[49] At one stroke the Supreme Court discarded and virtually overruled all of its decisions upon the "due process" clause from *Lochner* v. *New York* to *Tyson* v. *Banton*. Without much ado it reversed its settled convictions of a quarter of a century and calmly announced that now "the phrase 'affected with a public interest' . . . means no more than that an industry, for adequate reasons, is subject to control for the public good." Again, to use the Court's language, the phrase "affected with a public interest" is the equivalent of "subject to the police power", and, as far as the police power is concerned, "the Fifth Amendment in the field of federal activity, and the Fourteenth, as respects State action, do not prohibit governmental regulation for the public welfare." By its decision in the *New York Milk Case* the Supreme Court swept aside every vestige of distinction between price-fixing and police-power regulation and gave back to the state legislatures their former power to regulate industry and private property so long as the regulation was not arbitrary or discriminatory but was calculated to serve the public good. A note harmonious with the New Deal philosophy was sounded when the Court asserted that "equally fundamental with the private right is that of the public to regulate it in the common interest." The following is perhaps the most significant passage of the majority opinion, which was delivered by Mr. Justice Roberts, particularly when compared to the constitutional law expounded in such cases as *Lochner* v. *New York* and *Tyson* v. *Banton*:[50]

> If the law-making body within its sphere of government concludes that the conditions or practices in an industry make un-restricted competition an inadequate safeguard of the consumer's interests, produce waste harmful to the public, threaten ultimately to cut off the supply of a commodity needed by the public or portend the destruction of the industry itself, appropriate statutes passed in an honest effort to correct the threatened consequences may not be set aside because the regulation adopted fixes prices reasonably deemed by the legislature to be fair to those engaged in the industry and to the consuming public. And this is especially so where, as here, the economic maladjustment is one of price, which threatens harm to the producer at one end of the series and the consumer at the other. The Constitution does not secure to anyone liberty to conduct his business in

such fashion as to inflict injury upon the public at large, or upon any substantial group of the people. Price control, like any other form of regulation, is unconstitutional only if arbitrary, discriminatory, or demonstrably irrelevant to the policy the legislature is free to adopt. . . .

The foregoing pronouncement carries far-reaching economic significance. It eliminates the doctrine of "emergency" as the basis of power to regulate a private right[51] and places the power squarely upon the fact of economic maladjustment. Having stated the proposition that economic maladjustment is adequate reason for the exertion of state power, the Court proceeded calmly to tear down the limitations upon price-fixing which it had set up during the past few decades; and so naïvely as almost to give the impression that such limitations had never existed:

> We may as well say at once that the dairy industry is not, in the accepted sense of the phrase, a public utility. We think the appellant is also right in asserting that there is in this case no suggestion of any monopoly or monopolistic practice. . . . But if, as must be conceded, the industry is subject to regulation in the public interest, what constitutional principle bars the state from correcting existing maladjustments by legislation touching prices? We think there is no such principle. The due process clause makes no mention of sales or of prices any more than it speaks of business or contracts or buildings or other incidents of property. The thought seems nevertheless to have persisted that there is something peculiarly sacrosanct about the price one may charge for what he makes or sells, and that . . . the state is incapable of directly controlling the price itself. This view was negatived many years ago. *Munn* v. *Illinois* 94 U.S. 113.

In reaching the above conclusion the Court, it will be noted, relied on the old case of *Munn* v. *Illinois,* which had been previously overruled. It thus gave judicial recognition to the pressing economic realities which required the substitution of managed economy in the place of unrestricted laissez faire. The reversal of the Court's position is brought out most strikingly in the following passage from Mr. Justice Roberts' opinion:

> So far as the requirement of due process is concerned, and in the absence of other constitutional restriction, a state is free to adopt whatever economic policy may reasonably be deemed to promote public welfare, and to enforce that policy by legislation adapted to its purpose. The courts are without authority either to declare such policy, or, when it is declared by the legislative arm, to override it. If the laws passed are seen to have a reasonable relation to a proper legislative purpose, and are neither arbitrary nor discriminatory, the requirements of due process are satisfied. . . . "Whether the free operation of the normal laws of competition is a wise and wholesome rule for trade and commerce is an economic question which this court need not consider or determine." And it is equally clear that if the legislative policy be to curb unrestrained and harmful competition by measures which are not arbitrary or discriminatory it does not lie with the courts to determine that the rule is unwise. With the wisdom of the policy adopted, with the adequacy or practicability of the law enacted to forward it, the courts are both incompetent and unauthorized to deal.

As far as the states are concerned, the *New York Milk Case* put constitutional law exactly where it stood when *Munn* v. *Illinois* and *Mugler* v. *Kansas* were decided. What, then, does the Fourteenth Amendment mean when it says that a state shall not deprive any person of life, liberty or property without due process of law? Precisely what the Supreme Court thinks it should mean in a given economic and political situation. As Chief Justice Hughes once said: "We are under a Constitution, but the Constitution is what the Judges say it is."

A series of momentous decisions which began less than a year after the *Nebbia Case* were to prove the truth of this statement. The same Court which had upheld the New York Milk Law and the Minnesota Moratorium Law with such dexterous avoidance of constitutional guarantees of individual rights, went back to *Adkins* v. *Children's Hospital* in order to invalidate a minimum-wage law of the same state and thus to restore the "due process" clause in all its erstwhile rigor.[52] And the majority opinion in this latest reversal was concurred in by Mr. Justice Roberts, the author of *Nebbia* v. *New York!*[53]

"The Fifth Amendment, in the field of federal activity," Mr. Justice Roberts had said in deciding the *Nebbia Case,* "and the Fourteenth, as respects state action, do not prohibit governmental regulation for the public welfare. They merely condition the exertion of the admitted power, by securing that the end shall be accomplished by methods consistent with due process. And the guarantee of due process, as has often been held, demands only that the law shall not be unreasonable, arbitrary or capricious, and that the means selected shall have a real and substantial relation to the object sought to be attained." This then was to be the only valid constitutional test of whether or not a

[ 124 ]

given measure of social legislation violated due process; and the chief justice's vigorous dissent in the *New York Minimum Wage Case* was based on the conviction that this test had been successfully met by the New York Minimum Wage Law, and that it should therefore be spared the fate of the statute which had been invalidated in *Adkins* v. *Childern's Hospital.*

The average lay citizen may have found it difficult to grasp these fine legal distinctions. But the portentous import of the decision did not escape him. He saw that the Supreme Court, after having repeatedly invoked states' rights in order to halt federal action, was now immobilizing the states behind the barrier of the "due process" clause. He knew from the embarrassed silence or the open criticism of even the most conservative organs of opinion that the Court by a majority of one had condemned a method of social betterment which had found widespread acceptance in the nation. But he also knew—and he was not allowed to forget —which of the two major parties was more closely identified with the type of social legislation that was banned by the majority opinion. And on November 3, 1936, he registered his conclusions with unmistakable emphasis.

## CHAPTER VII

# Interstate Commerce—The Key to National Power

I<small>F</small>, IN ORDER to correct economic maladjustments, "a state is free to adopt whatever economic policy may reasonably be deemed to promote public welfare", may not the federal government under the Constitution enjoy a similar scope of freedom? If the National Industrial Recovery Act, the Guffey Coal Act and the Agricultural Adjustment Act were predicated upon a breakdown in industry and agriculture threatening "the producer at one end of the series and the consumer at the other", why did the Supreme Court declare that Congress was without power to act?[1] In *Nebbia* v. *New York*[2] the power of the states to relieve a local economic maladjustment by appropriate legislation was recognized. Yet similar power has since been denied to the federal government because manufacturing, mining and crop-producing have been declared to be local matters and, therefore, subject to the sole jurisdiction of the states. Even in the face of the contention that the breakdown in these "local" activities produced a nationwide crisis which demanded national regulation of production, prices, wages, hours of labor and trade prac-

[ 126 ]

tices, the Supreme Court maintained the stand that the Congress of the United States was powerless to intervene. This, then, may be called, pending modification, the orthodox judicial position on this momentous question. It may also be labeled the patriotic position, because it meets with the approval of many undeniably patriotic citizens who fear that further subjection of business enterprise to national control will destroy the economic and political foundations of the American system.

Yet from the time of James Wilson, who was appointed to the Bench by President Washington, to the present day, individual jurists have taken exception to a doctrine which denies to the federal government power to act where state action would be concededly ineffectual. The late Justice Holmes pointedly observed:[3]

> . . . It is not lightly to be assumed that, in matters requiring national action, "a power which must belong to and somewhere reside in every civilized government" is not to be found. . . . What was said . . . with regard to the powers of the States applies with equal force to the powers of the nation in cases where the States individually are incompetent to act. . . . With regard to that we may add that when we are dealing with words that also are a constituent act, like the Constitution of the United States, we must realize that they have called into life a being the development of which could not have been foreseen completely by the most gifted of its begetters. It was enough for them to realize or to hope that they had created an organism; it has taken a century and has cost their successors much sweat and blood to prove that they created a nation.

[ 127 ]

## The Supreme Court And The National Will

In a recent decision upholding the Guffey Coal Act, the Federal District Court of Kentucky ruled that if, in the judgment of Congress, a local activity, such as mining, affects the general welfare, the Court is without power to substitute a different judgment. Directly in point are the following words from the Court's opinion:[4]

> The people of the States intended to surrender all the rights they had to promote the general welfare that could not be done by the States acting independently. . . . In considering the future of the States of the Union, we must keep in mind the powers of government they can efficiently exercise. Modern technology has broken down barriers of space and time. Nation-wide organizations of every large industry in the United States, nation-wide advertisements of products over the radio, the construction of nation-wide highways, the development of the airplane, a rapid system of transportation and communication, have made the States helpless in controlling and regulating commerce. If we cling to the doctrine of States' Rights in the matter of commerce as it existed in the early days of the Republic, a palsied hand holds the power and decay will set in in our Nation before its time. If commerce is to be regulated and controlled for the public welfare in this country, it must be by the national government, because the States lack the power to make effective their own regulations.

The foregoing judicial views are premised upon the proposition that the national government should possess inherent power to act in all matters where the states are incapable of acting—whether it be war, foreign relations or internal economy. This view of national sovereignty, though implicit in Marshall's conception of the Constitution, has not been accepted by the Supreme Court. As a result, there has existed under the American system a more or less wide gap between the spheres of state and federal authority; and this gap explains the failure to realize the aspirations of American democracy whenever the federal government was unable to act because it had no constitutional sanction, while the states, though constitutionally competent, lacked the capacity for effective action.

The existence of this gap between the boundaries of state and federal jurisdiction has necessitated the compensatory enlargement of some of the powers expressly granted to the federal government by the Constitution. Among these powers, the so-called "commerce clause" has proved the most effective stopgap. Article I, Section 8 of the Federal Constitution, which authorizes Congress ". . . to regulate commerce with foreign nations, and among the several States", has been converted by judicial construction and affirmative federal legislation into an effective instrument for the integration and control of American economy during the period of its greatest expansion. Such major congressional enactments as the Interstate Commerce Act of 1887, the Sherman Antitrust Act of 1890, the Food and Drug Act of 1906, the Packers and Stockyards Act of 1921, the Grain Futures Act of 1922, the Air Commerce Act of 1926, and the Radio Act of 1927 have derived their constitutional sanction from the "commerce clause." The same clause also served as pivot, wholly or partially, for some of the most far-reaching legislation of President Franklin D. Roosevelt's first administration—such as the National Recovery Act,

[ 129 ]

the Securities and Exchange Act, the Public Utility Holding Company Act, and the Bituminous Coal Conservation Act. And while the Supreme Court balked at some of these attempts to expand national power, it had long since committed itself to the regulation, under the "commerce clause", not only of interstate commerce but of many primarily local activities to an extent unforeseen by the framers of the Constitution.

The original purpose of the "commerce clause" was to eliminate trade rivalries among the states and thus to secure economic peace and stability for the new nation and enable it to present a united economic front to the outside world. It was generally recognized that "a more perfect union" was unthinkable so long as the various states were free to raise discriminatory tariff walls against one another, and important states like New York, New Jersey, Connecticut and Pennsylvania pursued a policy of chronic fiscal retaliation which threatened at times to degenerate into civil war. "It may be doubted," said Chief Justice Marshall, "whether any of the evils proceeding from the feebleness of the federal government, contributed more to that great revolution which introduced the present system, than the deep and general conviction, that commerce ought to be regulated by Congress."[5] But when he added that, because of this conviction, the grant of power made by the "commerce clause" was "as extensive as the mischief, and should comprehend all foreign commerce, and all commerce among the States",[6] he was probably reading his strong nationalist beliefs into the intent of the framers. The "commerce clause" seems to have been meant to apply primarily to transportation by coastwise shipping—the only interstate commerce of consequence in those days. It was designed to invest Congress with power to regulate transportation to and from such maritime centers as Boston, New York City, Philadelphia and Charleston, and to give vessels of the several states the freedom of these ports. It was, in short, a Jeffersonian conception of interstate commerce that was prevalent during the early period of the Republic. And while, as we have seen, both Jefferson and his successors were frequently compelled to make concessions to national power, as late as 1822 President Monroe construed the "commerce clause" with the utmost strictness when he vetoed the Cumberland Road Act, which extended federal control over turnpikes within state boundaries. "Commerce between independent powers," he told Congress on that occasion, "is universally regulated by duties and imports. It was so regulated by the States before the adoption of this Constitution, equally in respect to each other and to foreign Powers. The goods and vessels employed in the trade are the only subject of regulation. It can act on none other. A power then to impose such duties and imports in regard to foreign nations and to prevent any on the trade between the States, was the only power granted."[7] It would startle Jefferson and his states' rights followers to know that the federal government has since derived from this grant of power over interstate commerce authority to regulate rates, wages and hours of labor; to dissolve monopolies, annul contracts, prescribe rules for the sale of securities and commodities, enjoin states in the collection of taxes; in brief, to establish a many-sided and effective control over business enterprise. And it would shock them even more, as strict-constructionists, to be told that all this was achieved without recourse to constitutional amendment, by judicial adaptation of the Constitution to an expanding and increasingly interdependent national economy.

The vast potentialities of the "commerce clause" were revealed for the first time by Chief Justice Marshall in *Gibbons* v. *Ogden*.[8] The case involved the validity of a New York law which gave to Robert R. Livingston and Robert Fulton the exclusive right of navigating the waters of that state by steamboat. Competing steamboat owners of New Jersey claimed the right to navigate New York waters by virtue of a federal coasting license issued pursuant to an act of Congress. The Livingston-Fulton monopoly obtained an injunction in the New York Courts against the New Jersey shipowners and the case came on appeal to the Supreme Court of the United States. The monopoly contended that the federal government could not interfere with the right of the state of New York to regulate commerce in the navigable waters within its own boundaries. Daniel Webster, as counsel for the opposing interests, made the then novel and extraordinary argument that Congress possessed exclusive authority to regulate commerce in all its forms on all navigable waters of the United States without any restraint from state legislatures. The case aroused intense interest. Idle capital, which was soon to be lured in increasing volume by the railroads, was waiting hopefully for an opportunity to be invested in steam navigation once the barriers of monopoly were removed.[9] Shippers of

merchandise had an equally heavy stake in the outcome
of the case, for the abolition of the steamboat monopoly would assure lower rates and higher profits. But
beyond these immediate interests, the development of
the United States as a coherent economic unit demanded
a liberal interpretation of the power of Congress over
interstate commerce. And such was the interpretation
made by Marshall's opinion, which, his biographer
claims, "has done more to knit the American people
into one indivisible nation than any one force in our
history excepting only war."

"Commerce," said the chief justice in a classic definition, ". . . undoubtedly, is traffic, but it is something
more: it is intercourse. It describes the commercial intercourse between nations, and parts of nations, in all
its branches, and is regulated by prescribing rules for
carrying on that intercourse. The mind can scarcely
conceive a system for regulating commerce between
nations, which shall exclude all laws concerning navigation, which shall be silent on the admission of the vessels of the one nation into the ports of the other, and
be confined to prescribing rules for the conduct of individuals, in the actual employment of buying and
selling, or of barter." It is "universally admitted", he
pointed out, that the words of the Constitution "comprehend every species of commercial intercourse between the United States and foreign nations"; and he
argued unanswerably that "if this be the admitted
meaning of the word, in its application to foreign
nations, it must carry the same meaning throughout the
sentence, and remain a unit, unless there be some plain
intelligible cause which alters it." After thus defining

international and interstate commerce, Marshall proceeded to an equally comprehensive definition of the power of Congress to regulate both. "This power," he said, "like all others vested in Congress, is complete in itself, may be exercised to its utmost extent, and acknowledges no limitations, other than are prescribed in the Constitution. . . . If, as has always been understood, the sovereignty of Congress, though limited to specified objects, is plenary as to those objects, the power over commerce with foreign nations, and among the several States, is vested in Congress as absolutely as it would be in a single government, having in its constitution the same restrictions on the exercise of the power as are found in the Constitution of the United States." He emphatically denied that the states possessed concurrent power over interstate and foreign commerce. He argued that the federal laws which had been adduced as proof that Congress believed in the existence of such power merely showed Congress to have been of the opinion "that the States retain powers enabling them to pass the laws to which allusion has been made, not that those laws proceed from the particular power which has been delegated to Congress." And he concluded that whereas when a state legislature and Congress exercise "the power of taxation, neither is exercising the power of the other", . . . "when a State proceeds to regulate commerce with foreign nations or among the several states, it is exercising the very power that is granted and is doing the very thing which Congress is authorized to do."

The decision in *Gibbons* v. *Ogden* is a salient example

of the adaptability of constitutional law to dominant economic trends and, incidentally, of Marshall's ability to anticipate the future. Steamboat monopolies granted by states were a "horse-and-buggy" anachronism at a time when the young nation was about to embark on its conquest of a continent. "But economic results of more far-reaching importance than the mere demolition of the monopoly were involved, which were not appreciated until later years. The opening of the Hudson River and Long Island Sound to the free passage of steamboats was the most potent factor in the building up of New York as a commercial center. The removal of danger of similar grants of railroad monopolies in other States promoted immensely the development of interstate communication by steam throughout the country; for the first railroad was built only five years later. The coal industry, then but an experiment, was developed through the growth of New England's manufacturing industries, made possible by cheap transportation of coal by water. In short, Marshall's opinion was the emancipation proclamation of American commerce."[10] To a greater extent perhaps than any of his other decisions, it translated Hamilton's economic nationalism into constitutional terms and thus hastened the economic and the political integration of the nation.

*Gibbons* v. *Ogden* established the rule that when Congress acts upon a matter dealing with interstate commerce, the states cannot exercise concurrent jurisdiction over the same matter. It left undecided, however, the question as to whether the states could regulate commerce in the absence of affirmative federal action with respect thereto. Marshall's constitutional convictions would doubtless have impelled him to declare that congressional authority over interstate commerce is exclusive and thus to bar the states from intermeddling with this most important source of national power. Such a declaration would probably have alarmed the South, where several states had already enacted laws regulating traffic in slavery; and Marshall, whose important decisions were invariably influenced by political considerations, deemed it wiser under the circumstances to curb his nationalist feelings. Three years later, however, in *Brown* v. *Maryland*,[11] he made no reference whatever to federal legislation when he declared that a Maryland statute imposing a license fee on importers was "hostile to the power given to Congress to regulate commerce" and, at the same time, denied that such a fee came within the scope of the taxing power of the states. "It is sufficient," he said, "for the present to say, generally, that when the importer has so acted upon the thing imported that it has become incorporated and mixed up with the general property in the country, it has, perhaps, lost its distinctive character as an import, and has become subject to the taxing power of the state; but while remaining the property of the importer, in his warehouse, in the original form of package . . . , a tax upon it is too plainly a duty on imports to escape the prohibition in the Constitution."

Marshall's decisions may be said to have expounded the "commerce clause" in its negative aspect—as a barrier against interference by the states with foreign and interstate commerce. In all his major opinions the great

chief justice placed the broadest possible construction
on the grants of power made by the Constitution to the
federal government, primarily in order to secure the
extrusion of the states from those fields rather than because he wanted to see national power exerted in positive fashion. With respect to the "commerce clause",
his concern was less that commerce should be regulated
than that it should not be regulated by the states. The
removal of the vexatious control of the states at a time
when the national economy was in its infancy was indeed "the emancipation proclamation of American
commerce." But with state regulation excluded and
federal regulation not yet forthcoming, the emanci-
pated infant might easily become—and did, in fact, become—a tyrannical and predatory giant. In short, *Gibbons* v. *Ogden* and *Brown* v. *Maryland,* like all of Marshall's great decisions, fostered both nationalism and
economic individualism; and, in the absence of action
by the national government, they tended to place economic enterprise beyond the reach of governmental
authority.

A corrective to this situation was imperatively
needed; yet the Supreme Court, even though under
Chief Justice Taney it was preponderantly favorable
to states' rights, was unable for a long time to determine clearly the field within which the states could exercise their regulatory powers in the absence of congressional action. It was not until *Cooley* v. *Port Wardens,*[12] involving the validity of a pilotage fee statute
of the state of Pennsylvania, that by a five-to-three decision a new doctrine was formulated which drew a
fairly distinct line between congressional and state jur-

isdiction with respect to the regulation of commerce.
". . . The grant of commercial power to Congress,"
said Justice Curtis, speaking for the majority of the
Court, "does not contain any terms which expressly
exclude the states from exercising any authority over
its subject matter. . . . The power to regulate commerce embraces a vast field, containing not only many,
but exceedingly various subjects, quite unlike in their
nature; some imperatively demanding a single uniform
rule, operating equally on the commerce of the United
States in every port; and some, like the subject now in
question, as imperatively demanding that diversity,
which alone can meet the local necessities of navigation.
Either absolutely to affirm, or deny that the nature of
this power requires exclusive legislation by Congress,
is to lose sight of the nature of the subjects of this
power, and to assert concerning all of them what is
really applicable but to a part. Whatever subjects of
this power are in their nature national, or admit only
of one uniform system or plan of regulation, may justly
be said to be of such a nature as to require exclusive
legislation by Congress." Laws for the regulation of
pilotage, the Court contended, did not belong to this
category, and the states could not be deprived of their
traditional right to legislate on this particular subject
merely because of an abstraction—i.e., the nature of
the power granted to Congress by the "commerce
clause." "This would be," continued the majority
opinion, "to affirm that the nature of the power is in
any case something different from the nature of the subject to which, in such cases, the power extends, and that

the nature of the power necessarily demands, in all cases, exclusive legislation by Congress, while the nature of one of the subjects of that power, not only does not require such exclusive legislation, but may be best provided for by many different systems enacted by the States, in conformity with the circumstances of the ports within their limits." The line of demarcation, then, between federal and state action with respect to interstate commerce depends, according to this doctrine, not on the nature of the power to regulate but on the nature of the subject to be regulated. Hence, while Congress can act competently on subjects which are "in their nature national", the states retain regulatory powers over commerce where "the nature of the subject when examined is such as to leave no doubt of the superior fitness and propriety, not to say absolute necessity, of different systems of regulation, drawn from local knowledge and experience and conformed to local wants."

The doctrine of *Cooley* v. *Port Wardens* enabled the states to regulate commerce at a time when the instrumentalities of transportation and communication were undergoing rapid development and thus to tap new sources of revenue and power. When the formula of the "superior fitness and propriety" of state regulation could not apply because the subjects were "in their nature national", the Court, as a rule, sustained state action on the basis of federal inaction. This warrant for state regulation of interstate commerce was couched quite unambiguously in the following excerpt from Chief Justice Waite's opinion in *Peik* v. *North-*

*western Ry,*[13] which upheld a Wisconsin statute regulating the rates and fares of an interstate carrier:

> The suits present the single question of the power of the legislature of Wisconsin to provide by law for a maximum of charge by the Chicago & Northwestern Railway Company for fare and freight upon the transportation of persons and property carried within the State, or taken up outside the State and brought within it or taken up inside and carried without. . . . As to the effect of the statutes as a regulation of interstate commerce. The law is confined to State commerce, or such interstate commerce as directly affects the people of Wisconsin. Until Congress acts in reference to the relations of this Company in interstate commerce, it is certainly within the power of Wisconsin to regulate its fares, etc. so far as they are of domestic concern. With the people of Wisconsin this Company has domestic relations. Incidentally, these may reach beyond the State. But certainly, until Congress undertakes to legislate for those who are without the State, Wisconsin may provide for those within, even though it may indirectly affect those without.

On the basis of the principle that the states were constitutionally competent in fields where state regulation was of "superior fitness and propriety" and with respect to subjects which, though "in their nature national", had not yet been dealt with by Congress, the states were able to exercise considerable control over interstate commerce. They regulated the rates of common carriers, granted anew monopolies of land and water transportation as well as of telegraphic communications, and wielded the taxing power upon instrumentalities of interstate commerce both for purposes of revenue and for the convenience of the public. This type of regulation was generally sustained by a divided Court until the middle eighties, when the "commerce clause" felt the impact of the same economic forces which were perverting the Fourteenth Amendment into an edict of noninterference by the states with the freedom of economic enterprise.

The turning point was reached in 1886 when the case of *Wabash Ry.* v. *Illinois* was decided against the sharp dissent of Chief Justice Waite and Justices Gray and Bradley. The case involved the validity of an Illinois law, passed "to prevent extortion and unjust discrimination in the rates charged for the transportation of passengers and freight" by the railroads within the state.[14] The Court, though unable to establish a substantial distinction between the Illinois statute and the Wisconsin statute which had been upheld ten years earlier in *Peik* v. *Northwestern Ry.,* declared, nevertheless, that the former was repugnant to the "commerce clause" despite the fact that its subject matter—common carrier rates—had not been regulated by Congress. The reasoning of the majority opinion, which was delivered by Justice Miller, ran as follows:

> It cannot be too strongly insisted upon that the right of continuous transportation from one end of the country to the other is essential in modern times to that freedom of commerce from the restraints which the State might choose to impose upon it, that the commerce clause was intended to secure. The clause, giving to Congress the power to regulate commerce among the States and with foreign nations, as the Court has said before, was among the most important of the subjects which prompted the formation of the Consti-

tution. . . . And it would be a very feeble and almost useless provision, but poorly adapted to secure the entire
freedom of commerce among the States which was deemed
essential to a more perfect Union by the framers of the
Constitution, if at every stage of the transportation of goods
and chattels through the country, the State within whose
limits a part of the transportation must be done could impose regulations concerning the price; compensation or taxation, or any other restrictive regulation interfering with or
seriously embarrassing this commerce.

Justice Bradley, dissenting, adduced the decision in
*Peik* v. *Northwestern Ry*. "We do not see," he said,
"how this can be distinguished from that now under
consideration." He was right. The two cases could not
be distinguished in point of fact; and if the doctrine of
*stare decisis* were to be followed, the Illinois statute
should have been sustained. But in the dynamic America of the late nineteenth century legal precedent had
to yield when it did not conform to the prevailing public sentiment generated by the unprecedented expansion
of business enterprise. The railroads were one of the
most potent factors in this expansion; and it was becoming increasingly clear that, while they had to be regulated if they were not to become the masters of states
and nation, their attempted regulation by the states
tended to obstruct the development of the national
economy. The doctrine of states' rights with respect to
the regulation of commerce had been invoked in the
past by both the North and the South. In its name
Southern states had barred their ports to free Negroes; New York and Massachusetts had attempted to
tax entering immigrants; Rhode Island, Massachusetts

and New Hampshire had sought to restrict the importation of alcoholic beverages.[15] The vitality of the doctrine depended in every case upon the strength of the economic, cultural or political interests it was designed to serve. Now those who attempted to curb the railroads through state legislation had no sentimental attachment to states' rights. But in the face of congressional inaction and the resultant license of the railroad companies, they were apt to forget that the nation was becoming, through the instrumentality of these same railroads, increasingly an economic unit; that the bonds of interdependence were daily bringing closer the farmer of Wisconsin, the miner of Pennsylvania, and the merchant of New York; that there was, in short, only one interstate commerce and that it would be hopelessly crippled—and the prosperity of the states would, in the long run, be impaired—if it were to be regulated by the several states through which it passed. Justice Miller's opinion in the *Wabash Case* said, in effect, that whatever else the states might regulate, their assumption of regulatory powers in interstate railroad transportation, of all subjects the most national in its nature, was a contradiction in terms. It thus made the power of Congress over interstate commerce exclusive, at least so far as transportation was concerned. And this *reductio ad absurdum* of the authority of the states over common carriers was an invitation to Congress to implement the "commerce clause" by affirmative federal legislation.

The beginning of such legislation was the Interstate Commerce Act of 1887, which was designed to organize federal regulation of the railroads and thus placed the stamp of finality on the exclusion of the states from that field. But the effect of the Wabash decision extended beyond the prohibition of state interference with common carriers. It practically demolished state powers of regulation and taxation of all interstate commerce. Having started at the proper focal point—transportation—the Court proceeded by degrees to immunize from state control every type of business whose scope was fundamentally interstate in character. The stream and flow of interstate commerce must not be obstructed—that was the cue. Therefore, any state regulation or tax which tended to burden, impede or discriminate against interstate commerce was banned by the "commerce clause", notwithstanding congressional dormancy on the subject. Insulation from state reach was thus afforded to pipe-line corporations, to communications companies, to natural-gas and electric-power transmission systems, to importers of goods who resold them in the original "unbroken packages"—in short, to all persons or companies engaged in the business of conducting an interstate commerce.[16] "A State cannot lay a tax on interstate commerce in any form," said Mr. Justice Sutherland. "The protection against imposition of burdens . . . is practical and substantial and extends to whatever is necessary to the complete enjoyment of the right protected."[17] And Justice Bradley, one year after his dissent in the *Wabash Case*, laid it down as "an axiom in our constitutional jurisprudence" that a state regulation of interstate commerce is "in conflict with the exclusive powers of Congress under the Constitution."[18] The merciless demolition of state legislation found an echo even in the state

[ 144 ]

courts. "The power to regulate commerce between the States," succinctly remarked Judge Andrews of the New York Court of Appeals, "is vested exclusively in Congress and the fact that Congress has not acted, confers no power of state regulation."[19] The pendulum now swung to the extreme opposite of the doctrine enunciated in *Cooley* v. *Port Wardens;* and the reaction against states' rights was carried to such lengths that a corporation, for instance, whose plants, equipment and funds were located almost entirely within the jurisdiction of a single state was permitted to escape state taxation merely because it may have had a section of a pipe line protruding a few odd miles beyond the state boundary.[20]

Caught by the "commerce clause" where the business was interstate and by the "due process" clause where it was local,[21] the states lost effective control of American industry. Corporate enterprise, which had bent and twisted the law to its purposes and had come to dominate the legal profession and to mold its thinking, found in these clauses, as interpreted by the Supreme Court, an almost impenetrable armor against state interference. With the states thus effectively barred, the next move had to be made by Congress. The courts had clearly stated that the control of commerce was its exclusive prerogative; and the language of the judicial decisions was a challenge to the national legislature to exercise the power vested in it by the "commerce clause" in order to protect the public against the untrammeled freedom of business enterprise and, at the same time, to hasten the integration of the national economy. The Interstate Commerce Act of 1887 was the first response to this challenge; and the second was made in 1890 when Congress passed the Sherman Antitrust Act, "to protect trade and commerce against unlawful restraints and monopolies."

The case of *United States* v. *E. C. Knight Co.,* which arose out of the government's attempt to dissolve the powerful Sugar Trust, provided the first important test of the adequacy of the Sherman Act as a protection of the consumer and the small businessman against monopoly.[22] In its suit the government charged that the American Sugar Refining Company, by its purchase of a group of refineries, had acquired complete control of the manufacture of refined sugar within the United States; and that, in entering into the contracts of purchase, the trust had conspired to restrain trade and commerce in refined sugar among the several states, contrary to the Sherman Antitrust Act. The allegation of monopoly was admitted by the defendant and the case went to the Supreme Court on the power of Congress to suppress it.

To the astonishment of those who believed that the Court had forbidden the states to regulate commerce because it had been nurturing the "commerce clause" as an instrument of national economic direction, Chief Justice Fuller[23] handed down an opinion dismissing the government's suit. The transaction impugned, he held, was the creation of a monopoly in manufacture bearing no direct relation to commerce; a local activity, if you please, hence outside the orbit of federal influence. The following excerpt from the Court's opinion shows the extent to which the Sherman Act was emasculated by judicial decision only five years after its passage:

[ 146 ]

Commerce succeeds to manufacture, and is not a part of it. The power to regulate commerce is the power to prescribe the rule by which commerce shall be governed, and is a power independent of the power to suppress monopoly. . . . The fact that an article is manufactured for export to another State does not of itself make it an article of interstate commerce. . . . Contracts, combinations or conspiracies to control domestic enterprise in manufacture, agriculture, mining, production in all its forms, or to raise or lower prices or wages, might unquestionably tend to restrain external as well as domestic trade, but the restraint would be an indirect result, however, inevitable and whatever its extent . . . Slight reflection will show that if the national power extends to all contracts and combinations in manufacture, agriculture, mining, and other productive industries, whose ultimate result may affect external commerce, comparatively little of business operations and affairs would be left for State control. It was in the light of well-settled principles that the act of July 2, 1890, was framed. Congress did not attempt thereby to assert the power to deal with monopoly directly as such; or to limit and restrict the rights of corporations created by the States or the citizens of the States in the acquisition, control, or disposition of property; or to regulate or prescribe the price or prices at which such property or the products thereof should be sold.

This decision is a flagrant example of the power of the Judiciary to legislate through its unrestricted reading of the laws and the Constitution. For when the Court declared that "Congress did not attempt . . . to assert the power to deal with monopoly directly", it read into the Sherman Act a public policy which was quite the reverse of the plain intent of Congress. If combinations or conspiracies to monopolize manufacture and trade on a national scale, touching at every point the producer, merchant and consumer, do not directly affect the national commerce, what type of commercial activity, then, was a statute enacted under the "commerce clause" intended to reach? If, as the Court said, "commerce succeeds to manufacture", then it merely involves the movement of goods after they have been manufactured—i.e., transportation. "The power to regulate . . . is the power to prescribe the rule." Hence, all that Congress can do under the "commerce clause" is to fix the rules of transportation. This stunted conception of national power with respect to commerce was more applicable to conditions in 1787 than to the economic realities of 1895. It was based on the same "horse-and-buggy" view of interstate commerce to which President Roosevelt alluded forty years later in his caustic criticism of the decision in the *Schechter Poultry Case*. It was aggravated, moreover, by the palpable inconsistency which marked judicial interpretation of the "commerce clause"; while it was made to embrace interstate commerce in any form when applied as a ban upon the exercise of state power, it was construed very strictly when the national government undertook regulatory action.

As a result, the Interstate Commerce Act[24] and the Sherman Act were whittled down by judicial interpretation during the last decade of the nineteenth century, and big business was placed beyond the effective reach of national as well as of state control. The states could not regulate, because state regulation interfered with interstate commerce or violated due process; but neither could the federal government regulate, because as soon as federal regulation was attempted the activities aimed at were declared to be local and the exercise of national power was barred as violative of states' rights. Thus big business was able to play the states against the national government and the national government against the states. When attacked by the states it became Hamiltonian and scurried for protection to national power; when assailed by the federal government it became Jeffersonian and sought refuge in states' rights. By playing both ends against the middle it achieved in its relations with government a closer approximation to laissez faire than at any time before or since.

The judicial decisions of the eighteen-nineties accorded with what were, in spite of strong movements of criticism and protest, the dominant economic interests and doctrines of the period. The last quarter of the nineteenth century was the climax of an era in which the pursuit of happiness, effectively served by steam and the prodigal exploitation of natural resources, had been converted into gigantic private fortunes. The law of the Constitution inevitably conformed to the economics and the ethics of this eminently acquisitive society, and the courts gave such effective protection to private property and private enterprise that the United States seemed, to many observers, to have reconciled democracy with dynamic capitalism and to have become safe for plutocracy. While anxiously envisaging the menace of popular government, Sir Henry Maine, that eminently conservative philosopher of law and history, could derive considerable comfort from "the powers and disabilities attached to the United States and to the several States by the Federal Constitution." The "beneficent prosperity" of the United States, he said, "reposes on the sacredness of contract and the stability of private property; the first the implement, and the last the reward of success in the universal competition." Hence, he singled out the prohibition against state legislation impairing the obligation of contracts as "the bulwark of American individualism against democratic impatience and socialistic fantasy."[25] The English scholar's diagnosis was borne out by unambiguous judicial pronouncements.[26] And it was this deep-rooted philosophy of the sanctity of private property which led Arthur T. Hadley, an orthodox exponent of railroad economics, to conclude that the position of property-holders in the United States was well-nigh impregnable. "The general status of the property-owner under the law," he said, "cannot be changed by the action of the legislature, or of the executive, or the people of a state voting at the polls, or all three put together. It cannot be changed without either a consensus of opinion among the judges, which should lead them to retrace their old views, or an amendment of the Constitution of the United States by the slow and cumbersome machinery provided for that purpose, or, last— and I hope most improbable—a revolution."[27] In an atmosphere so favorable to capitalist expansion, decisions of the Supreme Court similar to that handed down in the *Sugar Trust Case* stimulated industrial activity and speculation. They attracted not only domestic capital but vast foreign investments eager to enjoy the economic opportunities of America and the security offered by our constitutional limitations against

governmental encroachment.[28] The prodigious development of the American continent from 1875 to 1900 is
due to many factors—vast accumulations of capital,
cheap immigrant labor, unmatched natural resources,
an immense free-trade area, an ever-expanding home
market, a spirit of pioneer enterprise and resourceful-
ness, and the rapid progress of science and technology.
But as powerful as any of these was a political system
which, by means of judicial review, its most distinctive
feature, offered to private property and private business constitutional safeguards against the repressive or
regulatory velleities of democracy.

Yet it would be a mistake to think of American
democracy as consistently antiplutocratic. In an era of
capitalistic expansion, the ethics, the economics, the politics and the jurisprudence of the Gilded Age had a peculiar attraction even for the common man. For they
reflected the general intellectual climate of the period.
A popularized, and hence inevitably distorted, brand of
Darwinism transferred such scientific concepts as natural selection, survival of the fittest, evolution and progress to the eminently unscientific domain of social and
international relations. As a result, predatory capitalism and imperialism were invested in the eyes of many
who were not even remotely touched by their material
benefits with the sanctity of natural laws and cosmic
processes. Moreover, this kind of social Darwinism
was especially intelligible in post-Civil War America,
where the pioneers of the seventies had become the
plutocrats of the nineties through a technique of
acquisition which followed the classic pattern of "pre-
emption, exploitation and progress."[29] The builders of

[ 151 ]

industrial empires were convinced—and this conviction
was shared by millions of their fellow-citizens—that
while they were enriching themselves they were also
opening up a continent, raising America to the status of
a world power, and keeping pace with the inexorable
forward march of history. There were, to be sure,
voices of dissent—a Henry George, showing that the
reverse of the glittering medal of Progress was Poverty; an Edward Bellamy, "looking backward" in the
accepted fashion of utopia-builders and envisaging the
ethics, the society and the state that would make progress possible without poverty; a Eugene Debs, attempting to redefine the right to life, liberty and the pursuit
of happiness for those who tended the engines of production in an increasingly mechanical civilization. But
these were voices crying in the wilderness of an essentially individualistic and capitalistic and incurably opti-
mistic America. Sectional movements of protest, most
of which were variations of Jacksonian agrarianism,
arose during years of adversity only to decline with returning prosperity. A great political leader like La
Follette was able to assert within a single state the
right of democratic government to control business. A
potent orator like Bryan succeeded for a brief moment
in dramatizing popular discontent by the use of Chris-
tian symbolism. But in the last analysis it was the fluctuations of the business cycle that gave direction and
coherence to these sporadic or ephemeral trends and
helped them to crystallize on anything like a national
scale.

By the turn of the century the American people, pon-
dering the lessons of recurrent depression and pros-

perity, were coming to realize that big business wielded greater influence on the course of their lives than their supposedly sovereign government. They began to suspect that there was something wrong with an economy which permitted a group of private citizens to create, almost at will, either panic or binge. Above all, with monopoly taking a steady toll on farmer, factory, worker, consumer and small businessman, the conviction spread that American business was no longer free or genuinely competitive. The political revolt against "the curse of bigness" was epitomized during the first decade of the twentieth century in the activities of a strong congressional bloc, whose most prominent member was La Follette, and, with more striking effect on the popular mind, in the antitrust campaign of Theodore Roosevelt. President McKinley's successor repudiated the easy optimism of the "full dinner pail." He understood that American industry in the twentieth century could not be effectively regulated by the states. He knew that government regulation, which was urgently needed both in order to integrate the national economy and to serve social justice, must be undertaken on a national scale. Yet he had seen such federal control as had been attempted in the past largely circumvented by judicial interpretation, assisted to a considerable extent by the inadequacy or the vagueness of the regulatory enactments. His agitation was, therefore, directed toward a more precise redefinition and further expansion of the powers of the federal government under the "commerce clause"[30] and against the usurpation of legislative functions by the Supreme Court. He did not hesitate to question the infallibility

[ 153 ]

of judges, and he referred irreverently to "some members of the judicial body who have lagged behind in their understanding of these great and vital changes in the body politic, whose minds have never been opened to the new applications of the old principles made necessary by the new conditions."[31] Moreover, he advanced his own interpretation of the Constitution. He believed that "an inherent power rested in the Nation, outside of the enumerated powers conferred upon it by the Constitution, in all cases where the object involved was beyond the power of the several States."[32] He presented vividly to the American people the tragic dilemma created by the dominant trend of judicial interpretation. "The legislative or judicial decisions of which I complain," he said, "do not leave to the States power to deal with corporate wealth in business . . . and any action or decision that deprives the Nation of the power to deal with it, simply results in leaving the corporations absolutely free to work without any effective supervision whatever; and such a course is fraught with untold danger to the future of our whole system of government, and, indeed, to our whole civilization."[33] Finally, he capped his campaign by advocating the recall of judicial decisions in cases involving the nullification of social legislation.[34]

This critical temper could not but influence the course of judicial statesmanship. Already, before the turn of the century, the Supreme Court had made important concessions to antimonopoly sentiment. It had declared the Sherman Act to apply to agreements between competitive railroads tending to restrain trade, or between corporations, engaged in the same business, barring

competition in certain areas.[35] But the decisive landmark was the *Beef Trust Case,*[36] wherein the government sought to restrain a combination of some 60 per
cent of the nation's meat packers from carrying out
an agreement made between themselves "to arbitrarily
and from time to time raise, lower and fix prices and to
maintain uniform prices at which they will sell." The
obvious purpose of the agreement was to destroy competition by regulating prices and thereby to allow the
contracting parties to monopolize the meat industry.
The defendants contended that the fixing of prices and
the buying and selling of meat all took place within
the boundaries of the state of Illinois; that the activities complained of were purely local and, therefore,
could not be reached by the Sherman Act, whose scope,
they asserted, was limited to restraints upon interstate
commerce. They admitted the scheme and relied for
immunity upon the similar *Sugar Trust Case,* which in
fact and in law was directly in their favor. But the Supreme Court, responding to the new political environment and mindful of an antitrust movement of national
proportions, failed to see similarity in the two cases. It
politely "distinguished" the *Sugar Trust Case,* out of
deference, one would suppose, to Chief Justice Fuller,
and held that the alleged local acts in the *Beef Trust
Case* were "constituent elements" of a "scheme" which
"affected" interstate commerce and hence were within
reach of the commerce power. Said the Court, speaking
through Justice Holmes:

> The scheme as a whole seems to us to be within reach of the
> law. The constituent elements, as we have stated them, are

enough to give the scheme a body and, for all that we can say, to accomplish it. . . . It is suggested that the several acts charged are lawful and that intent can make no difference. But they are bound together as the parts of a single plan. The plan may make the parts unlawful. The statute gives this proceeding against combinations in restraint of commerce among the States and against attempts to monopolize the same. . . . Although the combination alleged embraces restraint and monopoly of trade within a single State, its effect upon commerce among the States is not accidental, secondary, remote or merely probable. . . . Commerce among the States is not a technical legal conception, but a practical one, drawn from the course of business. When cattle are sent for sale from a place in one State, with the expectation that they will end their transit, after purchase, in another, and when in effect they do so, with only the interruption necessary to find a purchaser at the stockyards, and when this is a typical constantly recurring course, the current thus existing is a *current of commerce among the States,* and the purchase of the cattle is a part and incident of such commerce.

The interpretation of interstate commerce made in *Swift and Co.* v. *United States* revived the conception of the Constitution as a living organism capable of meeting the exigencies of an expanding national life. It refuted the anachronistic view, propounded in the *Sugar Trust Case,* that commerce is confined to transportation, and revealed the "commerce clause" as the key to the richest source of national authority over the intricate ramifications of modern enterprise. The reading of the Constitution by judges is something like the reading of the scriptures by clergymen; a passage that is commonplace to one may appear a revelation to another. Justice Holmes, in whom common sense was articulated by the subtlest logic and expressed in the most cogent language, could not conceive that a national government was without power in matters requiring national action. And he won assent to his conviction that interstate commerce did require national action by defining it as something more than the mere physical movement of goods across state lines: as "a current of commerce among the states", the tributaries of which are the local business transactions. It follows from this definition that when a local act done within a single state clogs the stream, it affects the current of commerce, and Congress may remove the congestion under the constitutional power conferred by the "commerce clause."[37]

This broad construction of the "commerce clause" disclosed new potentialities for the affirmative exertion of national power over American industry. In the light of this interpretation the commerce power conferred authority not only to prescribe rules and regulations for commerce—to "control and restrain"—but to "foster" and "protect" it as well. The orthodox view had been that the Constitution must be preserved against the dangers of broad construction. But the Supreme Court seemed to recognize at last that the gravest menace to the Constitution was the kind of strict construction that favored the concentration of economic power and tended to abolish economic freedom. Hence, the new trend of judicial statesmanship was toward shifting the burden of constitutional limitations from government to business. But the Court also seemed to realize that the American economic structure in the twentieth century was the aggregate of numerous complicated and sensitive parts, most of which were of local origin and habitat; that the failure of any of the parts to function properly threw out of gear the whole structure; that the conceptions of commerce and local activity prevailing in the "horse-and-buggy" days were no longer applicable to an age of electricity; and that a balanced national prosperity required national co-ordination and direction above and beyond the scope of national power as originally conceived by the framers of the Constitution.

With the *Swift Case* as the starting point, the Supreme Court made successive extensions of the commerce power. In one case after another it permitted Congress to reach heretofore sacrosanct "local activities" whenever they impeded the free flow of the current of commerce. *Gibbons* v. *Ogden* had defined what the States could not do by virtue of the "commerce clause"; but the *Swift Case* and those that followed developed constructively, for the first time, what Congress could do. In *Southern Ry.* v *United States*,[38] the Court held that Congress could remove any danger to interstate commerce arising from any source, and sustained the validity of the Safety Appliance Acts, which applied to all vehicles used both in interstate and intrastate commerce. Asserting that the commerce power is plenary, it held that "it is no objection to such an exertion of this power that the dangers intended to be avoided arise, in whole or in part, out of matters connected with intrastate commerce." In the *Second Employers' Liability Cases*, the Employers' Liability Act of 1910, regulating the relations of carriers to their employees, was sustained with the argument that it is the "effect upon interstate commerce" and not "the source of the injury" which is "the criterion of Congressional power."[39] In the *Shreveport Case*[40] the power of the Interstate Commerce Commission to fix the intrastate rates of an interstate carrier was affirmed on the broad principle that "the authority of Congress is at all times adequate to meet the varying exigencies that arise and to protect the national interest by securing the freedom of interstate commercial intercourse from local control." In *Ferger* v. *United States*[41] the Court, upholding the right of Congress to punish a conspiracy to forge bills of lading, declared that the commerce power, "if it is to exist, must include the authority to deal with obstructions to interstate commerce, and with a host of other acts which, because of their relation and influence upon interstate commerce, come within the power of Congress to regulate, although they are not interstate commerce in and of themselves." This principle was restated three years later by Chief Justice Taft in the following terms: "Commerce is a unit and does not regard state lines, and while, under the Constitution, interstate and intrastate commerce are ordinarily subject to regulation by different sovereignties, yet when they are so mingled together that the supreme authority, the Nation, cannot exercise complete effective control over interstate commerce without incidental regulation of intrastate commerce, such incidental regulation is not an invasion of state authority or a violation of the proviso."[42] This was, of course, giving national power no more than its due. For to deny Congress the right to regulate where interstate and intrastate commerce are "inextricably commingled" would be to give that right to the state or states involved and, hence, to make the states, and not the nation, supreme in the national field.[43]

These decisions involved cases which tested the constitutionality of an imposing volume of federal legislation enacted since the Interstate Commerce Act of 1887 with a view to implementing the "commerce clause." Of these laws, the Adamson Act of 1916, which prescribed an eight-hour day for railroad employees and curbed the employers' power to decrease wages, was the first attempt to use the "commerce clause" as a means of infringing upon "freedom of contract." It was passed as an emergency measure to prevent a threatened strike of railroad trainmen, and it was chiefly in the guise of compulsory arbitration designed to meet an emergency that it was sustained in the sharply contested case of *Wilson* v. *New*.[44] Chief Justice White's majority opinion in this case made a notable extension of the meaning of interstate commerce in terms of the national government's regulatory powers. After asserting that "emergency may not call into life a power which has never lived", the chief justice declared:

> If acts which, if done, would interrupt, if not destroy interstate commerce may be by anticipation legislatively prevented, by the same token the power to regulate may be exercised to guard against the cessation of interstate commerce threatened by a failure of employers and employees to agree as to the standard of wages, such standard being an essential prerequisite to the uninterrupted flow of interstate commerce.

Another milestone in the extension of the commerce power was the case of *Stafford* v. *Wallace*,[45] which sustained the Packers and Stockyards Act of 1921. This act regulated stockyard facilities, the purchase and care of livestock, the activities of livestock dealers, the rates and charges of commission men and stockyard owners, all of whom were required to register with the secretary of agriculture and to submit to rules and practices prescribed by him. It was attacked as an unconstitutional attempt by the federal government to regulate a wholly intrastate business, but the Court, speaking through Chief Justice Taft, replied:

> The stockyards are not a place of rest or final destination. Thousands of head of livestock arrive daily by carload and trainload lots, and must be promptly sold and disposed of and moved out to give place to the constantly flowing traffic that presses behind. The stockyards are a throat through which the current flows and the transactions which occur therein are only incidents to this current from the West to the East, and from one State to another. Such transactions cannot be separated from the movement to which they contribute and necessarily take on its character. The Commission men are essential in making the sales without which the flow of the current would be obstructed, and this, whether they are made to packers or dealers. The dealers are essential to the stock farmers and feeders. The sales are not, in this aspect, merely local transactions. They create a local change of title, it is true, but they do not stop the flow; they merely change the private interests in the subject of the current, not interfering with, but, on the contrary, being indispensable to its continuity. The origin of the livestock is in the West, its ultimate destination known to, and intended by, all engaged in the business is in the Middle West and

East, either as meat products or stock for feeding and fattening. This is the definite and understood course of business. The stockyards and the sales are necessary factors in the middle of this current of commerce.

In thus expanding the meaning of the "commerce clause", the Supreme Court also conceded to Congress the exercise of the police power which does not figure among the enumerated grants made to the federal government. The police power gives the states authority to care for the health, safety, morals and welfare of the people subject to the limitations imposed by both the state and federal constitutions. Yet despite the Tenth Amendment, the Supreme Court decided that "when the United States exerts any of the powers conferred upon it by the Constitution, no valid objection can be based upon the fact that such exercise may be attended by the same incidents which attend the exercise by a State of its police power, or that it may tend to accomplish a similar purpose."[46] The question, then, whenever it is contended that Congress has encroached upon the state police power, is whether it has done so while exercising one of the powers conferred on it by the Constitution. It is because Congress was declared to be acting within its authority over interstate commerce that the Supreme Court sustained such ostensible encroachments on the police power as the prohibition of transportation from one state to another of lottery tickets,[47] of impure foods,[48] of diseased animals,[49] and of women for purposes of prostitution.[50] On the other hand, the Child Labor Act of 1916, prohibiting transportation in interstate commerce of articles manufac-

[ 162 ]

tured by child labor, was invalidated by a divided Court.[51] Justice Day, speaking for the majority, declared: "In our view the necessary effect of this act is, by means of a prohibition against the movement in interstate commerce of ordinary commercial commodities, to regulate the hours of labor of children in factories and mines within the States, a purely state authority." Justice Holmes, however, with the concurrence of three more dissenters, argued that "it is not for this Court to pronounce when prohibition is necessary to regulation . . . to say that it is permissible as against strong drink but not as against the product of ruined lives."

While the Supreme Court was developing the "commerce clause" constructively as a source of national power, it was using the "due process" clause as a barrier against state regulation of economic activity. This general trend of judicial statesmanship toward nationalism conformed, on the whole, to the economic and political realities of twentieth-century America. Technological progress, which within a short time made possible the automobile, the airplane and the radio, in addition to the railroad, enabled Americans to master the immensities of a continent and accelerated that process of standardization which the outside world has come to regard as peculiarly American. At the same time, the World War, apart from its contribution to the emotional content of nationalism, necessitated the concentration of power in the hands of the federal government and accustomed the American people to look more and more to Washington, rather than to the states, for governmental guidance and control. More than at any

[ 163 ]

time since it was founded, the union of states was a united nation.

But the same forces which have promoted nationalism within the United States have also made for internationalism by increasing the economic interdependence among nations. The tragedy of the present-day world is largely due to the fact that this truth, though almost universally recognized, has not been acted upon; and that, as a result, the nationalistic politics of the postwar era have been at loggerheads with its economic realities. But it should be clear by now, even to the most inveterate isolationists, that, while America can remain tolerably free from political entanglements, economic isolation in an integrated and interdependent world economy is unthinkable. This economic solidarity makes it more than ever imperative that the policies which the United States chooses to pursue—whether co-operative or isolationist—should be formulated and applied by a centralized authority. Such events or conditions abroad as financial collapse in Austria, a Trade Pact within the British Empire, deflationary policies in France, abandonment of the gold standard by Britain, debt repudiation by Germany, or currency devaluation in Japan, necessitate compensatory readjustments in our own economy which must be made on a national scale. When constitutional limitations interpose obstacles to effective action in the face of such worldwide developments, whatever the ostensible grounds, the real issue is no longer national authority against states' rights but, as has been well said, "national authority versus no authority."

The Roosevelt Administration was confronted in

March 1933 with a breakdown of the national economy
the more menacing because it was partly the repercussion of a worldwide crisis. It, therefore, had to make
the utmost use of its constitutional powers; and it naturally sought in the "commerce clause"—the most potent of these powers—the requisite authority for the
most drastic of the measures it initiated for meeting
the national emergency. But it was unfortunate that
the National Industrial Recovery Act was so drawn
that when it came up for the inevitable judicial test it
was unanimously invalidated because it involved an improper delegation of the legislative power.[52] Chief
Justice Hughes, after pointing out that though "extraordinary conditions may call for extraordinary
remedies" . . . they "do not create or enlarge constitutional power", put his finger on the basic weakness of
the act—namely, the legislative character of the codes
of fair competition. ". . . The statutory plan," he
said, "is not simply one for voluntary effort. It does
not seek merely to endow voluntary trade or industrial
associations or groups with privileges or immunities.
It involves the coercive exercise of the law-making
power. The codes of fair competition . . . are codes
of laws. If valid they place all persons within their
reach under the obligation of positive law, binding
equally those who assent and those who do not assent.
Violations of the provisions of the codes are punishable
as crimes." Since, then, the codes were in effect laws,
were they enacted by a proper delegation of the law-
making power? After a searching inquiry the chief
justice answered with an emphatic negative. "Section 3
of the Recovery Act," he concluded, "is without prec-

edent. It supplies no standards. . . . It does not undertake to prescribe rules of conduct to be applied to particular states of fact determined by appropriate administrative procedure. Instead of prescribing rules of conduct, it authorizes the making of codes to prescribe them. . . . We think that the code-making authority thus conferred is an unconstitutional delegation of legislative power." Or, in the suggestive words of Mr. Justice Cardozo's concurring opinion, "the delegated power of legislation which has found expression in this code is not canalized within banks that keep it from overflowing. It is unconfined and vagrant."

Had the Court confined itself to this issue it would have rendered a sound decision, and the demolition of the N.R.A. would have been none the less complete. But the unfortunate choice of the *Schechter Case* as a test of the constitutionality of the statute tempted the Court into a narrowing redefinition of the concept of interstate commerce. The *Schechter Case* involved a commodity consumed at the point of destination. The poultry shipped from other states came to a dead rest in New York; it did not go back into the current of commerce either in the original or in any altered form. Accordingly, the prices charged by the Schechters and the wages and hours of labor they fixed were deemed too remote or indirect in their effect upon interstate commerce. Local transactions, the Court ruled, may be regulated by Congress if their effect upon interstate commerce is direct; but if the effect is indirect, then they "remain within the domain of state power." And the chief justice added that "the distinction between direct and indirect effects of intrastate transactions upon interstate commerce must be recognized as a fundamental one, essential to the maintenance of our constitutional system."

Not content with having killed the goose, the Court proceeded to dissect it and, in so doing, created abounding confusion. "For the confusion that has been introduced into this important constitutional issue," said a well-known commentator, "the courts must be held in considerable part responsible. No one can read certain passages in Chief Justice Hughes's opinion in the *Schechter Case* without getting the impression that while Congress is powerless to exert control over the Schechters' hours of labor, wages and local sales because they did not directly 'affect' interstate commerce, the state of New York might have exerted such control. This view was not set forth in so many words, but it was clearly implied in such a general utterance as this: 'But where the effect of intrastate transactions upon interstate commerce is merely indirect, such transactions remain within the domain of state power.' And the chief justice went on to say for the Court that if the commerce clause were construed as the government sought to have it interpreted, 'the authority of the state over its domestic concerns would exist only by sufferance of the federal government.' At another point, he spoke of the federal authority as 'overriding the authority of the states to deal with domestic problems arising from labor conditions in their internal commerce.' In other words, he voiced the view that Congress by the National Industrial Recovery Act had invaded the domain of state power, interfered with the states' authority over its domestic concerns, meddled with its domestic problems. . . . The chief justice knows as well as any other competent student of constitutional law that such matters are not, under the Constitution of the United States as interpreted and applied by the Court itself, subject to unrestricted state control, if indeed to any state control at all."[53]

This strict construction of interstate commerce was maintained by the Supreme Court, despite the differences between poultry and coal, when it invalidated the Guffey Coal Act.[54] "The government's contentions in defense of the labor provisions," said Mr. Justice Sutherland for the majority, "are really disposed of adversely by our decision in the *Schechter Case*. The only perceptible difference between that case and this is that in the *Schechter Case,* the federal power was asserted with respect to commodities which had come to rest after their interstate transportation; while here, the case deals with commodities at rest before interstate commerce has begun. That difference is without significance. The federal regulatory power ceases when interstate commercial intercourse ends; and, correlatively, the power does not attach until interstate commercial intercourse begins."[55] Chief Justice Hughes, in a separate opinion, agreed that "production—in this case mining—which precedes commerce, is not commerce; and that the power to regulate commerce among the several states is not a power to regulate industry within the State." But he argued that the invalidity of the labor provisions did not also invalidate the provisions "for the regulation of the prices of bituminous coal sold in interstate commerce", and insisted that the expressed intent of Congress to keep the two parts of the act separable should be respected by the Court. In his dissenting opinion Mr. Justice Cardozo agreed with the chief justice concerning the separability of the price-fixing from the labor provisions. But while he upheld the validity of the former "as applied to transactions in interstate commerce and to those in intrastate commerce where interstate commerce is directly or intimately affected", he avoided extending the same broad construction to the latter. Thus the lengthy debate of the Guffey Coal Act by the justices did not materially advance the applicability of the commerce power to industry declared to be intrastate beyond the unsatisfactory stage where it was left by the *Schechter Case*.

To recapitulate, the "commerce clause", so far as it applies to interstate commerce, was conceived primarily as a means of regulating coastwise traffic; but its potentialities as a builder and unifier of the national economy were revealed by Marshall. Under Taney and the "states' rights" influences of his day, a fruitful distinction was made between the "commerce power" in the abstract and the subjects on which it can be exercised; and on the basis of this distinction the commerce power was divided between Congress and the states. With the ascendancy of nationalism and laissez faire during the post-Civil War era, the states were completely foreclosed from asserting any rights in matters of commerce, while at the same time Congress was cramped in its attempted broader use of the power. At the turn of the century, however, the Court, yielding to the sway of popular antagonism to trusts and monopolies, lifted its restrictions upon Congress and began to forge the "commerce clause" into an effective weapon of national authority. Encouraged, Congress tapped the commerce power at every source and successfully asserted the national authority in fields where the states once claimed exclusive jurisdiction. This expansion was halted by the Supreme Court during the second part of the first Roosevelt Administration. But the history of the "commerce clause" and the popular verdict of 1936 warrant the belief that this contraction of the commerce power cannot be permanent.

## CHAPTER VIII

# The Government and the People's Money

RESISTANCE TO TAXATION, as every schoolboy knows, has been a powerful factor in English and American history. In conjunction with the religious question, it precipitated in seventeenth-century England the long revolution which ultimately established the sovereignty of Parliament; and it was the vital issue in the conflict between the landowning and commercial oligarchy of England and the thirteen colonies which led to their armed secession and the eventual independence of the United States of America. Yet despite this strong tradition, and a Constitution so framed and interpreted as to afford the maximum protection to private property, in no other field is the authority of the federal government less encumbered by constitutional limitations than in taxing, spending, coining money and regulating its value. It is true that the power to tax and its derivative, the power to spend, as well as the power "to coin money" and "regulate the value thereof", are deemed subject to the Fifth Amendment, which decrees, among other things, that the federal government shall not deprive any person of his liberty or property without due process of law. But the efficacy of the "due process" clause as a curb on these particular powers and a safeguard of fiscal security has been inferior to its restrictive effect on the other substantive powers of Congress. The following discussion will attempt to substantiate this thesis and to appraise briefly its far-reaching implications.

The taxing power, the first in the list of powers expressly delegated to Congress, is couched in the following language:

> The Congress shall have power to lay and collect taxes, duties, imposts and excises to pay the debts and provide for the common defense and general welfare of the United States; but all duties, imposts and excises shall be uniform throughout the United States.[1]

It has been argued by staunch nationalists that this provision gave to Congress two separate and distinct substantive powers: (1) the power to lay and collect taxes, and (2) the power to provide for the common defense and general welfare of the United States. The opponents of this view, however, have pointed to the syntax and punctuation of the provision, and to the intent of its framers as disclosed by the proceedings of the Constitutional Convention. They have contended, moreover, that the reading of an independent grant of power into the "general welfare" clause would be inconsistent with the fundamental purpose of the Constitution, for it would tend to create a national government vested with general and unlimited powers. "Congress," said Jefferson, "are not to lay taxes *ad libitum,* for any purpose they please; but only to pay the debts or provide for the welfare of the Union. In like manner they are not to do any thing they please, to provide for the general welfare; but only to lay taxes for that purpose. To consider the latter phrase, not as describing the purpose of the first, but as giving a distinct and independent power to do any act they please, which might be for the good of the Union, would render all the preceding and subsequent enumerations of power completely useless. It would reduce the whole instrument to a single phrase, that of instituting a congress with power to do what ever would be for the good of the United States; and, as they would be the sole judges of the good or evil, it would also be a power to do whatever evil they pleased."[2]

Hence, the words "and provide for the common defense and general welfare", read in sequential conjunction with "to pay the debts", have come to be construed as specifying the second and third of the purposes of federal taxation, and, therefore, as a limitation on the taxing power. According to Justice Story's illuminating paraphrase, the subsection in question should be understood to say that "the Congress shall have power to lay and collect taxes . . . *in order* to pay the debts, and to provide for the common defense and general welfare of the United States."[3] This reading leaves no doubt as to the dependence of the "general welfare" clause on the part of the subsection immediately preceding it. In the words of the same authoritative commentator: "A power to lay taxes for any purposes whatever is a general power; a power to lay taxes for certain specified purposes is a limited power. A power to lay taxes for the common defense and general welfare . . . is not

[ 173 ]

in common sense a general power. It is limited to those objects."[4]

With this much conceded, it is obvious that the extent to which Congress may tax and spend in order to provide for the *general welfare* depends on the meaning of these two words. As was to be expected, the strict-constructionists have advocated such an interpretation as would confine taxing and spending under the "general welfare" clause to those activities which the Constitution specifically delegates to the national legislature. "Whenever . . . money has been raised by the general authority," said Madison, "and is to be applied to a particular measure, a question arises whether the particular measure be within the enumerated authorities vested in Congress. If it be, the money requisite for it may be applied to it. If it be not, no such application can be made."[5] This narrow interpretation, however, would have precluded any expenditure from the national treasury for roads, canals and other internal improvements; and it was therefore practically abandoned by Madison's successor.[6] When Justice Story wrote his Commentaries, he was describing the actual "practice of the government" when he said: "Appropriations have never been limited by Congress to cases falling within the specific powers enumerated in the Constitution, whether those powers be construed in their broad or in their narrow sense. And in an especial manner appropriations have been made to aid internal improvements of various sorts, in our roads, our navigation, our streams, and other objects of a national character and importance."[7]

With the Supreme Court following presidential and

congressional leadership to a greater extent in the domain of taxing and spending than in any other department of constitutional law, the taxing power has come to be qualified only in the sense that it must be exercised for the purpose of providing for the *general* welfare. This means, in theory at least, that Congress cannot collect taxes from all or part of the people and apply them for the private benefit of individuals or groups. But if taxes are collected for a *public* purpose, there is no limit to the taxing power, regardless of whether it is exercised for the purpose of revenue, regulation or even destruction of the thing taxed. This is true despite Chief Justice Marshall's dictum that "the power to tax is the power to destroy", which can be construed as a limitation on the taxing power only when torn from its context. "But this reasoning," said the Court in *Knowlton* v. *Moore*,[8] referring to Marshall's celebrated aphorism, "has no application to a lawful tax, for if it had there would be an end to all taxation; that is to say, if a lawful tax can be defeated because the power which is manifested by its imposition may when further exercised be destructive, it would follow that every lawful tax would become unlawful, and therefore no taxation whatever could be levied." This was an elaboration of the principle that the destructive potentialities of a given tax do not constitute any limitation of the taxing power. In the concise language of Justice Swayne, "the right of taxation where it exists, is necessarily unlimited in its nature. It carries with it inherently the power to embarrass and destroy."[9]

The constitutional muniments of private property

have been of relatively little avail against this all-embracing scope of the taxing power, and there is no clearer evidence of this fact than the decisions of the Court itself. The opinion rendered in *Veazie Bank* v. *Fenno*[10] was one of the earlier indications of the vast purview of this power. In that case the Supreme Court was called upon to review an act of Congress imposing a 10 per cent tax on the notes of state banks with a view to restraining their circulation and thus establishing a uniform national currency. The Veazie Bank contended that the imposition of this tax impaired its franchise, granted by the state; but the Court, while admitting the possible validity of this contention, refused to enjoin Congress by invoking the "contract" or "due process" clause. Chief Justice Chase proclaimed the supremacy of the congressional taxing prerogative in the following words:

> It is insisted, however, that the tax in the case before us is excessive, and so excessive as to indicate a purpose on the part of Congress to destroy the franchise of the bank, and is, therefore, beyond the constitutional power of Congress. The first answer to this is that the judicial cannot prescribe to the legislative departments of the government limitations upon the exercise of its acknowledged powers. The power to tax may be exercised oppressively upon persons, but the responsibility of the legislature is not to the courts, but to the people by whom its members are elected. So if a particular tax bears heavily upon a corporation, or a class of corporations, it cannot, for that reason only, be pronounced contrary to the Constitution.

The only constitutional barriers to the taxing power were defined by the same chief justice in the *License*

*Tax Cases*[11] as follows: "It is true that the power of Congress to tax is a very extensive power. It is given in the Constitution, with only one exception and only two qualifications. Congress cannot tax exports, and it must impose direct taxes by the rule of apportionment, and indirect taxes by the rule of uniformity. Thus limited, and thus only, it reaches every subject and may be exercised at discretion."

This means that the taxing power may be exercised not only despite the consequent impairment of contractual obligations but with scant regard to "due process." The deterrent effect of the Fifth and the Fourteenth Amendments upon federal and state interference with property rights has been repeatedly stressed in the preceding pages. With respect to the taxing power, however, "due process" has been shorn of its efficacy. The extent of its emasculation is made clear in the following excerpt from Justice White's opinion in *McCray* v. *United States*:[12]

> Whilst undoubtedly both the Fifth and Tenth Amendments qualify, insofar as they are applicable, all the provisions of the Constitution, nothing in those amendments operates to take away the grant of power to tax conferred by the Constitution upon Congress. . . . The right of Congress to tax within its delegated power being unrestricted, except as limited by the Constitution, it was within the authority conferred on Congress to select the objects upon which an excise should be laid. It therefore follows that, in exerting its power, no want of due process of law could possibly result. . . . The judicial power may not usurp the functions of the legislative in order to control that branch of the government in the performance of its lawful duties. . . . The judiciary is without authority to avoid an act of Congress exerting

the taxing power, even in a case where to the judicial mind it seems that Congress had in putting such power in motion abused its lawful authority by levying a tax which was unwise or oppressive, or the result of the enforcement of which might be to indirectly affect subjects not within the powers delegated to Congress.[13]

The spending power, though not expressly granted, is, paradoxically, even broader than the taxing power from which it is impliedly derived. Once the money collected by taxation goes into the treasury, there is no way to question by court action the validity of the method by which it is spent. And though the spending of public money may vitally affect contracts and property rights, there is no way by which the person affected may invoke the protection of "due process" or the "contract clause." It is true that attempts in this direction have been made, but the Court has repeatedly refused jurisdiction in such cases. Moreover, congressional spending without judicial restraint has been the practice for so long that it has become one of the firmly established conventions of the American system, and it is extremely doubtful that the Court at this late stage will attempt to disturb it. The principle of judicial noninterference with federal spending was stated most categorically in the case of *Massachusetts v. Mellon*,[14] which involved the so-called Maternity Act passed by Congress in 1921. The act was challenged and an attempt was made to restrain the appropriations provided therein on the ground that they were intended for local, and not for national, purposes and hence constituted an invasion of the powers reserved to the states under the Tenth Amendment. The Court, however, speaking through Mr. Justice Sutherland, dismissed the cases and refused to consider the constitutional issues involved with the following conclusive argument:

> The right of a taxpayer to enjoin the execution of a Federal appropriation act, on the ground that it is invalid and will result in taxation for illegal purposes, has never been passed upon by this Court. In cases where it was presented, the question has either been allowed to pass sub silentio, or the determination of it expressly withheld. . . . If one taxpayer may champion and litigate such a cause, then every other taxpayer may do the same, not only in respect to the statute here under review, but also in respect of every other appropriation act and statute whose administration requires the outlay of public money, and whose validity may be questioned. The bare suggestion of such a result, with its attendant inconveniences, goes far to sustain the conclusion which we have reached, that a suit of this character cannot be maintained. It is of much significance that no precedent sustaining the right to maintain suits like this has been called to our attention although since the formation of the government, as an examination of the acts of Congress will disclose, a large number of statutes appropriating or involving the expenditure of moneys for non-Federal purposes have been enacted and carried into effect.

The Court's readiness to seize almost any pretext in order to avoid the issue is a gauge of the unfettered power of Congress to spend for any purpose and the futility of attempting to frustrate this established and popular prerogative by judicial action. The Court has apparently made up its mind not to attempt to exercise any restraint beyond the constitutional limitation of Article I, Section 9, Subsection 7, which provides that "no money shall be drawn from the treasury, but in consequence of appropriations made by law." Once the appropriation has been duly made, Congress may draw upon the treasury for any purpose that the legislators may judge to be within the ambit of the general welfare. This was precisely the conception of the "general welfare" clause expounded by Hamilton. "The terms 'general welfare'," he said, "were doubtless intended to signify more than was expressed or imported in those which preceded; otherwise numerous exigencies incident to the force of a nation would have been left without provision. The phrase is as comprehensive as any that could have been used, because it is not fit that the constitutional authority of the Union to appropriate its revenues should have been restricted within narrower limits than the 'general welfare', and because this necessarily embraces a vast variety of particulars which are susceptible neither of specification nor of definition. It is therefore of necessity left to the discretion of the National Legislature to pronounce upon the subjects which concern the general welfare, and for which, under that description, an appropriation of money is requisite and proper."[15]

Though feints at challenge have been made, the Hamiltonian conception of the power to spend for the general welfare has never been upset by the Supreme Court, not even in the much misunderstood *Hoosac Mills Case* (*United States* v. *Butler, et al*), which invalidated the AAA. For while the Court outlawed the processing taxes, it was powerless to stop the spending contemplated by the Agricultural Adjustment Act, and the government continued its benefit payments to farmers, notwithstanding the nullification of the whole plan.

A careful analysis of the Court's decision bears out the contention that the *Hoosac Mills Case,* whatever else it may have done, did not contract the scope of the taxing power. It is true that Mr. Justice Roberts, speaking for the majority, denied that "the expropriation of money from one group for the benefit of another" was a tax "in the general understanding of the term, and as used in the Constitution", namely, "an exaction for the support of the Government." But while he contended that the processing tax was "a mere incident" of the regulation of agricultural production and the Agricultural Adjustment Act was not "an exertion of the taxing power", he did not affirm that the act was therefore void "or the exaction uncollectible." In order to determine whether or not the exercise of the taxing power for other than revenue-raising purposes was valid, he turned to another criterion— namely, the constitutional validity of the particular purpose to which the tax was to be applied. "To paraphrase what was said in the *Head Money Cases . . ."* he argued, "if this is an expedient regulation by Congress, of a subject within one of its granted powers, 'and the end to be attained is one falling within that power, the act is not void, because, within a loose and more extended sense than was used in the Constitution,' the exaction is called a tax." Having conceded as much, however, the Court fell back on the argument that regulation of agricultural production was outside the purview of congressional jurisdiction. "The Act," continued Mr. Justice Roberts, "invades the reserved rights of the states. It is a statutory plan to regulate and control agricultural production, a matter beyond the powers delegated to the federal government. The tax, the appropriation of the funds raised, and the direction of their disbursement, are but parts of the plan. They are but means to an unconstitutional end." This conclusion ruled out the possibility of validation through appeal to the doctrine of "implied powers." For while, the Court argued, paraphrasing Marshall's celebrated dictum, "the power of taxation, which is expressly granted, may . . . be adopted as a means to carry into operation another power also expressly granted, . . . resort to the taxing power to effectuate an end which is not legitimate, not within the scope of the Constitution, is obviously inadmissible."

This position was maintained against the government's contention that the Agricultural Adjustment Act was constitutional because its taxing and spending features did not conduce to compulsion but to voluntary co-operation. "The regulation," said the Court, "is not in fact voluntary. The farmer, of course, may refuse to comply, but the price of such refusal is the loss of benefits. The amount offered is intended to be sufficient to exert pressure on him to agree to the proposed regulation. The power to confer or withhold unlimited benefits is the power to coerce or destroy."[16] But even assuming the voluntary and co-operative character of the plan, the majority opinion held that it would still be invalid; for whether federal funds were used to engender "coercion by economic pressure" or to purchase compliance, they were the means by which the Agricultural Adjustment Act sought to achieve an unconstitu-

tional end—"federal regulation of a subject reserved
to the states."

Taking up the argument that Congress is entitled to
determine the conditions under which a federal grant
of money shall be expended, the Court distinguished
between "a statute stating the conditions upon which
moneys shall be expended and one effective only upon
assumption of a contractual obligation to submit to a
regulation which otherwise could not be enforced";
for example, between a congressional appropriation in
aid of education accompanied by stipulations concerning the uses to which the money shall be put, and "an
appropriation to an educational institution which by its
terms is to become available only if the beneficiary enters
into a contract to teach doctrines subversive of the Constitution." The Court warned (a) that "an affirmance
of the authority of Congress so to condition the expenditure of an appropriation would tend to nullify all
constitutional limitations upon legislative power"; (b)
that "if, in lieu of compulsory regulation of subjects
within the states' reserved jurisdiction, which is prohibited, the Congress would invoke the taxing and
spending power as a means to accomplish the same end,
Clause 1 of Section 8 of Article 1 would become the
instrument for total subversion of the governmental
powers reserved to the individual states"; and (c) that
if the Agricultural Adjustment Act "is a proper exercise of the federal taxing power, evidently the regulation of all industry throughout the United States may
be accomplished by similar exercises of the same power"
—i.e., by exacting money from one branch of an industry and paying it to another branch "in every field of

activity which lies within the province of the states."

Stripped of its elaborate argument and its somewhat extreme and alarmist speculations, the majority opinion in the *Hoosac Mills Case* said, in effect, that if a particular tax is identified with an appropriation for its spending and the spending is for an unlawful end—i.e. encroachment by the federal government upon the domain reserved to the states—then the tax becomes unlawful too. The dissenting opinion undertook to refute this basic contention. "The power cf Congress to spend," said Mr. Justice Stone, with the concurrence of Mr. Justice Brandeis and Mr. Justice Cardozo, "is inseparable from persuasion to action over which Congress had no legislative control. Congress may not command that the science of agriculture be taught in state universities. But if it would aid the teaching of that science by grants to state institutions, it is appropriate, if not necessary, that the grant be on the condition, incorporated in the Morrill Act, . . . that it be used for the intended purpose. Similarly it would seem to be compliance with the Constitution, not violation of it, for the government to take and the university to give a contract that the grant would be so used. It makes no difference that there is a promise to do an act which the condition is calculated to induce. Condition and promise are alike valid since both are in furtherance of the national purpose for which the money is appropriated." To regard these "incidents of the authorized expenditure of money" as a limitation on the taxing and spending power would be to reverse the principle that "the granted power includes all those which are incident to it" and to rephrase the classic

Marshallian dictum as follows: "Let the expenditure be to promote the general welfare, still, if it is needful in order to insure its use for the intended purpose to influence any action which Congress cannot command because within the sphere of state government, the expenditure is unconstitutional."

But this limitation of the taxing and spending power, argued Mr. Justice Stone, would be rank discrimination. For "Congress through the Interstate Commerce Commission has set aside intrastate railroad rates. It has made and destroyed intrastate industries by raising or lowering tariffs. These results are said to be permissible because they are incidents of the commerce power and the power to levy duties on imports. . . . The only conclusion to be drawn is that results become lawful when they are incidents of those powers but unlawful when incident to the similarly granted power to tax and spend." Moreover, "such a limitation is contradictory, . . . destructive of the power to appropriate for the public welfare . . . and . . . incapable of practical application" . . . because it must "lead to absurd consequences", such as the following:

> The government may give seeds to farmers, but may not condition the gift upon their being planted in places where they are most needed or even planted at all. The government may give money to the unemployed but may not ask that those who get it shall give labor in return, or even use it to support their families. It may give money to sufferers from earthquake, fire, tornado, pestilence or flood, but may not impose conditions—health precautions designed to prevent the spread of disease, or induce the movement of population to safer or more sanitary areas. All that, be-

[ 185 ]

cause it is purchased regulation infringing state powers, must be left for the states, who are unable or unwilling to supply the necessary relief. . . . Do all its activities collapse because, in order to effect the permissible purpose, in myriad ways the money is paid out upon terms and conditions which influence action of the recipients within the states, which Congress cannot command?

This reasoning could lead to but one conclusion: "If the expenditure is for a national public purpose, that purpose will not be thwarted because payment is on condition which will advance that purpose. . . . If appropriation in aid of a program of curtailment of agricultural production is constitutional, and it is not denied that it is, payment to farmers on condition that they reduce their crop average is constitutional. It is not any the less so because the farmer at his own option promises to fulfill the condition." Nor were the three dissenting justices frightened by the possible abuses of the spending power which the majority opinion had conjured up with considerable imaginative verve. "The power to tax and spend," concluded Mr. Justice Stone, "is not without constitutional restraints. One restriction is that the purpose must be truly national. Another is that it may not be used to coerce action left to state control. Another is the conscience and patriotism of Congress and the Executive." And as a corrective to the tendency of the Bench to abuse judicial power, he quoted Justice Holmes to the effect that "legislators are the ultimate guardians of the liberties and welfare of the people in quite as great a degree as the courts."[17]

Despite the invalidation of the Agricultural Adjustment Act, the decision in the *Hoosac Mills Case* followed the broad Hamiltonian definition of the power to spend for the general welfare rather than the strict construction of Madison which confined taxing and spending only to the fields covered by the enumerated powers delegated to Congress. The Court did not deny to Congress the right to lay processing taxes on manufacturers of farm products and to spend the money thus collected for the general welfare. Nor did it assert that the federal government lacked power to appropriate and spend moneys in aid of agriculture by crop curtailment or otherwise. To the contrary, it clearly intimated that once the money collected by taxation was in the national treasury, its appropriation and expenditure could not be restrained by taxpayers. But while the majority opinion made no substantial inroads on the taxing and spending power, it taught Congress a lesson in legislative procedure; namely, that it should not identify a given tax with the specific purpose to which it is to be applied. It is clear that Congress could lawfully re-enact the very same processing taxes that were invalidated by passing an amendment to the Revenue Act without reference to benefit payments for crop curtailment. It is equally clear that Congress could thereafter lawfully appropriate funds in the general treasury for payment to farmers for crop, hog or any other form of restriction on production or livestock raising; for there would be no possible way of identifying the money collected from processing taxes as part of the money appropriated to the farmers, once those taxes are commingled with the general revenues. In short, if the processing tax had been dissociated from the bounties paid to induce curtailment of production, if, in other words, the taxing power had been exercised separately from the spending power, it is a reasonable inference from the language of the majority opinion that the Court would have been powerless to interfere and the Agricultural Adjustment Act would have been sustained.

Now while the only constitutional limitation on indirect taxation is the rule of uniformity with respect to direct taxation the taxing power was originally restricted by the provisions that "representatives and direct taxes shall be apportioned among the several states which may be included within this Union, according to their respective members . . .", and "no capitation or other direct tax shall be laid, unless in proportion to the census or enumeration herein before directed to be taken."[18] If the rule of apportionment was designed to safeguard wealth against numbers in a society which combined a capitalistic economy with political democracy, its efficacy would obviously depend to a great extent on the interpretation which the courts would choose to place upon the term "direct taxes." As early as 1796 a federal carriage tax imposed without apportionment was not regarded as a direct tax and was therefore upheld, the Court ruling that the only direct taxes were the capitation tax and a tax on land.[19] This definition was generally accepted during the next hundred years. In *Pacific Insurance Co. v. Soule*[20] a unanimous Court held that a federal tax upon the receipts of insurance companies from premiums and assessments, and upon all sums made or added during the year to their surplus or contingent funds, was not a direct tax, but a duty or excise, and therefore valid. In

*Scholey* v. *Rew*[21] the Court upheld a federal inheritance tax imposed by an act of 1864 which provided that a duty "shall be paid at the time when the successor, or any person in his right or on his behalf, shall become entitled in possession to his succession, or to the receipt of the income and profits thereof." Chief Justice Chase, speaking for the Court, declared: "Taxes on houses, land and other permanent real estate have always been deemed to be direct taxes, and capitation taxes, by the express words of the Constitution, are within the same category; but it has never been decided that any other legal exactions for the support of the Federal Government fall within the condition that unless laid in proportion to numbers the assessment is invalid."

An even more decisive pronouncement was made in 1881 when the Supreme Court, accepting the ruling made in *Hylton* v. *United States,* unanimously upheld the constitutionality of an act of Congress which taxed income derived from every kind of property and from every trade, profession or employment.[22] Before rendering its decision the Court made a conscientious effort to determine the intent of the framers relative to the precise kind of taxation that was to be subjected to the rule of apportionment. The Court's opinion, after summarizing the results of this historical research, reaffirmed its previous conclusion "that *direct taxes,* within the meaning of the Constitution, are only capitation taxes, as expressed in that instrument, and taxes on real estate", and that the income tax under review "is within the category of an excise or duty."

But the legislative and judicial trend which had prevailed in the field of direct taxation since 1796 was destined to be reversed by the impact of the economic forces that were shaping the course of American history toward the close of the nineteenth century. The turning point came in the case of *Pollock* v. *Farmers' Loan and Trust Co.*[23] on a test of the constitutionality of "an Act to reduce taxation", passed in 1894, which levied taxes on income from real estate and income from personal property including municipal bonds. In the first decision, handed down on April 8, 1895, the Court held that the tax on income from real estate was a direct tax, hence invalid without apportionment, while the tax on income from municipal bonds was void because of lack of power to tax the source. With regard to the other questions involved, including taxation of income from personal property, the Court, being equally divided, was unable to render a decision.

A petition for a rehearing having been granted, a shift of one of the justices to the opposition brought forth, on May 20, 1895, a five-to-four decision to the effect that taxes on the income of personal property were likewise direct taxes and hence void because not apportioned. The prevailing opinion, written by Chief Justice Fuller, ignored the precedents made, among others, in *Hylton* v. *United States, Springer* v. *United States, Pacific Insurance Co.* v. *Soule* and *Scholey* v. *Rew,* and placed its chief reliance on the opinion of Madison, who thought that the *Hylton Case* had been badly decided. In other words, the Court adopted Madison's strict-constructionist views and rejected Hamilton's broad interpretation of the taxing power with respect to direct taxation despite the fact that it was the Hamiltonian viewpoint that had consistently molded previous decisions in this field. Both precedent and the popular will were set aside by the chief justice in the following passage, which was ominously reminiscent of the dictum in the *Dred Scott Case* that the Constitution "speaks . . . with the same meaning and intent with which it spoke when it came from the hands of the framers":

> We know of no reason for holding otherwise than that the words "direct taxes", on the one hand, and "duties, imposts, and excise", on the other, were used in the Constitution in their natural and obvious sense. Nor, in arriving at what those terms embrace, do we perceive any ground for enlarging them beyond, or narrowing them within, their natural and obvious import at the time the Constitution was framed and ratified.

But how was this view to be reconciled with the decision in the *Hylton Case,* which had set a precedent for nearly a century? "The Act of June 5, 1794," said the Court, "laying duties upon carriages for the conveyance of persons was enacted at a time of threatened war. Bills were then pending in Congress to increase the military force of the United States, and to authorize increased taxation in various directions. It was, therefore, as much a part of a system of taxation in war times, as was the income tax of the War of the Rebellion." Proceeding to examine the equity of direct taxation, the Court argued that a tax on income—i.e., the beneficial use of property—does not differ from a direct tax on property, since property in itself is a fiction unless beneficially used. "Whatever the speculative views of political economists or revenue reformers may be," said Chief Justice Fuller, "can it be properly held that the Constitution . . . authorizes a general unapportioned tax on the products of the farm and the rent of real estate, although imposed merely because of ownership . . . as belonging to a totally different class from that which includes the property from whence the income proceeds?" The five justices' characteristic answer to this question was: "We do not think so."

The chorus of protest against the invalidation of the federal income-tax law of 1894 was led by the four dissenting justices who, in as many vigorous opinions, did not shrink from emphasizing the political and social consequences of their colleagues' action. Indeed, the prevailing and dissenting opinions in this case read like a fiery parliamentary debate on a great question of social reform rather than a judicial decision. "The practical effect of the decision . . .", said Justice Harlan, "is to give to certain kinds of property a position of favoritism and advantage inconsistent with the fundamental principles of our social organization, and to invest them with power and influence that may be perilous to that portion of the American people upon whom rests the larger part of the burdens of the government, and who ought not to be subjected to the dominion of aggregated wealth any more than the property of the country should be at the mercy of the lawless." Justice Jackson denounced the decision because it disregarded "not only . . . the great principle of equality in taxation, but the further principle that in the imposition of taxes for the benefit of the government the burdens thereof should be imposed upon those having most *ability* to bear them." He charged that the Court's ruling would lead to a "directly opposite result"; for it would relieve "the citizens having the greater *ability,* while the burdens of taxation are made to fall most heavily and oppressively upon those having the least ability", and it would lighten "the burden upon the larger number, in some states subject to the tax" while placing it "most unequally and disproportionately on the smaller number in other states." And he concluded by characterizing the decision as "the most disastrous blow ever struck at the constitutional power of Congress."

Referring to the possibility of enlarging the constitutional power of Congress by amending the Constitution, Justice White, in his dissenting opinion, made the following trenchant observations:

> The suggestion that if the construction now adopted by the Court brings about hurtful results, it can be cured by an amendment to the Constitution instead of sustaining the conclusion reached, shows its fallacy. The Hylton case was decided more than one hundred years ago. The income tax laws of the past were enacted also years ago. At the time they were passed, the debates and reports conclusively show that they were made to conform to the rulings in the Hylton case. Since all these things were done, the Constitution has been repeatedly amended. These amendments followed the Civil War, and were adopted for the purpose of supplying defects in the national power. Can it be doubted that if an intimation had been conveyed that the decisions of this court would or could be overruled, so as to deprive the government of an essential power of taxation, the amendments would have rendered such a change of ruling impossible? The adoption of the amendments, none of which repudiated

the uniform policy of the government, was practically a ratification of that policy and an acquiescence in the settled rule of interpretation theretofore adopted.

It is, I submit, greatly to be deplored that, after more than one hundred years of our national existence . . . , this court should consider itself compelled to go back to a long repudiated and rejected theory of the Constitution by which the government is deprived of an inherent attribute of its being, a necessary power of taxation.

When four justices could be stirred to such vehement and devastating criticism of their brethren, there was little left for the politicians to add. Justice Brown's characterization of the decision as a possible "first step toward the submergence of the liberties of the people in a sordid despotism of wealth" could not be improved on by William Jennings Bryan. "If you want criticism," said the latter, "read the dissenting opinions of the Court." And he voiced what millions of Americans thought of judicial review at that moment when he added: "The income tax was not unconstitutional when it was passed. It was not unconstitutional when it went before the Supreme Court for the first time. It did not become unconstitutional until one judge changed his mind, and we cannot be expected to know when a judge will change his mind."[24] It was probably this last circumstance—the fact that a vital federal law was invalidated because of a single judge's shift of position—that helped more than any other to dramatize the issue and to make the Supreme Court appear as the inveterate defender of property rights against the national will. Nor was this popular conception belied by the record of the Court during the time when

American politics was dominated by big business and the doctrines of laissez faire. The Court's decisions in the *Sugar Trust Case,* the *Debs Case* and the *Pollock Case,* all of which were handed down in the single year 1895, contributed powerfully to that movement of protest which found political expression in the capture of the Democratic party by the Populists and the hard-fought election of 1896. Despite the Republican victory the clamor for the democratization of the American government did not cease. It was heeded by the Supreme Court even before the turn of the century; it soon penetrated into the Republican party itself; and it gave impetus to a wave of reform which left its impress on the political life of America. In the economic and fiscal field this reform movement contributed in 1913, as the repercussion and remedy of the decision in the *Pollock Case,* the Sixteenth Amendment, which empowers Congress to "lay and collect taxes on incomes, from whatever source derived, without apportionment among the several states, and without regard to any census or enumeration."

In addition to the taxing and spending powers which, as we have seen, confer on the federal government what amounts to inherent sovereignty over property, Congress has the power "to coin money" and "regulate the money thereof."[25] Now while the power to tax and spend is also possessed by the several states and is exercised concurrently with the federal government, authority over the currency, which by legislative fiat and judicial interpretation has also become the power of the "printing press", is exclusively a national prerogative.[26] The federal government is neither expressly authorized nor expressly forbidden to issue paper money which is not convertible into specie; but the Constitution specifically enjoins that "no state shall . . . make anything but gold and silver coin a tender in payment of debts."[27] In *Hepburn* v. *Griswold* the Supreme Court held that Congress also had no authority to make anything but specie legal tender in payment of debts contracted prior to the passage of the Legal Tender Acts, and that such authority could not properly be implied from the powers expressly granted. But *Knox* v. *Lee,* it will be recalled, soon afterward reversed this position and held that inconvertible paper money—i.e., greenbacks—was legal tender as to all contracts for the payment of money, the power to create such money being derived from the power to wage war and to preserve the Union. It was not, however, until 1884, by the decision in *Juilliard* v. *Greenman,*[28] that the power to issue fiat money became virtually limitless. In this case the Court went one step beyond *Knox* v. *Lee* and held that Congress had the power to make inconvertible treasury notes legal tender in payment of private debts whenever, in its judgment, the exigencies required it, whether in time of peace or in time of war. The decision read by Justice Gray is so sweeping an affirmation of national power that it places a severe strain on the conception of the government of the United States as one of limited powers.

> The breath and comprehensiveness of the words of the Constitution are nowhere more strikingly exhibited than in regard to the powers over the subjects of revenue, finance and currency. . . . It appears to us to follow as a logical and necessary consequence, that Congress has the power to

issue the obligations of the United States in such form, and
to impress upon them such qualities as currency for the purchase of merchandise and the payment of debts, as accord
with the usage of sovereign governments. . . . The power
of making the notes of the United States a legal tender in
payment of private debts, being included in the power to
borrow money and to provide a national currency, is not
defeated or restricted by the fact that its exercise may affect
the value of private contracts. . . . Such being our conclusion in matter of law, the question whether at any particular
time, in war or in peace, the exigency is such, by reason of
unusual and pressing demands on the resources of the government, or of the inadequacy of the supply of gold and
silver coin to furnish the currency needed for the uses of
the government and of the people, that it is, as a matter of
fact, wise and expedient to resort to this means, is a political
question to be determined by Congress when the question
of exigency arises, and not a judicial question, to be after-
wards passed upon by Congress.

The implications flowing from the Court's language
cannot be more aptly described than by quoting the
last paragraph from the dissenting opinion of Justice
Field:

From the decision of the Court I see only evil likely to follow. There have been times within the memory of all of us
when the legal tender notes of the United States were not
exchangeable for more than one half of their nominal value.
The possibility of such depreciation will always attend paper
money. This inborn infirmity no mere legislative declaration
can cure. If Congress has the power to make the notes a legal
tender and to pass as money or its equivalent, why should
not a sufficient amount be issued to pay the bonds of the
United States as they mature? Why pay interest on the mil-

lions of dollars of bonds now due, when Congress can in one day make the money to pay the principal? And why should there be any restraint upon unlimited appropriations by the government for all imaginary schemes of public government, if the printing press can furnish the money that is needed for them?

But though the *Juilliard Case* went far, the Gold Clause decisions of 1935 went a decisive step further. "A contract to pay a sum in money," Justice Gray had remarked in *Juilliard* v. *Greenman*, "without any stipulation as to the kind of money in which it shall be paid, may always be satisfied by the payment of that sum in any currency which is lawful money at the place and time at which payment is to be made." This statement implied that if an agreement stipulated payment in gold or other metallic coin, the tender of inconvertible paper currency would not discharge the obligation, and that Congress presumably could not legislate so as to make such tender in such cases lawful. Now while the Constitution does not specifically prohibit the federal government, as it does the states, from impairing the obligation of contracts, it has always been assumed that contract rights, being property rights, are protected with equal efficacy by the Fifth Amendment. This view, however, is hardly tenable after the Court's most recent pronouncements. In the case of *Norman* v. *Baltimore & Ohio R. R. Co.*,[29] decided in February 1935, the Court was called upon to decide the validity of the Joint Resolution of Congress, of June 5, 1933, which nullified the "gold clauses" in existing contractual obligations. The resolution provided that "every provision contained in . . . any obligation which purports to give the obligee a right to require payment in gold" is "against public policy", and that every such obligation, "whether or not any such provision is contained therein . . . shall be discharged upon payment, dollar for dollar, in any coin or currency which at the time of payment is legal tender for public and private debts." By this simple resolution Congress at one stroke reduced the value of existing contracts by many billions of dollars; and by upholding its validity, the Court, in effect, eliminated the Fifth Amendment as a limitation upon legislative interference with vested rights. In deciding the case favorably to the government, the Court clearly established the proposition that Congress, in the exercise of its delegated powers, may impair or even destroy private obligations without compensation whenever the enforcement of such private obligations would tend to interfere with the exercise by Congress of its constitutional powers.

Nor is this conclusion applicable to the revenue powers only. The comprehensive argument made by Chief Justice Hughes, who wrote the prevailing opinion, covered the exercise of every congressional power and touched contracts of every description save those made by the United States. After citing the *Legal Tender Cases* as illustrations of the power of Congress to impair private obligations in the exercise of its money powers, the chief justice said:

> The instant cases involve contracts between private parties, but the question necessarily relates as well to the contracts or obligations of States and municipalities, or of their political subdivisions, that is, to such engagements as are within the reach of the applicable national power. . . . Contracts,

however express, cannot fetter the constitutional authority of the Congress. Contracts may create rights of property, but when contracts deal with a subject matter which lies within the control of the Congress, they have a congenital infirmity. Parties cannot remove their transactions from the reach of dominant constitutional power by making contracts about them. This principle has familiar illustration in the exercise of the power to regulate commerce. If shippers and carriers stipulate for specified rates, although the rates may be lawful when the contracts are made, if Congress through the Interstate Commerce Commission exercises its authority and prescribes different rates, the latter control and override inconsistent stipulations in contracts previously made. This is so, even if the contract be a charter granted by a State and limiting rates, or a contract between municipalities and carriers. . . . The reason is manifest. To subordinate the exercise of the Federal authority to the continuing operation of previous contracts would be to place to this extent the regulation of inter-State commerce in the hands of private individuals and to withdraw from the control of the Congress so much of the field as they might choose by "prophetic discernment" to bring within the range of their agreements. The Constitution recognizes no such limitation. The same reasoning applies to the constitutional authority of the Congress to regulate the currency and to establish the monetary system of the country. If the gold clauses now before us interfere with the policy of the Congress in the exercise of that authority, they cannot stand.

In the case of *Perry* v. *United States*,[30] decided on the same day, the Court said that the same reasoning does not apply to United States government obligations. This is so, said the Court, because the sovereign cannot use a power—i.e., the power to "coin money"—in a way to destroy what it had already done under another power—i.e., the power to borrow money "on the credit of the United States." But because the export or possession of gold was unlawful, continued the Court, "the question of value, in relation to transactions legally available to the plaintiff, would require a consideration of the purchasing power of the dollars which the plaintiff could have received." Thus, while theoretically denying to the government the right to abrogate the gold clause in its obligations, it prevented the claimant from recovering the difference between the depreciated and the former standard gold dollars by changing the legal meaning of the term "value." The term previously meant gold of a certain weight and fineness; but the Court, in order to avoid an impossible situation, now declared that value meant purchasing power and that plaintiff could not recover damages because he could not prove that he sustained a loss of purchasing power.

The Gold Clause decisions then are another striking example of the Court's willingness and ability to adjust constitutional law to dominant political and economic realities. The President, supported by Congress, and acting to meet the exigencies of a grave domestic and international situation, abandoned the gold standard and depreciated the currency. The repercussions of these acts affected drastically not only our own national economy but world markets and the fiscal policies of other nations. The Court was, therefore, confronted with a *fait accompli* which it knew it could not upset. Moreover, it knew that no decision it could make or dare to make could restore the *status quo* which existed before the executive and legislative branches had caused

abandonment of the gold standard; and it probably
realized that any attempt to do so might result in the
impairment of its own power and prestige. The
majority of the Court wisely subordinated the constitutional issues involved to these paramount considerations; and, following the precedent established during
the Civil War, it upheld the measures initiated by the
President and Congress with overwhelming popular
support in order to meet a comparable national emergency.

The *Perry Case,* which involved government obligations, illustrates the Court's ability to bow to expediency
and to impart new meanings to legal terms in order to
meet an unalterable *de facto* situation. The *Norman
Case,* on the other hand, which involved private contracts, hit at the very heart of the Fifth Amendment.
As Mr. Justice McReynolds said in his dissenting
opinion, "the Fifth Amendment limits all governmental
powers." It qualifies all the substantive powers of Congress and the powers implied from them. If Congress
by direct action—the joint resolution abrogating the
gold clauses—can destroy contract rights, of what
efficacy is "due process"? "Contracts, however express," said the chief justice, "cannot fetter the constitutional authority of the Congress." It would seem
to follow then that Congress may exert its lawful
powers notwithstanding the effect upon vested rights.
And if this is so, the Fifth Amendment, as a muniment
of property, has been reduced to a mere shadow.

The analysis attempted in this chapter leads to the
conclusion that the taxing, spending and money powers
are exercisable without any effective limitation, and

that they wield a more stringent control on private property than any of the other substantive powers of the federal government. Though "due process" under the Fifth Amendment has been an obstacle to Congress in the enactment of price-fixing, maximum-hour, minimum-wage and other regulatory legislation designed to promote social well-being, it has been powerless to check the national will with regard to taxation, spending and matters pertaining to money. And yet it is arguable that the social and regulatory legislation against which "due process" has been successfully invoked cannot effect property rights and property values as drastically as tax and money legislation and spending appropriations over which the power of Congress is virtually unfettered. If Congress can tax so as to destroy, spend without judicial restraint, expand or contract credit, inflate or deflate the currency at will and regardless of consequences to individuals, then of what value is the constitutional inhibition against deprivation of property without due process of law and without compensation? The virtual abdication of the Supreme Court in this field increases proportionately the responsibility of the other two branches of the government and ultimately of the people themselves. Professor Corwin's assertion that "the vital question" is not "that of the relationship of judicial review to governmental expenditure, but that of the proper relationship of the executive and the legislature in this field of power"[31] is very much to the point. In his opinion, vigorously endorsed by Mr. Walter Lippmann, a "proper relationship" would be established between the two branches by the complete restoration of the principle

[ 203 ]

that all proposals for governmental expenditure must originate with the Executive and that the rôle of Congress should be "merely that of allowance or disallowance." This is a sound suggestion, even though it may err on the side of optimism. For it must be borne in mind that the English system of budgetary control, while undoubtedly more efficient and responsible than the congressional "pork barrel", postulates an Executive able to limit himself to "the *necessary* expenditures of the national government" and to resist both the raids of pressure groups on the treasury and the temptation to use the power of the purse for largely political purposes.

But the increase of executive and legislative responsibility which results from the emasculation of judicial review with regard to taxing and spending extends beyond the budgetary field. The New Deal can accomplish by indirection—through taxing, spending and the control of money—what it could not do directly because of the prohibitions of "due process" and the inadequacies of the "commerce clause." An act of Congress, for instance, to compel corporations, under penalty, to pay certain dividends out of specified earnings would clearly violate "due process" and be beyond the reach of the commerce power. Yet Congress accomplishes this precise object through the Revenue Act of 1936 which imposes a steep graduated tax on undistributed profits. Under the new revenue measure the federal government substitutes its own judgment for the judgment of the management of private companies as to what fiscal policies shall be pursued. This is unmistakable governmental interference with liberty and property, and if attempted directly, it would be barred by the Fifth Amendment; but because it is effected through the use of the taxing power, it cannot be successfully challenged. The idea of redistribution of wealth through governmental action is utterly foreign to our constitutional conceptions and anathema to "due process." Yet, though indirectly, a process of wealth redistribution is taking place every day through taxation; for, in practical effect, Congress can collect money from one group and give it to another, so long as it separates the spending appropriation from the tax legislation. "While unconstitutional exercise of power by the executive and legislative branches of the government," Mr. Justice Stone wisely observed in his dissent from the AAA decision, "is subject to judicial restraint, the only check upon our own exercise of power is our own sense of self-restraint." Precisely because in the field of taxing, spending and regulating the value of money the Supreme Court has heeded this admonition almost to the point of surrendering judicial review, it behooves the executive and the legislative branches to practice self-restraint in their turn if our government is to remain one of limited powers and, at the same time, use its power over the people's money in order to promote the *general* welfare.

# CHAPTER IX

# Judicial Review and
# Constitutional Government

THE DISCUSSION of the preceding chapters has been based on the assumption that the trend of judicial statesmanship, from *Marbury* v. *Madison* to the latest decision of the Supreme Court, cannot be properly appraised if it is dissociated from the general course of American history. This span of over one hundred and thirty years may be conveniently divided into successive periods which can be described briefly, or characterized by some suggestive term that seems to epitomize each. We must bear in mind, however, that when we thus generalize we oversimplify and, hence, to a certain extent distort. For example, though the election of 1800 marked the annihilation of the Federalist party, nationalism, its dominant doctrine, did not wither away under Jefferson, the defender of states' rights, and his presumably like-minded successors. Again, Chief Justice Marshall was the archexponent of nationalism throughout his long incumbency. Yet his exaltation of national power at the expense of states' rights was often basically inconsistent with his equally vigorous defense of property rights. His decision in the *Dartmouth College Case,* which upheld the sanctity of contractual obligations against interference by a state legislature, had it been allowed to stand, would unquestionably have obstructed the economic development of America, without which the concept of national power would have remained a constitutional fiction. And it was Marshall's successor, Taney, the reputedly systematic enemy of national power, who reversed this decision in the *Charles River Bridge Case* against the dissent of Justice Story, the heir to Marshall's nationalistic mantle. As a matter of fact, when Taney, in his truly historic opinion, upheld the new against the old, defended the rights of investors in railroads and canals against turnpike companies, and envisaged an America made over by technological progress, he was preaching much the same nationalistic doctrine as Marshall in *Gibbons* v. *Ogden* though from different constitutional premises— and with much the same consequences. Many more illustrations could be adduced to show that it is not quite accurate to think of the two successive phases in the history of the Supreme Court which were dominated respectively by Marshall and Taney in terms of a sharp contrast—an abrupt transition from national power and property rights to states' rights and interference with contractual obligations.[1] And if this is true of the Court under Marshall and Taney, it is much more valid with respect to the more complex and less easily delimited period since the Civil War.

Yet, with this emphatic reservation in mind, it is still possible to divide the history of the Supreme Court into fairly distinguishable periods, to discern the prevalent temper of each, and to learn something about the connection between the dominant social and political forces and the contemporaneous course of judicial statesmanship. We may then recapitulate and summarize the course of judicial review since its establishment in the first decade of the nineteenth century as follows:

1. Marshall addressed himself primarily to the development of the concept of national power at a time when, though economic forces were making for nationalism, political thought and action in America were still dominated by the strong tradition of states' rights. To this end he applied and expanded the affirmative powers conferred by the Constitution on the national government and, at the same time, he invoked with consistent rigor the prohibitions imposed on the states. Because in his day interference with the rights of individuals was largely attempted by the states, he was able, by restraining state action, both to increase the powers of the national government and to strengthen the security of contractual obligations and of private property. Thus, both as a nationalist and as an economic individualist, he laid the constitutional groundwork for an economy based on private enterprise and capable of developing on a national and continental scale.

2. Jacksonian democracy—a transfusion of new blood into Jeffersonian democracy twenty-eight years after the "revolution of 1800"—was a combination of the planter interests of the South and the agrarian populism of the pioneer West against the capitalism of the East which had been nurtured both by the nationalism and the economic individualism of Mar-

shall. The Supreme Court under Taney came in time to reflect the new social and political environment, and molded the Constitution accordingly. It halted the deterioration of states' rights by developing the concept of the state police power as an antidote to the inviolability of contracts and private property and as a constitutional warrant for the enactment by the states of urgently needed regulatory health and public welfare legislation. But with the aggravation of the "irrepressible conflict", Taney's Court tended to align itself with the politically dominant South in an attempt to consolidate by political and constitutional means a social system which was doomed to be superseded by the expanding free economy of the North and West. The culmination of this effort was the Dred Scott decision, which combined a drastic denial of national power with an equally extreme affirmation of property rights in one particular kind of property.

3. The profound upheaval of the Civil War and Reconstruction was inevitably reflected in the policies of the Supreme Court. During the war, and especially after Taney's death and the accession of Chase to the chief-justiceship, the Court practically permitted the Constitution to be held in abeyance and interposed no obstacles to the exercise of almost absolute power by the President in coping with the gravest emergency in the nation's history. It also yielded for a time to the virtual congressional dictatorship established during Johnson's incumbency and did not seriously interfere with the measures designed to consolidate the gains of victory. But before the end of the Reconstruction period it resumed its constitutional function and called a halt

to the rampant nationalism of the militant congressional majority.

4. Under Chief Justice Waite this revolt against nationalism assumed the form of a revival of states' rights and a refusal to allow them to be submerged by the Fourteenth Amendment. The extension of the police power to economic enterprise clothed with a public interest, combined with a broad definition of the latter concept, permitted the enactment of state legislation designed to curb big business during the lusty postbellum phase of its expansion.

5. During Fuller's chief-justiceship this trend was decisively reversed. The Fourteenth Amendment, broadly construed as a protection of private property against the states, enabled the Court to invalidate state legislation directed against business enterprise. At the same time, when the national government attempted the regulation and control forbidden to the states, either the scope of the "commerce clause" was contracted so as to render the regulation ineffectual, or the "due process" clause of the Fifth Amendment was invoked to paralyze its action. By reviving Marshall's conception of contractual obligations and property rights while, at the same time, refusing to follow the Marshallian doctrine with respect to national power, the Supreme Court translated laissez faire into constitutional terms and gave big business, then at the height of its dominance, the maximum protection against governmental interference.

6. The democratic reaction against the sovereign power of business is discernible in the trend of judicial statesmanship since the close of the nineteenth century.

During the last thirty years judicial interpretation has tended unmistakably to increase national power by expanding the "commerce clause", by giving the federal government, through its control of interstate commerce, the analogue of the state police power, and by construing the taxing and spending power with increasing liberality. At the same time, private property and business have continued to find refuge in the "due process" clause against social legislation by the states and have been protected against similar federal action by the Court's refusal to permit too indirect recourse to the "commerce clause."

7. The most daring of the experiments in economic regimentation made since March 1933 have been invalidated by the Supreme Court through the revival of the doctrine of states' rights and the consequent contraction of national power with respect to interstate commerce. On the other hand, after a number of contradictory decisions, it is not yet clear how much is left of the barrier erected on the "due process" clause against regulatory and social legislation by the states.

It is evident from this brief survey that the interpretation of the Constitution has been a process as continuous, though possibly less obviously dynamic, as the parallel development of American civilization during the last hundred and thirty years. It is true, of course, that this ceaseless modification has not been entirely the work of the Judiciary. For example, the powers of the states were irretrievably impaired after the enactment of the Fourteenth Amendment, even though the extent of the impairment has been variously determined by judicial decision; the "commerce clause" was implemented, and its efficacy as an instrument of federal control was enhanced, by the Interstate Commerce Act and the antitrust laws; and the Sixteenth Amendment deprived the Supreme Court of its discretion in determining what constitutes direct taxation. Yet though the Constitution has been materially altered by congressional legislation, by political usage and by occasional recourse to the amending process, by far the greatest contribution to its development has been made by judicial review. Indeed, the letter of the Constitution has undergone relatively slight modification. But by invoking its affirmative or prohibitory provisions in order to uphold or to invalidate state and federal legislation, the Supreme Court has so modified its meaning that, except for the tragic interlude of the Civil War, the stupendous growth of American society has taken place within its framework. "It is generally recognized," writes a thoughtful student, "that the development of the country has led to the creation of new doctrines, and the modification of old by the Supreme Court. By processes of innovation, distinction and overruling, adjustments have been made in the rules of law administered by the Justices."[2]

These adjustments have involved constant revision of what Mr. Justice Cardozo calls "the great generalities of the Constitution" and redefinition of their "content and significance."[3] The more general these generalities the wider has been the range of modification and hence of judicial discretion. The Constitution being what the judges say it is, the meaning of its most pregnant generalities, such as the "supremacy" clause, the "necessary and proper" clause, the "due process"

[ 212 ]

clause, the "general welfare" clause and the "commerce clause", has always been provisional. A brief glance at some of the most striking shifts of position in the history of the Court will help to illustrate this fluidity of constitutional interpretation and to throw some light on the nature of judicial review.

The rigid doctrine of the *Dartmouth College Case,* whereby corporate charters were placed under the protection of the "contract" clause, was reversed by the *Charles River Bridge Case,* which decided, in effect, that a state did not alienate its sovereignty when it granted a charter to a private corporation. *Gibbons* v. *Ogden* and *Brown* v. *Maryland* construed the grant of the commerce power to the federal government as though tantamount to a prohibition to the states; but the barrier thus erected against any state legislation in this field was partially demolished by the *License Cases,* the most important of which was "distinguished" from *Brown* v. *Maryland* and its "original package" doctrine because it did not involve foreign commerce; and the way was cleared for regulatory legislation by the states when *Cooley* v. *Port Wardens* laid down the principle that the nature of the subject to be regulated rather than the allegedly exclusive character of the commerce power in the abstract should be the criterion of jurisdiction.

*Hepburn* v. *Griswold* held that the issuance of inconvertible paper currency was not "an appropriate and plainly adapted means for carrying on war", and that, hence, the Legal Tender Acts impaired the obligation of contracts; but this decision was expressly reversed by *Knox* v. *Lee,* which affirmed that the authority to issue legal tender notes was derived impliedly from the power to wage war, and denied that either the "contract" clause or the "due process" clause afforded the individual any protection against such action by the federal government. *Munn* v. *Illinois* invoked the concept of property and business "clothed with a public interest" in order to uphold state legislation prescribing elevator and storage rates; but though railroads are certainly no less clothed with a public interest than grain elevators, this precedent was not held binding by the majority of the Court thirteen years later in the *Minnesota Rate Case,* which, in effect, reversed *Munn* v. *Illinois* and recognized the "due process" clause as a bar to state legislation tending to interfere with the rights of property. Again, while in *New State Ice Co.* v. *Liebmann* "due process" was considered a barrier to the regulation of the ice business by the state of Oklahoma, in *Nebbia* v. *New York* it was not allowed to interfere with the fixing of the price of milk.

The police power of the states, which had been developed under Taney as a counterweight to the protection afforded to private property by the "contract" clause, was successfully invoked in 1887 in *Mugler* v. *Kansas* against the "due process" clause; and though a state was thus allowed to prohibit the manufacture and sale of liquor, the Court decided eighteen years later in *Lochner* v. *New York* that the police power did not include regulation of work in bakeries because such work did not affect the health, morals or welfare of the public. *Muller* v. *Oregon* and *Bunting* v. *Oregon* in effect reversed *Lochner* v. *New York* by deciding that the freedom of contract included in the liberty which is

[ 214 ]

guaranteed by the "due process" clause does not prohibit regulation of maximum hours by state legislation. Yet six years later, in *Adkins* v. *Children's Hospital,* a minimum-wage law for women in the District of Columbia was invalidated over Chief Justice Taft's protest that the *Bunting Case* had overruled the *Lochner Case "sub silentio"* and that he failed to see the "substance of the distinction between a minimum of wages and a maximum of hours in the limiting of liberty to contract." Despite the *Nebbia Case,* which ignored "due process" as an obstacle to state legislation in the field of price-fixing, the Court reverted to the *Adkins Case* when in the *New York Minimum Wage Case* it vetoed the fixing of a minimum wage by the state of New York. But in its latest decision in this field, handed down on March 29, 1937, it upheld, by a five-to-four vote made possible by Mr. Justice Roberts' shift, the Washington State Minimum Wage Law for Women and held that "the case of *Adkins* v. *Children's Hospital* should be and is overruled."

The Interstate Commerce Act and the Sherman Antitrust Act were practically shorn of all efficacy by the Court's early decisions—the *Maximum Freight Rate Case*[4] and the *Sugar Trust Case.* But by a series of subsequent decisions the scope of interstate commerce was expanded to include the fixing of rates in intrastate commerce as well, while the decision in the *Sugar Trust Case* "gradually lost its force by the process of distinction"[5] and was, in effect, overruled by *Swift and Co.* v. *United States.* Beginning with *Standard Oil Co.* v. *United States,* however, the Court developed the doctrine of the "rule of reason" in interpreting the Sherman Antitrust Act. On the basis of this doctrine and contrary to its decision in *United States* v. *Trans-Missouri Freight Assoc.* and subsequent cases, which held that *all* combinations in restraint of trade were unlawful, it thereafter construed the Sherman Act as aimed only at *"undue"*, or *"unreasonable"*, restraints of trade, notwithstanding the plain intent of Congress to outlaw *all* restraints and its refusal to limit the act, by amendment, to undue or unreasonable combinations.

The "commerce clause", as we have seen, was also expanded by judicial decision so as to give the federal government, under the guise of regulating interstate commerce, the equivalent of the state police power.[6] Yet though all kinds of activities were thus prohibited by congressional mandate, the Court, in *Hammer* v. *Dagenhart,* refused to extend the prohibition to the transportation of articles manufactured by child labor. Finally, in the field of taxation the most resounding judicial reversal was presented by *Pollock* v. *Farmers' Loan and Trust Co.,* which rejected the principle laid down a century earlier in the *Hylton Case* and thereby necessitated the enactment of the Sixteenth Amendment.

From the thumbnail characterizations of successive phases in the history of the Supreme Court, which were attempted in the first part of this chapter, and from the examples of striking modifications and reversals presented in the second we may now draw the following conclusions:

The Supreme Court has departed materially from the common-law tradition and method of binding precedents. "The English system," wrote Brooks Adams a generation ago, ". . . brings society almost to a stand when applied to the most vital functions of government, with no means at hand to obtain a corrective. For the Court of last resort having once declared the meaning of a clause of the Constitution, that meaning remains fixed forever, unless the Court either reverses itself, which is a disaster, or the Constitution can be amended by the states, which is not only difficult, but which, even if it be possible, entails years of delay."[7] As a matter of fact, the cumbersome process of constitutional amendment would probably have been resorted to much more frequently if the Court had regarded reversing itself as a "disaster" and had shrunk from modifying previous decisions. Its revisionist doctrine has been repeatedly formulated by some of its most eminent members. "After such opinions, judicially delivered," said Chief Justice Taney in his dissent in the *Passenger Cases,* "I had supposed that question to be settled so far as any question upon the construction of the Constitution ought to be regarded as closed by the decision of the court. I do not, however, object to the revision of it, and am quite willing that it be regarded hereafter as the law of this court, that its opinion upon the construction of the Constitution is always open to discussion when it is supposed to have been founded in error, and that its judicial authority should hereafter depend altogether on the force of the reasoning by which it is supported." The same thought was expressed more tersely by Justice Field. "It is more important," he declared, "that the Court should be right upon later and more elaborate consideration of the cases than consistent with previous declarations. Those doctrines will eventually stand which bear the strictest examination and the test of experience."⁸ In a famous dissenting opinion⁹ Mr. Justice Brandeis cogently argued against the validity of precedent when it cannot stand the test of experience. "Under the rule of *Gillespie* v. *Oklahoma,*" said he, "vast private incomes are being given immunity from state and federal taxation. I agree with Mr. Justice Stone that that case was wrongly decided and should now be frankly overruled. Merely to construe strictly its doctrine will not adequately protect the public revenues. . . . *Stare decisis* is not, like the rule of *res judicata,* a universal, inexorable command. 'The rule of *stare decisis,* though one tending to consistency and uniformity of decision, is not inflexible. Whether it shall be followed or departed from is a question entirely within the discretion of the Court, which is again called upon to consider a question once decided.' . . . *Stare decisis* is usually the wise policy, because in most matters it is more important that the applicable rule of law be settled than that it be settled right. . . . This is commonly true even where the error is a matter of serious concern, provided correction can be had by legislation. But in cases involving the Federal Constitution, where correction through legislative action is practically impossible, this Court has often overruled its earlier decisions. The Court bows to the lessons of experience and the force of better reasoning, recognizing that the process of trial and error, so fruitful in the physical sciences, is appropriate also in the judicial function. . . . The judgment of the Court in the earlier decision may have

[ 218 ]

been influenced by prevailing views as to economic or social policy which have since been abandoned. In cases involving constitutional issues of the character discussed, this Court must, in order to reach sound conclusions, feel free to bring its opinions into agreement with experience and with facts newly ascertained, so that its judicial authority may, as Chief Justice Taney said, 'depend altogether on the force of the reasoning by which it is supported.' "

Judicial review as practiced by the Supreme Court is a legislative as well as a judicial function. It attempts to find in the "great generalities" of the Constitution a sanction or a prohibition for the legislative measures submitted to its scrutiny, and the results of this search determine what the law shall be. Thus, the Supreme Court does not merely declare the law; it makes law by determining the applicability of general constitutional principles laid down a century and a half ago to specific and ever-changing conditions. "The judge," says Mr. Justice Cardozo, ". . . legislates only between gaps." But under the American system the gaps between constitutional principle and legislative enactment are so wide that in order to fill them the judges are given a degree of discretion which amounts to lawmaking even when they avoid conscious substitution of their will for that of the legislature. "The chief law makers in our country," said Theodore Roosevelt, "may be, and often are, the judges, because they are the final seat of authority. Every time they interpret contract, property, vested rights, due process of law, liberty, they necessarily enact into law parts of a system of social philosophy; and as such interpretation is fundamental, they give direction to all lawmaking. The decisions of the courts on economic and social questions depend upon their economic and social philosophy; and for the peaceful progress of our people during the twentieth century we shall owe more to those judges who hold to a twentieth-century economic and social philosophy and not to a long outgrown philosophy, which was itself the product of primitive economic conditions."[10] In other words, it is the "personality of the judge" that determines the manner in which the gap between the general principles of the Constitution and particular laws is to be filled. When the "free decision" of a judge is guided by whatever ingredients of his personality happen to be dominant at the time, constitutional interpretation becomes a means to an end. "Alternative principles of construction and alternative lines of precedent," says Professor Corwin, "constantly vest the Court with a freedom virtually legislative in scope in choosing the values which it shall promote through its reading of the Constitution."[11]

Despite occasional and important deviations, every period in the history of the Supreme Court is dominated by a clearly discernible trend of judicial doctrine which impresses itself more or less on the interpretation of all the parts of the Constitution that may happen to come under judicial review. The trend of judicial doctrine, in turn, is decisively influenced by those forces which create the distinctive social environment and the political complexion of every period. There have been exasperating lags on the part of the Judiciary and recurrent headlong clashes with the other two branches of the government. But if we take the long view and

examine the history of the Supreme Court in its entirety,
we cannot but admit that it has translated the political
will into constitutional terms with remarkable fidelity
and has developed the Constitution by incorporating
in it the temper of successive periods in the nation's
history.

The fact that in the long run a concordance is established between the trend of judicial statesmanship and
the political will is partially accounted for by external
circumstances. The Supreme Court, after all, is subject
to constant renewal and rejuvenation. Since the justices
are nominated by the President and confirmed by the
Senate they can be presumed not to be alien or antag-
onistic to the political purposes dominant at the time
of their appointment and may even be said to reflect,
though very indirectly, important segments of public
sentiment. In short, judicial appointments, even when
their motives are not consciously political, are of political origin, and the Court is being constantly re-created
by Presidents in their own image.

This does not mean, however, that "a bench pur-
posely constructed to pass upon political questions must
be politically partisan."[12] It is true that during the bit-
ter duel between Marshall and Jefferson the motivation of every judicial appointment was almost exclusively partisan; yet as one Jeffersonian appointee after
another was converted to Federalism, it became clear
that party affiliations were destined to become the least
important factors in molding the personality of the justices and the collective temper of the Court. The Taney
Court was, of course, Democratic because the Democratic party was, on the whole, dominant during the

three decades which preceded the Civil War. But even
on the eve of that struggle, when the Court's political
preoccupations became most pronounced, it was not
narrowly partisan; nor is it at all certain that Jackson,
who was a Democrat but also a nationalist, would
have approved of its most fateful—and most political
—decision. Chase, Lincoln's appointee and a man of
notoriously political antecedents, displayed remarkable
nonpartisanship and independence after the crisis of the
Civil War and the acute phase of the Reconstruction
Era had passed; and in the *Legal Tender Cases* he
condemned, as chief justice, the great financial measures
which he had initiated as secretary of the treasury. In
the present Court Mr. Justice McReynolds, perhaps
the most consistent opponent of Mr. Roosevelt's policies, was appointed by President Wilson, a Democrat.
But so was Mr. Justice Brandeis, who has been friendly
to the New Deal. On the other hand, the other two of
the administration's most consistent supporters,
Mr. Justice Stone and Mr. Justice Cardozo, owe their
nominations to the Republican Presidents Coolidge and
Hoover respectively.

But while the Supreme Court is free from blind partisanship, there can be no doubt that political conviction plays an important part in determining its decisions. The great constitutional issues are, in the last
analysis, political issues, and a body which contributes
so decisively to their settlement cannot remain above
the battle. "The judges who will be called upon to pass
upon the validity of national and state legislation," says
Brooks Adams, summarizing Jefferson's case against
judicial review, "will be plunged in the most heated of

controversies, and in those controversies they cannot fail to be influenced by the same passions and prejudices which sway other·men. In a word they must decide like legislators, though they will be exempt from the responsibility to the public which controls other legislators."[13] This is less true under normal conditions, when a judge's bias resulting from his social philosophy may often be unconscious, than in times of crisis. It is when men's souls are sorely tried that all the ideas, loyalties and prejudices which constitute one's "world outlook" crystallize into passionate political conviction. In the history of our country the Civil War and the years immediately preceding and following it were pre-eminently such an emergency; and the course of the Supreme Court during that period on all questions that were related to the central issue of slavery and state sovereignty versus freedom and national unity was primarily shaped by the political faith of its members. "When . . ." says Professor Corwin of the *Dred Scott Case,* "the student finds six judges arriving at precisely the same result by three distinct processes of reasoning, he is naturally disposed to surmise that the result may have induced the processes rather than the processes compelled the result"; and he adds that after examination of the opinions this "suspicion becomes conviction."[14] During the most recent crisis in the nation's history the political temper of the Court was very much in evidence. Mr. Justice Roberts' elaborate opinion in the *Hoosac Mills Case,* for example, and Mr. Justice Stone's eloquent dissent were more than a constitutional argument. They were a political debate motivated by intense conviction, on behalf of which both sides mobilized all the instrumentalities of constitutional interpretation they could command.

Not only have particular decisions of the Supreme Court been shaped by the political convictions of its members, but its general course at times has been influenced by what seemed like a deliberate effort to assume political leadership. In the *Slaughterhouse Cases,* for instance, the Court's decision was probably dictated by its determination so to interpret the Fourteenth Amendment as to halt the rapid postwar progress of nationalism and, incidentally, to reaffirm its independence after a long period of acquiescence in presidential and congressional dictatorship. So far as the immediate issue was concerned, the decision confirmed an iniquitous monopoly granted by a corrupt state legislature; while the strict construction of the Fourteenth Amendment which emerged from it tended to deprive the Negroes and their newly won civil rights of all federal protection. Yet it was substantially the same strict construction of the same amendment which inspired the socially beneficent decision in *Munn* v. *Illinois,* and which, had it been adhered to, would have prevented the erection of the "due process" clause into an obstacle to state legislation against the license of unregulated business enterprise. These developments could not, of course, have been foreseen in the early seventies. The great issue of that day was essentially political. With national unity saved by the defeat of secession, the rescue of the federal structure from the policies of Reconstruction must have seemed equally urgent to many Americans. It was toward such a reorientation of national destiny, and in opposition to the momentarily dominant politi-

cal tendencies, that the Supreme Court provided much-
needed leadership by its strict construction of the
Fourteenth Amendment in the *Slaughterhouse Cases*
and throughout Waite's chief-justiceship.

A different and much more pronounced manifestation of political-mindedness was the adoption of the
"rule of reason" in interpreting the Sherman Antitrust
Act. This was undeniably a direct incursion of the
Supreme Court into the legislative field, the more
flagrant because it not only reversed previous decisions
but limited the scope of the act after the express refusal
of Congress to amend it in the same restrictive sense.
Brooks Adams, in his severe indictment of this assumption of the legislative prerogative by the Court, offers
the following analysis of the motives of its decision in
*Standard Oil Co. v. United States:* "To me this opinion, like Taney's opinion in the *Charles River Bridge
Case,* indicates that the tension had reached the breaking point, the Court yielding in all directions at once,
while the dominant preoccupation of the presiding
judge seemed to be to plant his tribunal in such a position that it could so yield, without stultifying itself
hopelessly before the legal profession and the public.
In striving to reach this position, however, I apprehend
that the Chief Justice, unreservedly, crossed the chasm
on whose brink American jurists had been shuddering
for ninety years. The task the Chief Justice assumed
was difficult almost beyond precedent. He proposed to
surrender to the vested interests the principle of *reasonableness* which they demanded, and which the tribunal he represented, together with Congress, had refused
to surrender for fifteen years. To pacify the public,

which would certainly resent this surrender, he was prepared to punish two hated corporations, while he strove to preserve, so far as he could, the respect of the legal profession and of the public, for the Court over which he presided, by maintaining a semblance of consistency."[15]

It should be added, however, that besides the vested interests, the legal profession which served them, and the public which clamored against the trusts, there may have been in the chief justice's mind the fear that indiscriminate "trust busting" might cripple American capitalism at a time when increasing integration was essential to its development. Precisely because "the tension had reached the breaking point", the Court may have felt that it was its duty to point the way to a less drastic solution than that provided by the inclusive terms of the Sherman Act. Indeed, the fact that the purposes envisaged more than twenty years later by the National Industrial Recovery Act necessitated the suspension of the antitrust laws would seem to indicate that they were not the last word as instruments of governmental control or social justice. In view of the fact that the Court also resisted enforcement of the Clayton Act, it may be said that the intent of Congress had been frustrated by judicial review. On the other hand, when we consider that the intellectual and political environment at the time of Theodore Roosevelt's ascendancy was very different from that of President Harding's administration, and that the antitrust crusade was only a memory during the twenties, we may hesitate to assert positively that the Court was out of harmony with prevailing public sentiment on this issue.

In the light of these precedents of political-mindedness in the history of the Court, its attitude toward President Franklin D. Roosevelt's first administration becomes perhaps more intelligible. The rapid succession of negative decisions which demolished the most far-reaching measures of the New Deal had the effect of making the public, and particularly the critics of the Court, forget that it had upheld many of the administration's policies. As a matter of fact, with due allowance for the inaccuracy inherent in generalizations, the Court may be said to have sustained those measures of the New Deal that made for recovery and nullified those that were designed to effect drastic reform. The Gold Clause decisions clearly belong to the first category, while the *Schechter Case* and the *Hoosac Mills Case* belong to the second. The pro-New Deal phase of the Supreme Court corresponded roughly to the early part of President Roosevelt's administration—the period of his unquestioned ascendancy—and also included approval of state legislation (the *Minnesota Moratorium Case* and the *Nebbia Case*) which was in harmony with his general objectives. The anti-New Deal phase, on the other hand, synchronized with the re-emergence of a critical spirit in the nation and went to such lengths that another piece of progressive state legislation, the New York Minimum Wage Law, was crushed under its accumulated momentum.

Apart from this manifestation of extremism, which indicated that the Court was not immune to the mounting political temperature, the decisions on important administration measures seemed to be inspired by a settled policy. The Court, under the guidance of a chief justice who also has the background and temper of a statesman, seemed determined not to interfere with the President's effort to bring about recovery, the more so because this effort enjoyed practically universal support and was made in pursuance of the most unambiguous part of the mandate he had received from the electorate. It must be remembered that the Supreme Court did not invalidate the N.R.A. until after it had achieved a degree of recovery and both its oppressive features and its destructive implications for the American system began to be increasingly felt and resented. For apart from the people's bidding to end the depression, the President had no mandate on specific issues. The Democratic platform was such a mandate, but it was discarded because its specifications did not fit the emergency. The President was thus left with a blank check, which he proceeded to fill with a series of measures, some of which, whatever one may think of their merits, eventually provoked opposition from increasingly large and articulate segments of the nation. The objections to these measures were that they tended to alter the fundamentals of the American system, that the issues they raised had not been sufficiently debated or understood by the people, that, hence, the President had no mandate for such drastic and permanent reform, and that the contribution of Congress to this far-reaching legislation had been negligible.

The validity of this last contention was unquestionable. What was functioning in Washington at the time when these measures were enacted was not congressional government but a presidential dictatorship founded on consent, acquiescence or mere tolerance. The major instruments of recovery and reform were inspired by, or directly emanated from, the White House and the various executive departments; and Congress had practically abandoned both its legislative initiative and its constitutional rôle as a counterweight to the Executive. It was this virtual abdication of Congress that must have made the Court feel that its intervention was imperative, particularly with respect to those basic reforms of the national economy on which the country was becoming increasingly divided. As early as the *Minnesota Moratorium Case* the chief justice laid the foundation for a critical examination of these New Deal measures when he denied that the existence of an emergency warrants virtual suspension of the Constitution. "Emergency," he said, "does not create power. . . . The Constitution was adopted in a period of grave emergency. Its grants of power to the Federal Government and its limitations of the power of the States were determined in the light of emergency and they are not altered by emergency. . . ."[16] At the same time, the sedulous care with which he avoided testing the constitutionality of the disputed aspects of T.V.A. showed that he had his ear to the ground and was anxious not to lower the prestige of the Court by the appearance of systematic obstruction and by invalidating a measure which had already left its mark on the American landscape.[17]

While one may agree or disagree with specific decisions, and the writer disagrees with several, the advocates of judicial review can claim that the Supreme

Court, by acting as a political body, by causing important measures to be thoroughly debated and resubmitted to the electorate, and by exercising a check on Congress and the Executive at a time when they no longer checked one another, has helped to restore constitutional government. At the same time, the fact that the specific issues raised by the Court's decisions were not thoroughly debated during a presidential campaign which generated much heat is indicative of the inveterate tendency of the American people to become politically conservative with returning prosperity. So far as his commitments were concerned, the President's check in 1936 was even blanker than it was in 1932. His triumphant re-election was his reward for conquering the emergency; and it testified to the American people's faith in his leadership and their expectation that he would continue to pursue his general objectives.

Whether or not "the American constitutional system breeds in the judge a conviction that he is superior to the legislator",[18] it is now generally conceded that it has expanded judicial review into a legislative and a political function. The doctrine of the separation of powers was an eighteenth-century abstraction which was adopted by the founders as a safeguard of the individual citizen against governmental authority. But just as subsequent developments, of which the growth of political parties was perhaps the most crucial, have made the separation of the Executive from the Legislature largely illusory, so judicial review has played havoc with the notion that the Judiciary is governed by disembodied legal intelligence, and is concerned not with the substance of the laws but merely with whether or not the general principles of the Constitution have been observed in their enactment. This expansion of the judicial function has not taken place without resistance. Throughout the history of the Court there have been justices who have adhered, or have endeavored to adhere, to the strict judicial ideal; so much so that "politically-minded" and "judicially-minded", or more and less "politically-minded", might be a more suggestive classification for them than the current designation "liberal" and "conservative."

To those who make the latter distinction, a "liberal" member of the Court is one who tends to make social welfare rather than vested rights his criterion in filling the gap between constitutional principle and a given statute, or refuses to substitute his judgment for that of the legislator with respect to laws designed to promote the social welfare. Political-mindedness, on the other hand, makes for greater discretion either in a "liberal" or in a "conservative" direction and is, at its best, an exercise of statesmanship based on a conscientious appraisal of the exigencies of the public welfare. In his severe arraignment of "American Courts as Legislative Chambers", Brooks Adams deservedly commends Justice Bradley for his dissent in the *Minnesota Rate Case* and for his refusal to turn the Bench "from a tribunal which should propound general rules applicable to all material facts, into a jury to find verdicts on the reasonableness of the votes of representative assemblies."[19] At the same time, he compares this dissent, as well as Justice Bradley's judicial temper and procedure, to that of Justice Story in the *Charles River Bridge Case.* From the point of view of the public welfare, however,

[ 231 ]

it is undeniable that the dissent inspired by adherence to the strict judicial ideal was as liberal in the *Minnesota Rate Case* as it was reactionary in the *Charles River Bridge Case*. Similarly, Justice Peckham, who is praised because in the *Trans-Missouri Case* he "laid down a general principle in conformity to the legislative will",[20] construed "due process" so broadly in *Allgeyer* v. *Louisiana* as to make it a barrier against state regulation of insurance companies. And Justice Harlan, a consistent opponent of judicial interference with the substance of legislation, obtained results far from liberal when he based his decision in *Adair* v. *United States*[21] on the antiquated notion that a contract between an employer and an individual employee involves the exercise of equal freedom by the contracting parties. Likewise, Justice Holmes's consistent application of the judicial ideal often led him to concur with reactionary decisions, to the bewilderment of his liberal followers. These examples would seem to indicate that adherence to the strict judicial ideal does not invariably produce liberal decisions. Indeed, in view of the power conferred by judicial review on the Supreme Court, a degree of political-mindedness in its members is highly desirable provided it is exercised by great judges and scholars who are also endowed with "insight into social values" and "suppleness of adaptation to changing social needs"[22]—in short, with the intellectual equipment and the temper of statesmen.

Precisely because the Supreme Court, by means of judicial review, has come to exercise political power, it must sedulously avoid even the appearance of playing politics. As a judicial body, it tends, by its very nature, to be more conservative on economic and social issues than state legislatures or Congress, though it must not be forgotten that on questions involving civil liberty— freedom of thought, speech, the press, assembly, teaching—and the other individual rights guaranteed by the Constitution, it has been far more liberal than legislative bodies, which are all too often subject to group pressures and mass passions. But the Court's inherent conservatism must not be allowed to crystallize into permanent identification with those groups, classes or parties which are obdurately opposed to social change. Such identification would lower the Court's prestige and in the long run endanger its existence. Conservative institutions, especially in times of social crisis, must know how to bend in order not to break. Because it yielded at the last moment on the Reform Bill of 1832, which admitted the upper middle class to the franchise, the House of Lords retained its legislative prerogatives despite the gradual democratization of British politics during the nineteenth century. But when, at the beginning of the twentieth, it permanently allied itself with the Conservative party, systematically obstructed democratic reform, ignored the verdict of successive general elections, and resisted the national will expressed through the House of Commons, it was deprived of much of its power by the Parliament Act of 1911 and has been rapidly declining ever since.

The French *Parlements,* and the part they played on the eve of the French Revolution, present perhaps a more striking analogy. They functioned as courts of appellate jurisdiction and, at the same time, they had traditionally converted the edicts of the king into law through the formality of registration. It was this latter function which they sought to expand into the power of judicial review after they had been restored to power at the beginning of the reign of Louis XVI. Politically, this claim had an appearance of liberalism, since it tended to curb the king's absolute power and to give an independent body a share in the legislative function. Socially, however, the *Parlements'* claim was reactionary, for it was advanced as a means of thwarting urgently needed fiscal and social reform at the expense of the privileged orders. For the *Parlements* were as privilege-minded as the most recalcitrant of the nobility and the upper clergy. Recruited from the so-called "nobility of the robe", they were the apex of a magistracy in which offices were purchased and inherited. As the owners of vast property and the beneficiaries of hereditary privilege, the members of the *Parlements* were the staunchest defenders of the social order. "The magistrates had come to believe," writes a French historian, "that their functions were more political than judicial; and that since the monarchy leaned toward despotism and the nation dreamed of liberty, it was their duty to play between the two the rôle of arbiter."[23] Now the "despotism" of the king, which they feared and resented, meant the measures introduced by such enlightened ministers as Turgot and Necker in order to meet an acute budgetary crisis. Claiming the power of judicial review, the *Parlements* consistently obstructed social reforms because of their social incidence. They took the stand that, "however they might sympathize with the lower classes," as courts of justice, "charged with the duty of safeguarding the rights of all the orders," they could not "dispose of the property of the rich for the benefit of the poor" but were bound to "protect the real and feudal property founded on custom and possession."[24] In order to protect "custom and possession", they invoked the ancient constitution of France and its checks against royal absolutism. And having successfully revived one of these checks, they pressed for the convocation of the States-General, another institution associated with the régime of limited monarchy. That proved their undoing. For on the crucial question of the organization of the States-General, they showed their true colors and held out obstinately against the fusion of the three orders into a National Assembly. They thus aligned themselves with the most reactionary of the nobles and upper clergy and lost the popularity they had fleetingly enjoyed. Having opposed both the national and the liberal trend of the revolution, they were soon leveled out of existence by its forward march. "As they did not have with them either public sentiment or material force, they succumbed with the institutions which they were powerless to defend."[25]

We need not press the analogy any further than stressing the crucial importance of public opinion. No institution can survive the loss of public confidence, particularly when the people's faith is its only support. The Supreme Court has survived many storms and much more or less merited obloquy because, in the last analysis, the American people have faith in it and in the beneficence of judicial review. It is admittedly a conservative institution. But a conservative institution at its best is of unquestioned social utility. It can be a bulwark against revolution and dictatorship—its inevitable concomitant; especially against revolution from the Right, due to the resistance of large and powerful sections of the community to what they consider hasty and drastic innovation. At such a critical juncture a conservative institution like the Supreme Court may, by a wise use of its suspensive veto, either secure revision or facilitate the consolidation and clearer expression of the national will and, hence, the eventual acquiescence of the protesting minority. It can thus help to bring about social change by consent and, at the same time, preserve the framework, the machinery and the *habit* of free government. This is a high and an eminently political mission. And the first requisite for its successful accomplishment is frank recognition of the political implications of judicial review. Such recognition might, for one thing, influence executive and senatorial policy with respect to appointments. It might also help to effect such modifications in the Court's powers and procedure as will make judicial review more compatible with democratic government.

# Epilogue

CHAPTER VII of this book, which deals with interstate commerce, after discussing the invalidation of the National Recovery Act and the Guffey Coal Act by the Supreme Court, concluded as follows: "But the history of the 'commerce clause' and the popular verdict of 1936 warrant the belief that this contraction of the commerce power cannot be permanent." This expectation has since been largely fulfilled. After the manuscript had gone to press, the Supreme Court handed down its affirmative decisions in all of the five cases submitted to it under the Wagner National Labor Relations Act of 1935. In the *Motor Bus Case*,[1] a unanimous Court found that the Washington, Virginia and Maryland Coach Company came under the jurisdiction of the act because it was "an instrumentality of interstate commerce." In the *Associated Press Case*[2] the Court held by a five-to-four decision that the collection and transmission of news is interstate commerce, and that the invocation of the Wagner Act by an employee of the Associated Press did not abridge the freedom of speech and of the press guaranteed by the First Amendment. More crucial in its implications was the five-to-four decision in the *Jones & Laughlin Case*, which was also extended to the *Fruehauf Case* and the *Friedman Case*.[3] The majority opinion, which was delivered by Chief Justice Hughes, after endorsing the findings of the National Labor Relations Board both with regard to the interstate nature of the steel company's business and its relations to its discharged employees, rejected the contention that the Wagner Act "has the fundamental object of placing under the compulsory supervision of the Federal Government all industrial labor relations within the nation." The term "affecting commerce", the chief justice contended, "is one of exclusion as well as inclusion. The grant of authority to the Board does not purport to extend the relationship between all industrial employees and employers. . . . It purports to reach only what may be deemed to burden or obstruct that commerce, and thus qualified, it must be construed as contemplating the exercise of control within constitutional bounds"; for "it is a familiar principle that acts which directly burden or obstruct interstate or foreign commerce, or its free flow, are within the reach of the congressional power."

The Court's decision, however, was based not only on the federal government's acknowledged power to remove obstructions to the free flow of commerce, but also on its "plenary" power to "protect" interstate commerce "no matter what the source of the dangers which threaten it." The Court contended that "industrial strife" leading to a stoppage of operations by a steel company engaged in "far-flung activities" was a prolific source of such dangers. "We are asked," said the chief justice, "to shut our eyes to the plainest facts of our national life and to deal with the questions of direct and indirect effects in an intellectual vacuum."

Whenever in the past the Court refused to adopt this myopic attitude, it sustained, as in the case of railroads, federal control of intrastate activities "by reason of close and intimate relation to interstate commerce." By the same token the chief justice rejected the decision in the *Schechter Case* as a binding precedent because "the effect there was so remote as to go beyond the Federal power [and because] to find 'immediacy or directness' there was to find it 'almost everywhere', a result inconsistent with our Federal system." On the other hand, the chief justice's dismissal of the decision in the *Carter Case* (Guffey Coal Act) was far less convincing. For while it is true that "the provisions of the statute relating to production were invalid upon several grounds", it is equally true that the Court gave a conspicuous place among these grounds to the alleged *intrastate* character of the coal-mining industry.

By sustaining the Wagner Labor Act, the Supreme Court has broadened the meaning of the "commerce clause" and has discovered in it national power to regulate industrial relations in manufacturing industries operating on a national scale with a view to obviating stoppages which demonstrably injure the national economy. It has thus demonstrated once more its ability to take into account economic and social realities, its responsiveness to the national will, and the elasticity of a Constitution which, in the words of Chief Justice Marshall, was "framed for ages to come", [and was] "designed to approach immortality as nearly as human institutions can approach it."

# Appendix

# Notes

## CHAPTER I

1 C. A. Beard, *An Economic Interpretation of the Constitution of the United States* (1925), p. 52.
2 *Documentary History of the Constitution,* Vol. IV, p. 30.
3 Robert L. Schuyler, *The Constitution of the United States,* pp. 59–60.
4 Beard, op. cit., p. 52.
5 Alexander Hamilton's view of the nature of the Union, expressed in 1780. C. W. Gerstenberg, *Constitutional Law,* p. 6.
6 Journal of the House of Delegates of the Commonwealth of Virginia, January 21, 1786, p. 153.
7 Quoted by Gerstenberg, op. cit., p. 9.

## CHAPTER II

1 Beard, op. cit., Ch.V.
2 The conflict of interest between large and small states was largely illusory. As Madison, that profound economic determinist, pointed out, the three large states of Virginia, Pennsylvania and New York were, culturally and economically, "as dissimilar as any three other states in the Union," and the natural alignment was between Northern and Southern states, rather than between large and small. A. C. McLaughlin, *A Constitutional History of the United States,* pp. 172–74.
3 Ibid., pp. 159–60.

4 Ibid., p. 167.

5 Ibid., p. 149.

6 No. 10 of the *Federalist.*

7 For the complete enumeration of powers delegated to the federal government and denied to the states, see Appendix, Article I, Sections 8 and 10 of the Constitution.

8 The separation of powers and the concomitant system of checks and balances were advocated as the surest safeguard of liberty by the French political philosopher Montesquieu, who thought (erroneously as Madison pointed out in No. 47 of the *Federalist*) that they were the basic principles of the British Constitution.

9 Beard, op. cit., pp. 161–62.

10 No. 50 of the *Federalist.*

11 No. 51 of the *Federalist.*

12 E. S. Corwin, *The Twilight of the Supreme Court,* pp. 9–10.


## CHAPTER III

1 A. V. Dicey, *Introduction to the Study of the Law of the Constitution,* p. 38, The Macmillan Co., London (1931).

2 James Bryce, *The American Commonwealth,* Vol. I, p. 374, The Macmillan Co., New York (1931).

3 Dicey, op. cit., p. 41.

4 H. L. McBain, *The Living Constitution,* p. 19, The Macmillan Co., New York (1928).

5 Bryce, op. cit., Vol. I, p. 361.

6 For a fuller discussion of constitutional conventions, cf. Bryce, op. cit., Vol. I, pp. 392–400; C. A. Beard, *American Government and Politics,* pp. 73–75, The Macmillan Co., New York (1910); McBain, op. cit., pp. 25–26.

7 Walter Bagehot, *The English Constitution,* pp. 1–29, Oxford University Press.

8 Ibid., p. 9.

# Notes

9 No. 78 of the *Federalist,* G. P. Putnam's Sons, New York (1888).

10 This was one of the suggestions made in the Virginia plan. It was rejected by the convention as not only dangerous but unnecessary because, as Roger Sherman of Connecticut said, "the courts of the states would not consider as valid any law contravening the authority of the Union." McLaughlin, op. cit., pp. 157, 181–83.

11 Address at a dinner of the Harvard Law School Association of New York, February 15, 1913.

12 No. 78 of the *Federalist.*

13 From opinion of Judge Hand in *United States of America* v. *A. L. A. Schechter Poultry Corp.* (U. S. Circuit Court of Appeals, 2nd Circuit.)

14 Some of the most momentous cases before the Supreme Court have been decided by a five-to-four vote.

15 1 Cranch, 137.

16 Original jurisdiction refers to cases which may be heard in the first instance by the Supreme Court without having been previously adjudicated in a lower Court. These cases are specifically mentioned in Article III of the Constitution. In all other cases the Supreme Court has appellate jurisdiction both as to Law and Fact, subject to such exceptions and under such regulations as the Congress shall make. The Constitution created only the Supreme Court and left to Congress the power to establish such inferior Federal Courts as from time to time it deemed necessary. The inferior Federal Courts which Congress has created have also assumed the power to set aside laws of Congress. Article III of the Constitution defines the scope of the federal judicial power but is silent as to how the Federal Courts shall conduct their business. The mechanics of federal judicial procedure have, therefore, been attended to by Congress through appropriate legislation commencing with the Judiciary Act of 1789. Under the Judiciary Act of 1925 an appeal to the Supreme Court as a matter of

right has been limited to cases involving constitutional law. In common-law and equity cases originating in the Lower Federal Courts, the litigant cannot appeal to the Supreme Court without first obtaining its permission through what is known as a *writ of certiorari.*

17 *Marbury* v. *Madison* in A. Doscow, *Historic Opinions of the Supreme Court,* The Vanguard Press, New York (1935).

18 McLaughlin, op. cit., p. 272.

19 McLaughlin, op. cit., p. 274.

20 Charles E. Hughes, *The Supreme Court of the United States,* pp. 1–2, Columbia University Press, N. Y. (1928).

21 For suggestions provoked by the Supreme Court's invalidation of major measures of the Roosevelt Administration, cf. Lloyd K. Garrison, "The Constitution and the Future," the *New Republic,* Vol. LXXXV, pp. 328–30, January 29, 1936; Max Lerner, "The State of the Supreme Court," the *Nation,* Vol. CXLII, pp. 379–81, March 25, 1935.

22 *Dred Scott* v. *Sanford,* 19 Howard, 393 (1857). This decision held that Congress did not possess power under the Constitution to abolish slavery in the territories of the United States. The decision accentuated the animosity between North and South which culminated in the Civil War.

23 But he immediately added: "Nor is there in this view any assault upon the Court or the Judges. It is a duty from which they may not shrink to decide cases properly brought before them, and it is no fault of theirs if others seek to turn their decisions to political purposes." Quoted in Charles Warren, *The Supreme Court in United States History,* Vol. II, p. 331, 2 volumes, Little, Brown & Co., Boston (1922).

24 *Adkins* v. *Children's Hospital,* 261 U.S., 525 (1923).

25 It is significant that the five-to-four decision in this case was invoked by the court against the vigorous dissent of Chief Justice Hughes and of Justices Stone, Brandeis and Cardozo, when it invalidated the New York Minimum Wage Law by another five-to-four decision. The majority

opinion in which Mr. Justice Sutherland concurred was read by Mr. Justice Butler.

26 *United States* v. *Butler et al, Receivers of Hoosac Mills Corp.,* 80 L.Ed., 287 (1936).

27 *Schechter Poultry Corp.* v. *United States,* 295 U.S., 495 (1935). See also *Louisville, etc. Bank* v. *Radford,* 295 U.S., 535.

28 *Railway Retirement Board* v. *Alton R. R. Co.,* 295 U.S., 330 (1935).

29 See note 26.

30 *Carter* v. *Carter Coal Co.,* 80 L.Ed., 749 (1936).

31 The first intimation of the President's intention to press the constitutional issue was given in his message to Congress on January 6, 1937, in which he said: "Means must be found to adapt our legal forms and our judicial interpretation to the actual present national needs of the largest progressive democracy in the modern world." A similar hint was contained in his second inaugural address, which stressed the necessity of harmony between the legislative and the judicial branches of the government.

32 Only the Socialist and Communist platforms spoke boldly on the Constitution. The former favored a Farmers' and Workers' Rights Amendment ending the usurped power of the Supreme Court to declare social legislation unconstitutional and granting the power to acquire and operate industries; the latter proposed a constitutional amendment "to put an end to the dictatorial and usurped powers of the Supreme Court." The *Nation,* Supplement, July 18, 1936.

33 Lincoln's views on the Court's power and on the possibility of reversing its decisions were clearly expressed in the course of his debates with Stephen Douglas. "We believe," he said, "as much as Judge Douglas (perhaps more) in obedience to, and respect for, the judicial department of government. We think its decisions on constitutional questions, when fully settled, should control not only the particular cases decided,

but the general policy of the country, subject to be disturbed only by Amendments of the Constitution, as provided in that instrument itself. More than this would be revolution. But we think the Dred Scott decision is erroneous. We know the Court that made it has often overruled its own decisions, and we shall do what we can to have it overrule this. We offer no resistance to it." Warren, op. cit., Vol. II, p. 330.

34 *Morehead* v. *New York Ex Rel. Tepaldo,* 80 L.Ed., 921 (1936).

35 The doctrine of inherent powers was first expounded by James Wilson of Pennsylvania, a member of the Philadelphia Convention, who was later appointed justice of the Supreme Court by President Washington. Wilson, who was one of the greatest jurists of his day, argued: "When a subject has neither been expressly excluded from the regulating power of the Federal Government nor necessarily left within the exclusive control of the States, it may be regulated by Congress if it be, or become, a matter the regulation of which is of general importance to the whole Nation, and at the same time a matter over which the States are, in practical fact, unable to exercise the necessary controlling power."

36 259 U.S., 120. This decision declared unconstitutional an Act of Congress of February 24, 1919 (40 Stat. 1138) which placed a tax on child-made-labor articles.

37 Westel Woodbury Willoughby, *The Constitutional Law of the United States,* 2 ed., Vol. I, p. 81, Baker Voorhis & Co., New York (1929).

38 *Missouri-Kansas-Texas R.R. Co.,* v. *May,* 194 U.S., 267, 270.

### CHAPTER IV

1 Appointed by President John Adams on January 20, 1801.
2 Charles A. Beard, *The Rise of American Civilization,* Vol. I, p. 388.

3 The verdict of the jury was: not guilty "by any evidence submitted to us." Burr and his counsel protested that the verdict was "irregular." Claude Bowers, *Jefferson in Power,* pp. 395, 396, 398–424, Houghton, Mifflin Co., Boston (1936).

4 McLaughlin, op. cit., pp. 324–30.

5 This is Professor McLaughlin's summary of the opinion of Albert Gallatin, secretary of the treasury, op. cit., p. 337.

6 Beard, op. cit., Vol. I, pp. 392–93.

7 4 Wheaton, 316 (1819).

8 1 Wheaton, 326 (1816). Opinion per Justice Story, colleague and disciple of Marshall, held that the Supreme Court could review decisions of state courts which involved federal rights.

9 6 Wheaton, 264.

10 4 Wheaton, 316 (1819).

11 *Trustees of Dartmouth College* v. *Woodward,* 4 Wheaton, 518 (1819).

12 Besides *Marbury* v. *Madison* and those already discussed, the following are the most important decisions of the period under review: *Fletcher* v. *Peck,* 6 Cranch 87; *Sturges* v. *Crowninshield,* 4 Wheaton, 117; *Osborne* v. *Bank of the United States,* 9 Wheaton, 738; *Gibbons* v. *Ogden,* 9 Wheaton, 1.

13 V. L. Parrington, *Main Currents of American Thought,* Vol. II, p. 23.

14 Cf. Ch. II.

15 Corwin, op. cit., p. 10.

16 *Democracy in America.* Quoted in Corwin, op. cit., p. 8.

17 Beard, op. cit., Vol. I, p. 653.

18 Ibid., p. 655.

19 Southern opposition developed against the tariffs of 1824 and 1828 ("the tariff of abominations").

20 According to Professor McLaughlin's summary of *A Century of Population Growth* (published by the Bureau of the

Census, 1909), "between 1820 and 1830 the population of New York was increased by 545,796, while the increase of the whole of the old South was less than 400,000. In that decade over 1,100,000 persons were added to the population of the Northern States, not including the new states west of the mountains, and that was over three times as much as the total growth of all the old states south of the Pennsylvania line. In 1790 South Carolina contained 107,094 slaves; forty years later, 315,401. Between 1820 and 1830 the slave population of the state increased 56,926 and the White population about 22,000. To the population of Pennsylvania in the same decade were added about 300,000 persons—more than three-fourths as many as the total increase in the old South, including both slave and free." Op. cit., p. 431.

21 J. C. Calhoun, *Works* (1874), Vol. I, p. 3; quoted in W. S. Carpenter, *The Development of American Political Thought,* p. 145, Princeton University Press (1930).

22 Ibid.

23 President Jackson's other appointees were: John McClean of Ohio, March 6, 1829; Henry Baldwin of Pennsylvania, January 4, 1830; James Monroe Wayne of Georgia, January 7, 1835; Philip Pendleton Barbour of Virginia, December 28, 1835. Taney, who was appointed on December 28, 1835, and confirmed on March 15, 1836, had served in Jackson's Cabinet as attorney general and as secretary of the treasury.

24 The New York *Courier* on July 9, 1835, wrote: "The liberties of a great people are put in peril by the departure of the most eminent of their conservators. . . . We tremble in the contemplation of the risque we run in his successor. . . ." Similar statements appeared in editorials throughout the North. Several speakers and writers, however, went to fanatical limits in their prediction of impending calamity. The Democratic press, on the other hand, hailed the advent of a new chief justice. On July 28, 1835, the Richmond *Enquirer* wrote: "The Court has done more to change the character

of that instrument and to shape, as it were, a new Constitution for us, than all the other departments of the Government put together. The President will nominate a Democratic Chief Justice, and thus, we hope, give us some opportunity for the good old State-Rights doctrines of Virginia of '98–99 to be heard and weighed on the Federal Bench. . . . We believe that Taney is a strong State-Rights man." Warren, op. cit., Vol. II, p. 9.

25 Warren, op. cit., Vol. II, p. 10.

26 President van Buren appointed John Catron of Tennessee and John McKinley of Alabama.

27 Warren, op. cit., Vol. II, p. 35.

28 *Trustees of Dartmouth College* v. *Woodward,* 4 Wheaton, 518 (1819).

29 *The Proprietors of Charles River Bridge* v. *The Proprietors of the Warren Bridge,* 11 Peters, 420.

30 For cases of similar import decided during this period, see *Briscoe* v. *Bank of Kentucky,* 11 Peters, 257, and *City of New York* v. *Milne,* 11 Peters, 102.


## CHAPTER V


1 Noah Haynes Swayne of Ohio, appointed January 22, 1862; Samuel Freeman Miller of Iowa, appointed July 15, 1862; David Davis of Illinois, appointed December 1, 1862; Stephen Johnson Field of California, appointed March 6, 1863; and Chief Justice Salmon Portland Chase of Ohio, appointed December 6, 1864.

2 Justice Field was a Democrat but a Unionist; and of the other Lincoln appointees only Chief Justice Chase had been actively in politics.

3 Letter to Erastus Corning, June 12, 1863, Warren, op. cit., Vol. II, p. 373.

## Appendix

4 George S. Boutwell, *Reminiscences of Sixty Years in Public Affairs;* Warren, op. cit., Vol. II, p. 400.

5 *Ex parte Merryman,* Fed. Cas. No. 9, 487 (1861).

6 1 Wallace, 243.

7 4 Wallace, 2.

8 *Prize Cases,* 2 Black, 635 (1863); also *Miller* v. *United States,* 11 Wallace, 268 (1871).

9 *Bank Tax Cases,* 2 Wallace, 200 (1865), *Pacific Insurance Co.* v. *Soule,* 7 Wallace, 433 (1869).

10 Warren, op. cit., Vol. II, p. 418.

11 *Mississippi* v. *Johnson,* 4 Wallace, 475. An attempt to enjoin the President and the military commander appointed by him in the state of Mississippi from executing the Reconstruction Acts of March 2 and 25, 1867.

12 *Georgia* v. *Stanton,* 6 Wallace, 50 (1867).

13 It was expected that the Reconstruction Acts would be held invalid by a closely divided Court. Prior to the Act of March 27, 1868, repealing the Court's appellate jurisdiction in *habeas corpus* cases, a bill had been introduced in the same session which provided that no act of Congress could be declared invalid without the affirmative vote of two thirds of the justices. Such attempts have not been uncommon where judicial frustration of a declared public policy appeared imminent. On May 14, 1935, eight days after the Railway Retirement Act of 1934 had been declared void by a five-to-four decision, a constitutional amendment was proposed in the House of Representatives, requiring a two-thirds vote of the Supreme Court to declare a law of Congress invalid. This proposed amendment would also vest in the Supreme Court exclusive jurisdiction over questions of constitutionality, thus barring inferior Federal Courts from deciding whether Congress had properly exercised its legislative powers.

14 *Ex parte McCardle,* 7 Wallace, 506 (1869).

15 7 Wallace, 700 (1869).

[ 252 ]

# Notes

16  See: *Crandall* v. *Nevada,* 6 Wallace, 35 (1867); *The Nine*
v. *Trevor,* 4 Wallace, 555 (1866).

17  8 Wallace, 603 (1870). This suit arose over a promissory
note which had become due and payable just prior to the
passage of the first Legal Tender Act of 1862. The maker,
having defaulted in payment at maturity, subsequently offered to pay the principal and interest in greenbacks. The
payee refused to accept this depreciated currency and demanded payment in gold. The question before the Court was
whether a debtor could discharge an obligation entered into
prior to the act by tendering inconvertible paper currency in
lieu of specie.

18  The chief justice justified his reversal in the following significant passage: "It is not surprising that amid the tumult of the
late civil war, and under the influence of apprehensions for
the safety of the Republic almost universal, different views,
never before entertained by American statesmen or jurists,
were adopted by many. The time was not favorable to con-
siderate reflection upon the constitutional limits of Legislative or Executive authority. If power was assumed from
patriotic motives, the assumption found ready justification
in patriotic hearts. . . . Not a few who then insisted upon
its necessity, or acquiesced in that view, have, since the return
of peace, and under the influence of the calmer time, reconsidered this conclusion."

19  The appointment was made pursuant to the Act of April 10,
1869, which increased the number of justices from seven to
nine.

20  12 Wallace, 457 (1871). Decided by a vote of five-to-four.
The four judges who constituted the prevailing majority in
*Hepburn* v. *Griswold* became the dissentient minority in
*Knox* v. *Lee.* See also *Juilliard* v. *Greenman,* 110 U.S., 421
(1884), where the Court later held that the reissue of inconvertible treasury notes in time of peace was a valid exercise
of congressional power. By this latter decision the power of

## Appendix

Congress to authorize fiat money and make it legal tender for payment of debts was rendered virtually unlimited.

21  16 Wallace, 36 (1873).

## CHAPTER VI

1  Section 2 aims to achieve indirectly the same purpose as Section 1 by threatening to reduce the electoral strength of those states which disfranchise their Negro citizens. Section 3 deprives federal and state office holders who joined the insurrection of the right to hold federal or state office. Section 4 repudiates the public debt of the Confederacy; and Section 5 provides for the implementing of the amendment by appropriate legislation.

2  Charles W. Collins, *The Fourteenth Amendment and the States;* Warren, op. cit., Vol. II, p. 540.

3  Dissenting opinion in the *Slaughterhouse Cases,* 16 Wallace, 36 (1873).

4  16 Wallace, 36 (1873).

5  94 U.S., 113. Decided in 1877.

6  Morrison R. Waite of Ohio was appointed chief justice by President Grant in 1874 to succeed Chief Justice Chase, who died in the preceding year. Unlike his predecessors, he ascended to the Bench without deep-rooted political convictions. He was an impartial magistrate of the law, and his opinion in *Munn* v. *Illinois,* perhaps his greatest, is deemed a landmark in American judicial history.

7  On the authority of *Munn* v. *Illinois,* the Court upheld several state statutes fixing maximum railway rates for freight and passengers. See *Peik* v. *Chicago & Northwestern Ry.,* 94 U.S., 164; *Chicago, Burlington & Quincy R.R.* v. *Iowa,* 94 U.S., 155.

8  123 U.S., 623. Decided 1887.

9  The *Civil Rights Cases,* decided in 1883, which declared the

[ 254 ]

# Notes

Civil Rights Act of March 1, 1875, unconstitutional. 109 U.S., 3.

10 Justice Miller in the *Slaughterhouse Cases.*

11 Bryce, op. cit., Vol I, p. 267.

12 *The Rise of American Civilization,* Vol. II, p. 178.

13 *Chicago, Milwaukee & St. Paul R.R.* v. *Minnesota,* 134 U.S., 418. Decided March 1890.

14 See *Davidson* v. *New Orleans,* 96 U.S., 97 (1878), where Justice Miller observed "that there exists some strange misconception" of the scope of the "due process" clause. "In fact, it would seem," said he, "from the character of many of the cases before us, and the arguments made in them, that the clause under consideration is looked upon as a means of bringing to the test of the decision of this Court the abstract opinions of every unsuccessful litigant in a State court of the justice of the decision against him, and of the merits of the legislation on which such a decision may be founded." By this statement Justice Miller implied that where a legislature acts pursuant to a conceded power, the Court will not review the merits of the legislation by virtue of the "due process" clause.

15 *Smyth* v. *Ames,* 169 U.S., 145 (1898) laid down the method of determining whether rates were confiscatory. It was there held that the basis of all calculations must be "the fair value" of the property being used by the company for the convenience of the public and upon this value the company was entitled to a fair return. In order to ascertain "fair value", the Court must consider the following relevant factors: (a) Original cost of construction; (b) Cost of improvements; (c) Cost of replacement; (d) Market value of outstanding securities; (e) Operating expenses. Such determination requires a broad inquiry into facts to which an appellate court does not always have ready or timely access. A legislature usually resorts to preliminary hearings where shippers, carriers and the public express their views and where qualified experts on both sides

testify as to the justification or economic advantages of the proposed rates. The composite result of this investigation is reflected in legislation which, in theory, at least, represents a desired public policy. Wherefore, presumably, Justice Bradley declared that the question of what is a reasonable charge "is pre-eminently a legislative one involving considerations of policy as well as of remuneration."

16 Per his opinion in *Hurtado* v. *California,* 110 U.S., 516 (1884).

17 198 U.S., 45. Decided in 1905.

18 Compare with *Holden* v. *Hardy,* 169 U.S., 366, which sustained an eight-hour law for persons working in mines, and with *Otis* v. *Parker,* 187 U.S., 606, which upheld a prohibition of sales of stock on margins or for future delivery. See also *Northern Securities Co.* v. *United States,* 193 U.S., 197, and *Jacobson* v. *Massachusetts,* 197 U.S., 11, which sustained legislative limitations on the liberty of individuals.

19 Supra, pp. 99–100.

20 Per his dissenting opinion in *Adkins* v. *Children's Hospital,* 261 U.S., 525 (1923).

21 See opinion of Judge Van Orsdel in 284 Fed., 613.

22 *Powell* v. *Pennsylvania,* 127 U.S., 678 (1888).

23 *Burns Baking Co.* v. *Bryan,* 264 U.S., 504 (1924).

24 For example: antitrust laws, the Interstate Commerce Commission, progressive state legislation, particularly in Wisconsin; and the Sixteenth, Seventeenth, Eighteenth and Nineteenth amendments.

25 *Muller* v. *Oregon,* 208 U.S., 412 (1908).

26 *Bunting* v. *Oregon,* 243 U.S., 426 (1917).

27 *N. Y. Central R.R. Co.* v. *White,* 243 U.S., 188 (1917).

28 *Adkins* v. *Children's Hospital,* 261 U.S., 525 (1923). It was a five-to-three decision. Chief Justice Taft dissented, with Justice Sanford concurring; Justice Holmes handed down a separate dissent; Mr. Justice Brandeis took no part in the case.

# Notes

29 *Chicago, Burlington & Quincy R.R. Co.,* v. *Iowa,* 94 U.S., 155 (1876).

30 See *Railroad Commission Cases,* 116 U.S., 307 (1886) ; also the *Minnesota Rate Case,* 134 U.S., 418.

31 273 U.S., 418. Decided February 28, 1927, by a five-to-four-vote.

32 *Wolff Packing Co.* v. *Kansas Industrial Court,* 262 U.S., 522.

33 See *German Alliance Insurance Co.* v. *Lewis,* 233 U.S., 389 (1914), where a Kansas statute regulating rates of fire-insurance companies was upheld by a divided Court.

34 *Home Building & Loan Assoc.* v. *Blaisdell,* 290 U.S., 398. Decided January 8, 1934.

35 Minnesota Laws of 1933, Ch. 339.

36 The decision was by a five-to-four vote. Chief Justice Hughes wrote the prevailing opinion and concurring with him were Justices Brandeis, Roberts, Cardozo and Stone. Justices Sutherland, McReynolds, Van Devanter and Butler dissented.

37 Quoted from Marshall's opinion in *McCulloch* v. *Maryland,* 4 Wheaton, 316 (1819). The organic or adaptive theory of interpretation was also advocated by Marshall's colleague and disciple, Justice Story. See *Martin* v. *Hunter,* 1 Wheaton, 326 (1816), wherein he said : "The instrument was not in-tended to provide merely for the exigencies of a few years, but was to endure through a long lapse of ages, the events of which were locked up in the inscrutable purposes of Provi-dence."

38 The same reasoning was applied by the Court a year later in upholding the congressional resolution which abrogated the "gold clause" in private contracts. *Norman* v. *Baltimore & Ohio R.R. Co.,* 294 U.S., 240 (1935).

39 Mr. Justice Sutherland, who wrote the dissenting opinion, attacked the views of the majority. Deprecating the adapta-tive interpretation employed by Chief Justice Hughes, he invoked the words uttered by Taney in the Dred Scott Decision: "that while the Constitution remains unaltered it

must be construed now as it was understood at the time of its adoption." In light of the facts of history, the attempted resurrection of this defunct Dred Scott doctrine seems incredible. However, the real significance of a decision is often gauged by the tenor of the dissent. Bewailing the "encroachments" upon the sanctity of private contracts, Mr. Justice Sutherland observed that "few questions of greater moment than that just decided have been submitted for judicial inquiry during this generation."

40 *Nebbia* v. *New York*, 291 U.S., 502. Decided March 5, 1934.

41 New York Laws of 1933, Ch. 158, sec. 312 (b).

42 *New State Ice Co.* v. *Liebmann*, 285 U.S., 262 (1932).

43 Ibid. See also *Fairmont Creamery Co.* v. *Minnesota*, 274 U.S., 1 (1927).

44 *Wolff Packing Co.* v. *Court of Industrial Relations*, 262 U.S., 522 (1923).

45 *Tyson & Bro.* v. *Banton*, 273 U.S., 418 (1927).

46 *Lochner* v. *New York*, 198 U.S., 45 (1905); *Williams* v. *Standard Oil Co. of La.*, 278 U.S., 235 (1929); *Ribnick* v. *McBride*, 277 U.S., 350 (1929).

47 *Ex parte Milligan*, 4 Wallace, 2; *U.S.* v. *L. Cohen Grocery Co.*, 255 U.S., 81.

48 *Wilson* v. *New*, 243 U.S., 332 (1917); *Block* v. *Hirsh*, 256 U.S., 135 (1921).

49 The decision was by a five-to-four vote. The division of justices was the same as in the *Minnesota Moratorium Case*. Mr. Justice Roberts read the prevailing opinion, Mr. Justice McReynolds the dissent.

50 Also compare Mr. Justice Roberts' opinion in *Nebbia* v. *New York* with opinions rendered in the cases cited in notes 45, 46 and 47.

51 See note 47.

52 *Morehead* v. *New York Ex Rel. Tepaldo*, 80 L.Ed., 921 (1936).

# Notes

53 On March 29, 1937, by a five-to-four majority made possible by Mr. Justice Roberts' shift, the Court reversed its decision in the *New York Minimum Wage Case* and held that the Minimum Wage for Women Act of the State of Washington was constitutional. No. 293, October Term 1936—*West Coast Hotel Co.* v. *Parrish.*

## CHAPTER VII

1 *Schechter Poultry Corp.* v. *United States,* 295 U.S., 495 (1935); *Carter* v. *Carter Coal Co.,* 80 L.Ed., 749 (1936); *United States* v. *Butler et al, Receivers of Hoosac Mills Corp.,* 80 L.Ed., 287 (1936).
2 Supra, ch. VI, p. 119.
3 *Missouri* v. *Holland,* 252 U.S., 416 (1920).
4 *R. C. Tway Coal Co.* v. *Glenn,* 12 Fed. Supp., 570 (1935).
5 *Brown* v. *Maryland,* 12 Wheaton, 419 (1827).
6 Ibid.
7 Warren, op. cit., Vol. I, p. 610.
8 22 U.S., 1; 9 Wheaton, 1 (1824).
9 Exclusive licenses or monopolies for steamboat navigation had also been granted by the legislatures of Louisiana, Georgia, Massachusetts and other states.
10 Warren, op. cit., Vol. I, p. 616.
11 12 Wheaton, 419 (1827).
12 53 U.S., 299 (1851).
13 94 U.S., 164 (1876). Decided by a divided Court. See also *Chicago, Burlington & Quincy R.R. Co.* v. *Iowa,* 94 U.S., 155 (1876).
14 *Wabash, St. Louis Pacific Ry.* v. *Illinois,* 118 U.S., 557.
15 The *Passenger Cases,* 7 Howard, 283 (1849); *The License Cases,* 5 Howard, 504 (1847).
16 *Philadelphia & S.S. Co.* v. *Pennsylvania,* 122 U.S., 326; *Ozark Pipe Line Corp.* v. *Monier,* 266 U.S., 555; *Willcuts*

v. *Bunn,* 282 U.S., 216; *Anglo-Chilean Nitrates Corp.* v. *Alabama,* 288 U.S., 218.

17 *Ozark Pipe Line Corp.* v. *Monier,* see note 16.

18 *Philadelphia & S.S. Co.* v. *Pennsylvania,* see note 16.

19 *People Ex Rel. Pennsylvania R.R.* v. *Wemple,* 138 N.Y., 1 (1893).

20 See note 17.

21 Perhaps the most extreme extension of the Fourteenth Amendment was made in *Allgeyer* v. *Louisiana,* 165 U.S., 578 (1897), in which it was decided that a state law regulating insurance companies violated the "due process" clause.

22 156 U.S., 1 (1895).

23 Melville Weston Fuller of Illinois was appointed chief justice by President Cleveland on May 2, 1888, to succeed Chief Justice Waite, who died on March 23, 1888. He came to the chief-justiceship without previous judicial experience and served for twenty-two years, until his death on July 4, 1910.

24 *Interstate Commerce Commission* v. *Cincinnati, N. O. & T. P. R. Co.,* 167 U.S., 497 (1897).

25 Sir Henry S. Maine, *Popular Government,* pp. 245–48, John Murray, London (1885).

26 "It should be remembered," said Mr. Judge Van Orsdel, "that of the three fundamental principles which underlie government, and for which government exists, the protection of life, liberty and property, the chief of these is property." Per his opinion in *Children's Hospital* v. *Adkins,* 284 Fed., 613. Note also the following words of Judge Van Orsdel from the same opinion: "Legislation tending to fix the prices at which private property shall be sold, whether it be a commodity or labor, places a limitation upon the distribution of wealth, and is aimed at the correction of the inequalities of fortune which are inevitable under our form of Government, due to personal liberty and the private ownership of property. . . . The history of civilization proves that, when the citizen is deprived of the free use and enjoyment of his prop-

# Notes

erty, anarchy and revolution follow, and life and liberty are without protection."

27 Charles A. and William Beard, *The American Leviathan,* p. 72.

28 According to approximate estimates of the International Economic Research Bureau of New York City, the total of foreign capital invested in the United States rose from 400 million dollars in 1860 to 1600 million in 1880, and in 1899 reached the then huge total of 3 billion 300 million.

29 These terms are used by V. L. Parrington in *Main Currents in American Thought,* Vol. III, Ch. I.

30 In 1906, under the President's energetic sponsorship, Congress overcame its scruples against delegating its legislative powers and passed a statute giving the Interstate Commerce Commission authority to fix maximum rates for common carriers.

31 Beard, *The Rise of American Civilization,* Vol. II, p. 598.

32 See Chapter III, note 37.

33 See note 32.

34 A typical reaction to Theodore Roosevelt's agitation is contained in the following excerpt from the *Commercial and Financial Chronicle:* "Political attacks against men of wealth and against organized capital; the serious advocacy of political and economic doctrines which would completely change the theory of our Government and revolutionize social relations—these and kindred matters had threatened the security and stability of investment values. . . . There were many manifestations of the President's [Theodore Roosevelt's] activities. . . . The remarkable special message which he sent to Congress on January 31, embodying propositions for new legislation and attacking men of wealth, was one of the most extraordinary documents ever sent to a legislative body." From the Annual Review of the *Commercial and Financial Chronicle* (1909).

35 *United States* v. *Trans-Missouri Freight Assoc.,* 166 U.S.,

290 (1897) ; *Addyston Pipe and Steel Co.* v. *United States,* 175 U.S., 211 (1899).

36 *Swift and Co.* v. *United States,* 196 U.S., 375 (1905).

37 The Court also sustained the application of the Sherman Act to the Standard Oil Trust, *Standard Oil Co.* v. *United States,* 221 U.S., 1 (1911), and to the American Tobacco Trust, *United States* v. *American Tobacco Co.,* 221 U.S., 106 (1911).

38 222 U.S., 20 (1912).

39 223 U.S., 1 (1912).

40 234 U.S., 342 (1914).

41 250 U.S., 199 (1919).

42 *Wisconsin Railroad Commission* v. *Chicago, Burlington & Quincy R.R. Co.,* 257, U.S., 563 (1922).

43 See also *Lemke* v. *Farmers Grain Co.,* 258 U. S., 50 (1922) ; *Coronado Coal Co.* v. *United Mine Workers,* 268, U.S., 295 (1925) ; and *Tagg Bros.* v. *United States,* 280 U.S., 420 (1930).

44 243 U.S., 332 (1917).

45 258 U.S., 495 (1922). To the same effect see *Board of Trade* v. *Olsen,* 262 U.S., 1. (1923), which sustained the Grain Futures Act of 1922. Under this act the commerce power was used to supervise the buying and selling of grain and grain futures on the various Boards of Trade.

46 *Hamilton* v. *Kentucky Distilleries Co.,* 251 U.S., 146 (1919).

47 *Lottery Case,* 188 U.S., 321 (1903).

48 *Hipolite Egg Co.* v. *United States,* 220 U.S., 45 (1911).

49 *Reid* v. *Colorado,* 187 U.S., 137 (1902).

50 *Hoke* v. *United States,* 227 U.S., 308 (1913). Similarly, Congress, acting within the scope of its war power, established wartime prohibition. *Hamilton* v. *Kentucky Distilleries Co.,* 251 U.S., 146 (1919).

51 *Hammer* v. *Dagenhart,* 247 U.S., 251 (1918).

52 *Schechter Poultry Corp.* v. *United States.* Supra, p. 126.

# Notes

53 "Who said States' Rights?" by Howard Lee McBain, *Today*, August 17, 1935. Mr. McBain's conclusion does not appear warranted in the light of the *New York Milk Case* but receives support in the New York Minimum Wage decision which followed it.

54 *Carter* v. *Carter Coal Co.* Supra, p. 126.

55 For a discussion of the Court's second argument against the act—unconstitutional use of the taxing power—see Ch. VIII, note 16.

## CHAPTER VIII

1 Constitution of U. S., Art. I, Sec. 8, Subsec. 1.

2 Jefferson's Correspondence, pp. 524–25; O. L. Phillips, "Constitutional Limitations on Social Legislation," *Proceedings of the Academy of Political Science,* Vol. XVI, No. 4.

3 Joseph Story, *Commentaries on the Constitution.* 3 volumes. 1833 ed., Vol. I, Sec. 905.

4 Ibid., Sec. 919.

5 Madison's "Report on the Virginia Resolutions", *Elliot's Debates,* Vol. IV, p. 552; O. L. Phillips, op. cit.

6 Monroe's Message of May 4, 1822, is quoted at length in Story's Commentaries, Vol. I, Sec. 977–87.

7 Ibid., Vol. I, Sec. 988.

8 178 U.S., 41 (1900).

9 *Austin* v. *The Aldermen,* 7 Wallace, 694 (1868). To the same effect see *Pacific Insurance Co.* v. *Soule,* 7 Wallace, 433 (1868).

10 8 Wallace, 533 (1869).

11 5 Wallace, 462 (1866).

12 195 U.S., 27 (1904).

13 See also *Treat* v. *White,* 181 U.S., 264 (1901) and *Patton* v. *Brady,* 184 U.S., 608 (1902). In the latter case Justice

# Appendix

Brewer observed: "It is not the province of the judiciary to inquire whether the exercise [of the taxing power] is reasonable in amount, or in respect to the property to which it is applied. These are matters in respect to which the legislative determination is final."

14 262 U.S., 447 (1922).

15 "Report on Manufactures," *The Works of Alexander Hamilton,* in 3 volumes. Vol. I, Official Reports, p. 231, Williams & Whiting, New York (1881).

16 The same point was made by Mr. Justice Sutherland with regard to the taxation provisions of the Bituminous Coal Conservation Act. "The so-called excise tax of 15 *percentum,"* he said, speaking for the majority in *Carter* v. *Carter Coal Co.,* ". . . is clearly not a tax but a penalty . . . to compel compliance with the regulatory provisions of the acts." The Hoosac Mills decision was cited, among others, in support of this view, which, however, was not pressed by the Court because the government had chosen to base the defense of the act on the "commerce clause." Supra, Ch. VII, p. 126.

17 *Missouri-Kansas-Texas R.R. Co.* v. *May,* 194 U.S., 267, p. 270.

18 Constitution of U. S., Art. I, Sec. 2, Subsec. 3, and Art. I, Sec. 9, Subsec. 4.

19 *Hylton* v. *United States,* 3 Dall., 171 (1796).

20 7 Wallace, 433 (1868). The tax involved in this case was imposed by an act of Congress passed in 1864 and amended in 1866.

21 23 Wallace, 331 (1875).

22 *Springer* v. *United States,* 102 U.S., 586 (1881). The tax involved was imposed by an act of Congress passed in 1864 and amended in 1865. The income in this case was from professional services and United States bonds.

23 157 U.S., 429 (1895); on rehearing, 158 U.S., 601 (1895).

24 Charles A. and William Beard, op. cit., p. 132.

25 Constitution of U. S., Art. I, Sec. 8, Subsec. 5.

26 "No State shall . . . coin money; emit bills of credit." The Constitution, Art. I, Sec. 10, Subsec. 1.

27 Ibid.

28 110 U.S., 421 (1884).

29 294 U. S., 240. Justices McReynolds, Van Devanter, Sutherland and Butler dissented in this and the other *Gold Clause Cases.*

30 294 U.S., 330. See also *Nortz* v. *United States*, 294 U.S., 317. Chief Justice Hughes wrote the prevailing opinion in these two cases.

31 Corwin, op. cit., p. 177.

## CHAPTER IX

1 "The Court under Chief Justice Taney did not in fact systematically decrease the protection given to private rights by the Constitution. . . . The protection of contracts for tax exemption made by corporations with states against impairment by subsequent legislation is a famous, controversial, and typical act of the Court, concurred in by Chief Justice Taney." Malcolm P. Sharp, "Movement in Supreme Court Adjudication", *Harvard Law Review.* Vol. XLVI, No. 3, p. 372.

2 Sharp, op. cit., p. 364.

3 Benjamin N. Cardozo, *The Nature of the Judicial Process,* p. 17. Yale University Press (1921).

4 *Interstate Commerce Com.* v. *Cincinnati, N.O. and T.P.R. Co.,* 167 U.S., 479 (1897).

5 Sharp, op. cit., p. 392.

6 Supra, Ch. VIII.

7 Brooks Adams, *The Theory of Social Revolution,* p. 83. New York (1913).

8 *Barden* v. *Northern Pacific R.R. Co.,* 154 U.S., 288. See

also disssenting opinion of Justice Miller in *Washington University* v. *Rouse,* 8 Wallace, 439.

9  *Burnet* v. *Coronado Oil and Gas Co.,* 285 U.S., 393–404.

10  Cardozo, op. cit., p. 171.

11  Corwin, op. cit., p. 117.

12  Adams, op. cit., p. 53.

13  Adams, op. cit., p. 50.

14  "The Dred Scott Decision," *American Historical Review,* Vol. XVIII, p. 52.

15  Adams, op. cit., p. 119.

16  *Home Building & Loan Assoc.* v. *Blaisdell,* 290 U.S., 398.

17  *Ashwander* v. *Tennessee Valley Authority,* 297 U.S., 288 (1936). The prevailing opinion was written by Chief Justice Hughes; Mr. Justice Brandeis concurred in a separate opinion and Mr. Justice McReynolds alone dissented.

18  Adams, op. cit., p. 125.

19  Adams, op. cit., p. 103.

20  Adams, op. cit., p. 116.

21  208 U.S., 161 (1908).

22  Cardozo, op. cit., p. 94.

23  Henri Carré, *La Fin des Parlements* (*1788–1790*), p. 19. Hachette and Co., Paris (1912).

24  Decision of the *Parlement* of Besançon. Ibid., p. 23.

25  Ibid., p. 57.

## EPILOGUE

1  *Washington, Virginia & Maryland Coach Co.* v. *N.L.R.B.* No. 469, October Term, 1936.

2  *The Associated Press* v. *N.L.R.B.* No. 365, October Term, 1936.

3  *N.L.R.B.* v. *Jones & Laughlin Steel Corp.*
*N.L.R.B.* v. *Fruehauf Trailer Co.*
*N.L.R.B.* v. *Friedman-Harry Marks Clothing Co. Inc.* Nos. 419, 420–21, 422–23, October Term, 1936.

# THE CONSTITUTION*
## OF THE
## UNITED STATES OF AMERICA

WE THE PEOPLE of the United States, in Order to form a more perfect Union, establish Justice, insure domestic Tranquility, provide for the common defence, promote the general Welfare, and secure the Blessings of Liberty to ourselves and our Posterity do ordain and establish this Constitution for the United States of America.

### ARTICLE I.

*Section 1.* All legislative Powers herein granted shall be vested in a Congress of the United States, which shall consist of a Senate and House of Representatives.

*Section 2.* The House of Representatives shall be composed of Members chosen every second Year by the People of the several States, and the Electors in each State shall have the Qualifications requisite for Electors of the most numerous Branch of the State Legislature.

No Person shall be a Representative who shall not have attained to the Age of twenty five Years, and been seven Years a Citizen of the United States, and who shall not, when elected, be an Inhabitant of that State in which he shall be chosen.

Representatives and direct Taxes shall be apportioned among the several States which may be included within this Union, according to their respective Numbers, which shall be determined by adding to the whole Number of free Persons, including those bound to Service for a Term of Years, and excluding Indians not

*Note:* The words "The Constitution of the United States of America" do not appear on the original.

[ 267 ]

taxed, three fifths of all other Persons. The actual Enumeration shall be made within three Years after the first Meeting of the Congress of the United States, and within every subsequent Term of ten Years, in such Manner as they shall by Law direct. The Number of Representatives shall not exceed one for every thirty Thousand, but each State shall have at Least one Representative; and until such enumeration shall be made, the State of New Hampshire shall be entitled to chuse three, Massachusetts eight, Rhode-Island and Providence Plantations one, Connecticut five, New-York six, New Jersey four, Pennsylvania eight, Delaware one, Maryland six, Virginia ten, North Carolina five, South Carolina five, and Georgia three.

When vacancies happen in the Representation from any State, the Executive Authority thereof shall issue Writs of Election to fill such Vacancies.

The House of Representatives shall chuse their Speaker and other Officers; and shall have the sole Power of Impeachment.

*Section 3.* The Senate of the United States shall be composed of two Senators from each State, chosen by the Legislature thereof, for six Years; and each Senator shall have one Vote.

Immediately after they shall be assembled in Consequence of the first Election, they shall be divided as equally as may be into three Classes. The Seats of the Senators of the first Class shall be vacated at the Expiration of the second Year, of the second Class at the Expiration of the fourth Year, and of the third Class at the Expiration of the sixth Year, so that one third may be chosen every second Year; and if Vacancies happen by Resignation, or otherwise, during the Recess of the Legislature of any State, the Executive thereof may make temporary Appointments until the next Meeting of the Legislature, which shall then fill such Vacancies.

No Person shall be a Senator who shall not have attained to the Age of thirty Years, and been nine Years a Citizen of the United States, and who shall not, when elected, be an Inhabitant of that State for which he shall be chosen.

The Vice President of the United States shall be President of the Senate, but shall have no Vote, unless they be equally divided.

The Senate shall chuse their other Officers, and also a President pro tempore, in the Absence of the Vice President, or when he shall exercise the Office of President of the United States.

The Senate shall have the sole Power to try all Impeachments. When sitting for that Purpose, they shall be on Oath or Affirmation. When the President of the United States is tried the Chief Justice shall preside: And no Person shall be convicted without the Concurrence of two thirds of the Members present.

Judgment in Cases of Impeachment shall not extend further than to removal from Office, and disqualification to hold and enjoy any Office of honor, Trust or Profit under the United States: but the Party convicted shall nevertheless be liable and subject to Indictment, Trial, Judgment and Punishment, according to Law.

*Section 4.* The Times, Places and Manner of holding Elections for Senators and Representatives, shall be prescribed in each State by the Legislature thereof; but the Congress may at any time by Law make or alter such Regulations, except as to the Places of chusing Senators.

The Congress shall assemble at least once in every Year, and such Meeting shall be on the first Monday in December, unless they shall by Law appoint a different Day.

*Section 5.* Each House shall be the Judge of the Elections, Returns and Qualifications of its own Members, and a Majority of each shall constitute a Quorum to do Business; but a smaller Number may adjourn from day to day, and may be authorized to compel the Attendance of absent Members, in such Manner, and under such Penalties as each House may provide.

Each House may determine the Rules of its Proceedings, punish its Members for disorderly Behaviour, and, with the Concurrence of two thirds, expel a Member.

Each House shall keep a Journal of its Proceedings, and from time to time publish the same, excepting such Parts as may in

[ 269 ]

their Judgment require Secrecy; and the Yeas and Nays of the Members of either House on any question shall, at the Desire of one fifth of those Present, be entered on the Journal.

Neither House, during the Session of Congress, shall, without the Consent of the other, adjourn for more than three days, nor to any other Place than that in which the two Houses shall be sitting.

*Section 6.* The Senators and Representatives shall receive a Compensation for their Services, to be ascertained by Law, and paid out of the Treasury of the United States. They shall in all Cases, except Treason, Felony and Breach of the Peace, be privileged from Arrest during their Attendance at the Session of their respective Houses, and in going to and returning from the same; and for any Speech or Debate in either House, they shall not be questioned in any other Place.

No Senator or Representative shall, during the Time for which he was elected, be appointed to any civil Office under the Authority of the United States, which shall have been created, or the Emoluments whereof shall have been encreased during such time; and no Person holding any Office under the United States, shall be a Member of either House during his Continuance in Office.

*Section 7.* All Bills for raising Revenue shall originate in the House of Representatives; but the Senate may propose or concur with Amendments as on other Bills.

Every Bill which shall have passed the House of Representatives and the Senate, shall, before it becomes a Law, be presented to the President of the United States; If he approve he shall sign it, but if not he shall return it, with his Objections to that House in which it shall have originated, who shall enter the Objections at large on their Journal, and proceed to reconsider it. If after such Reconsideration two thirds of that House shall agree to pass the Bill, it shall be sent, together with the Objections, to the other House, by which it shall likewise be reconsidered, and if approved by two thirds of that House, it shall become a Law. But in all such Cases the Votes of both Houses shall be determined by yeas and Nays, and the Names of the Persons voting for and against the Bill shall be entered on the Journal of each House respectively. If any Bill shall not be returned by the President within ten Days (Sundays excepted) after it shall have been presented to him, the Same shall be a Law, in like Manner as if he had signed it, unless the Congress by their Adjournment prevent its Return, in which Case it shall not be a Law.

Every Order, Resolution, or Vote to which the Concurrence of the Senate and House of Representatives may be necessary (except on a question of Adjournment) shall be presented to the President of the United States; and before the Same shall take Effect, shall be approved by him, or being disapproved by him, shall be repassed by two thirds of the Senate and House of Representatives, according to the Rules and Limitations prescribed in the Case of a Bill.

*Section 8.* The Congress shall have Power To lay and collect Taxes, Duties, Imposts and Excises, to pay the Debts and provide for the common Defence and general Welfare of the United States; but all Duties, Imposts and Excises shall be uniform throughout the United States;

To borrow Money on the credit of the United States;

To regulate Commerce with foreign Nations, and among the several States, and with the Indian Tribes;

To establish an uniform Rule of Naturalization, and uniform Laws on the subject of Bankruptcies throughout the United States;

To coin Money, regulate the Value thereof, and of foreign Coin, and fix the Standard of Weights and Measures;

To provide for the Punishment of counterfeiting the Securities and current Coin of the United States;

To establish Post Offices and post Roads;

To promote the Progress of Science and useful Arts, by securing for limited Times to Authors and Inventors the exclusive Right to their respective Writings and Discoveries;

To constitute Tribunals inferior to the supreme Court;

# Appendix

To define and punish Piracies and Felonies committed on the high Seas, and Offences against the Law of Nations;

To declare War, grant Letters of Marque and Reprisal, and make Rules concerning Captures on Land and Water;

To raise and support Armies, but no Appropriation of Money to that Use shall be for a longer Term than two Years;

To provide and maintain a Navy:

To make Rules for the Government and Regulation of the land and naval Forces;

To provide for calling forth the Militia to execute the Laws of the Union, suppress Insurrections and repel Invasions;

To provide for organizing, arming, and disciplining, the Militia, and for governing such Part of them as may be employed in the Service of the United States, reserving to the States respectively, the Appointment of the Officers, and the Authority of training the Militia according to the discipline prescribed by Congress;

To exercise exclusive Legislation in all Cases whatsoever, over such District (not exceeding ten Miles square) as may, by Cession of particular States, and the Acceptance of Congress, become the Seat of the Government of the United States, and to exercise like Authority over all Places purchased by the Consent of the Legislature of the State in which the Same shall be, for the Erection of Forts, Magazines, Arsenals, dock-Yards, and other needful Buildings;—And

To make all Laws which shall be necessary and proper for carrying into Execution the foregoing Powers, and all other Powers vested by this Constitution in the Government of the United States, or in any Department or Officer thereof.

*Section 9.* The Migration or Importation of such Persons as any of the States now existing shall think proper to admit, shall not be prohibited by the Congress prior to the Year one thousand eight hundred and eight, but a Tax or duty may be imposed on such Importation, not exceeding ten dollars for each Person.

The Privilege of the Writ of Habeas Corpus shall not be suspended, unless when in Cases of Rebellion or Invasion the public Safety may require it.

No Bill of Attainder or ex post facto Law shall be passed.

No Capitation, or other direct, Tax shall be laid, unless in Proportion to the Census or Enumeration herein before directed to be taken.

No Tax or Duty shall be laid on Articles exported from any State.

No Preference shall be given by any Regulation of Commerce or Revenue to the Ports of one State over those of another: nor shall Vessels bound to, or from, one State, be obliged to enter, clear, or pay Duties in another.

No Money shall be drawn from the Treasury, but in Consequence of Appropriations made by Law; and a regular Statement and Account of the Receipts and Expenditures of all public Money shall be published from time to time.

No Title of Nobility shall be granted by the United States: And no Person holding any Office of Profit or Trust under them, without the Consent of the Congress, accept of any present, Emolument, Office, or Title, of any kind whatever, from any King, Prince, or foreign State.

*Section 10.* No State shall enter into any Treaty, Alliance, or Confederation; grant Letters of Marque and Reprisal; coin Money; emit Bills of Credit; make any Thing but gold and silver Coin a Tender in Payment of Debts; pass any Bill of Attainder, ex post facto Law, or Law impairing the Obligations of Contracts, or grant any Title of Nobility.

No State shall, without the Consent of the Congress, lay any Imposts or Duties on Imports or Exports, except what may be absolutely necessary for executing its inspection Laws: and the net Produce of all Duties and Imposts, laid by any State on Imports or Exports, shall be for the Use of the Treasury of the United States; and all such Laws shall be subject to the Revision and Controul of the Congress.

No State shall, without the Consent of Congress, lay any Duty of Tonnage, keep Troops, or Ships of War in time of Peace, enter into any Agreement or Compact with another State, or with a foreign Power, or engage in War, unless actually invaded, or in such imminent Danger as will not admit of delay.

## ARTICLE II.

*Section 1.* The executive Power shall be vested in a President of the United States of America. He shall hold his Office during the Term of four Years, and, together with the Vice President, chosen for the same Term, be elected, as follows

Each State shall appoint, in such Manner as the Legislature thereof may direct, a Number of Electors, equal to the whole Number of Senators and Representatives to which the State may be entitled in the Congress: but no Senator or Representative, or Person holding an Office of Trust or Profit under the United States, shall be appointed an Elector.

The Electors shall meet in their respective States, and vote by Ballot for two Persons, of whom one at least shall not be an Inhabitant of the same State with themselves. And they shall make a List of all the Persons voted for, and of the Number of Votes for each; which List they shall sign and certify, and transmit sealed to the Seat of the Government of the United States, directed to the President of the Senate. The President of the Senate shall, in the Presence of the Senate and House of Representatives, open all the Certificates, and the Votes shall then be counted. The Person having the greatest Number of Votes shall be the President, if such Number be a Majority of the whole Number of Electors appointed; and if there be more than one who have such Majority, and have an equal Number of Votes, then the House of Representatives shall immediately chuse by Ballot one of them for President; and if no Person have a Majority, then from the five highest on the List the said House shall in like Manner chuse the President. But in chusing the President, the Votes shall be taken by States, the Representation from each State having one Vote; A quorum for this Purpose shall consist of a Member or Members from two thirds of the States, and a Majority of all the States shall be necessary to a Choice. In every Case, after the Choice of the President, the Person having the greatest Number of Votes of the Electors shall be the Vice President. But if there should remain two or more who have equal Votes, the Senate shall chuse from them by Ballot the Vice President.

The Congress may determine the Time of chusing the Electors, and the Day on which they shall give their Votes; which Day shall be the same throughout the United States.

No Person except a natural born Citizen, or a Citizen of the United States, at the time of the Adoption of this Constitution, shall be eligible to the Office of President; neither shall any Person be eligible to that Office who shall not have attained to the Age of thirty five Years, and been fourteen Years a Resident within the United States.

In Case of the Removal of the President from Office, or of his Death, Resignation, or Inability to discharge the Powers and Duties of the said Office, the same shall devolve on the Vice President, and the Congress may by Law provide for the Case of Removal, Death, Resignation or Inability, both of the President and Vice President, declaring what Officer shall then act as President, and such officer shall act accordingly, until the Disability be removed, or a President shall be elected.

The President shall, at stated Times, receive for his Services, a Compensation, which shall neither be encreased nor diminished during the Period for which he shall have been elected, and he shall not receive within that Period any other Emolument from the United States, or any of them.

Before he enter on the Execution of his Office, he shall take the following Oath or Affirmation:—"I do solemnly swear (or affirm) that I will faithfully execute the Office of President of the United States, and will to the best of my Ability, preserve, protect and defend the Constitution of the United States."

[ 275 ]

*Appendix*

*Section 2.* The President shall be Commander in Chief of the Army and Navy of the United States, and of the Militia of the several States, when called into the actual Service of the United States; he may require the Opinion, in writing, of the principal Officer in each of the executive Departments, upon any Subject relating to the Duties of their respective Offices, and he shall have Power to grant Reprieves and Pardons for Offences against the United States, except in Cases of Impeachment.

He shall have Power, by and with the Advice and Consent of the Senate, to make Treaties, provided two thirds of the Senators present concur; and he shall nominate, and by and with the Advice and Consent of the Senate, shall appoint Ambassadors, other public Ministers and Consuls, Judges of the supreme Court, and all other Officers of the United States, whose Appointments are not herein otherwise provided for, and which shall be established by Law: but the Congress may by Law vest the Appointment of such inferior Officers, as they think proper, in the President alone, in the Courts of Law, or in the Heads of Departments.

The President shall have Power to fill up all Vacancies that may happen during the Recess of the Senate, by granting Commissions which shall expire at the End of their next Session.

*Section 3.* He shall from time to time give to the Congress Information of the State of the Union, and recommend to their Consideration such Measures as he shall judge necessary and expedient; he may, on extraordinary Occasions, convene both Houses, or either of them, and in Case of Disagreement between them, with Respect to the Time of Adjournment, he may adjourn them to such Time as he shall think proper; he shall receive Ambassadors and other public Ministers; he shall take Care that the Laws be faithfully executed, and shall Commission all the Officers of the United States.

*Section 4.* The President, Vice President and all Civil Officers of the United States, shall be removed from Office on Impeachment for, and Conviction of, Treason, Bribery, or other high Crimes and Misdemeanors.

## ARTICLE III.

*Section 1.* The judicial Power of the United States, shall be vested in one supreme Court, and in such inferior Courts as the Congress may from time to time ordain and establish. The Judges, both of the supreme and inferior Courts, shall hold their Offices during good Behaviour, and shall, at stated Times, receive for their Services, a Compensation, which shall not be diminished during their Continuance in Office.

*Section 2.* The judicial Power shall extend to all Cases, in Law and Equity, arising under this Constitution, the Laws of the United States and Treaties made, or which shall be made, under their Authority;—to all Cases affecting Ambassadors, other public Ministers and Consuls;—to all Cases of admiralty and maritime Jurisdiction;—to Controversies to which the United States shall be a Party;—to Controversies between two or more States;—between a State and Citizens of another State;—between Citizens of different States,—between Citizens of the same State claiming Lands under Grants of different States, and between a State, or the Citizens thereof, and foreign States, Citizens or Subjects.

In all Cases affecting Ambassadors, other public Ministers and Consuls, and those in which a State shall be Party, the supreme Court shall have original Jurisdiction. In all the other Cases before mentioned, the supreme Court shall have appellate Jurisdiction, both as to Law and Fact, with such Exceptions, and under such Regulations as the Congress shall make.

The Trial of all Crimes, except in Cases of Impeachment, shall be by Jury; and such Trial shall be held in the State where the said Crimes shall have been committed; but when not committed within any State, the Trial shall be at such Place or Places as the Congress may by Law have directed.

*Section 3.* Treason against the United States, shall consist only in levying War against them, or in adhering to their Enemies, giving them Aid and Comfort. No Person shall be convicted of Treason unless on the Testimony of two Witnesses to the same overt Act, or on Confession in open Court.

The Congress shall have Power to declare the Punishment of Treason, but no Attainder of Treason shall work Corruption of Blood, or Forfeiture except during the Life of the Person attainted.

### ARTICLE IV.

*Section 1.* Full Faith and Credit shall be given in each State to the Public Acts, Records, and judicial Proceedings of every other State. And the Congress may by general Laws prescribe the Manner in which such Acts, Records and Proceedings shall be proved, and the Effect thereof.

*Section 2.* The Citizens of each State shall be entitled to all Privileges and Immunities of Citizens in the several States.

A Person charged in any State with Treason, Felony, or other Crime, who shall flee from Justice, and be found in another State, shall on Demand of the executive Authority of the State from which he fled, be delivered up, to be removed to the State having Jurisdiction of the Crime.

No Person held to Service or Labour in one State, under the Laws thereof, escaping into another, shall, in Consequence of any Law or Regulation therein, be discharged from such Service or Labour, but shall be delivered up on Claim of the Party to whom such Service or Labour may be due.

*Section 3.* New States may be admitted by the Congress into this Union; but no new State shall be formed or erected within the Jurisdiction of any other State; nor any State be formed by the Junction of two or more States, or Parts of States, without the Consent of the Legislatures of the States concerned as well as of the Congress.

The Congress shall have Power to dispose of and make all

needful Rules and Regulations respecting the Territory or other Property belonging to the United States; and nothing in this Constitution shall be so construed as to Prejudice any Claims of the United States, or of any particular State.

*Section 4.* The United States shall guarantee to every State in this Union a Republican Form of Government, and shall protect each of them against Invasion; and on Application of the Legislature or of the Executive (when the Legislature cannot be convened) against domestic Violence.

## ARTICLE V.

The Congress, whenever two thirds of both Houses shall deem it necessary, shall propose Amendments to this Constitution, or, on the Application of the Legislatures of two thirds of the several States, shall call a Convention for proposing Amendments, which, in either Case, shall be valid to all Intents and Purposes, as Part of this Constitution, when ratified by the Legislatures of three fourths of the several States, or by Conventions in three fourths thereof, as the one or the other Mode of Ratification may be proposed by the Congress; Provided that no Amendment which may be made prior to the Year One thousand eight hundred and eight shall in any Manner affect the first and fourth Clauses in the Ninth Section of the first Article; and that no State, without its Consent, shall be deprived of its equal Suffrage in the Senate.

## ARTICLE VI.

All Debts contracted and Engagements entered into, before the Adoption of this Constitution, shall be as valid against the United States under this Constitution, as under the Confederation.

This Constitution, and the Laws of the United States which shall be made in Pursuance thereof; and all Treaties made, or which shall be made, under the Authority of the United States, shall be the supreme Law of the Land; and the Judges in every State shall be bound thereby, any Thing in the Constitution or Laws of any State to the Contrary notwithstanding.

The Senators and Representatives before mentioned, and the Members of the several State Legislatures, and all executive and judicial Officers, both of the United States and of the several States, shall be bound by Oath or Affirmation, to support this Constitution; but no religious Test shall ever be required as a Qualification to any Office or public Trust under the United States.

## ARTICLE VII.

The Ratification of the Conventions of nine States, shall be sufficient for the Establishment of this Constitution between the States so ratifying the Same.

## AMENDMENTS TO THE CONSTITUTION OF THE UNITED STATES OF AMERICA

### AMENDMENT 1.

Congress shall make no law respecting an establishment of religion, or prohibiting the free exercise thereof; or abridging the freedom of speech, or of the press; or the right of the people peaceably to assemble, and to petition the Government for a redress of grievances.

### AMENDMENT 2.

A well regulated Militia, being necessary to the security of a free State, the right of the people to keep and bear Arms, shall not be infringed.

### Amendment 3.

No Soldier shall, in time of peace be quartered in any house, without the consent of the Owner, nor in time of war, but in a manner to be prescribed by law.

### Amendment 4.

The right of the people to be secure in their persons, houses, papers, and effects, against unreasonable searches and seizures, shall not be violated, and no Warrants shall issue, but upon probable cause, supported by Oath or affirmation, and particularly describing the place to be searched, and the persons or things to be seized.

### Amendment 5.

No person shall be held to answer for a capital, or otherwise infamous crime, unless on a presentment or indictment of a Grand Jury, except in cases arising in the land or naval forces, or in the Militia, when in actual service in time of War or public danger; nor shall any person be subject for the same offence to be twice put in jeopardy of life or limb; nor shall be compelled in any criminal case to be a witness against himself, nor be deprived of life, liberty, or property, without due process of law; nor shall private property be taken for public use, without just compensation.

### Amendment 6.

In all criminal prosecutions, the accused shall enjoy the right to a speedy and public trial, by an impartial jury of the State and district wherein the crime shall have been committed, which district shall have been previously ascertained by law, and to be informed of the nature and cause of the accusation; to be confronted with the witnesses against him; to have compulsory process for obtaining witnesses in his favor, and to have the Assistance of Counsel for his defence.

## AMENDMENT 7.

In Suits at common law, where the value in controversy shall exceed twenty dollars, the right of trial by jury shall be preserved, and no fact tried by a jury, shall be otherwise reexamined in any Court of the United States, than according to the rules of the common law.

## AMENDMENT 8.

Excessive bail shall not be required, nor excessive fines imposed, nor cruel and unusual punishments inflicted.

## AMENDMENT 9.

The enumeration in the Constitution, of certain rights, shall not be construed to deny or disparage others retained by the people.

## AMENDMENT 10.

The powers not delegated to the United States by the Constitution, nor prohibited by it to the States, are reserved to the States respectively, or to the people.*

## AMENDMENT 11.†

The Judicial power of the United States shall not be construed to extend to any suit in law or equity, commenced or

*The ratifications of the foregoing ten amendments were communicated by the President to Congress, from time to time as the several States notified him of their action.

†The eleventh amendment was declared by the President, in a message to Congress dated January 8, 1798, to have been ratified by three-fourths of the States.

prosecuted against one of the United States by Citizens of another State, or by Citizens or Subjects of any Foreign State.

## AMENDMENT 12.*

The Electors shall meet in their respective states, and vote by ballot for President and Vice-President, one of whom, at least, shall not be an inhabitant of the same state with themselves; they shall name in their ballots the person voted for as President, and in district ballots the person voted for as Vice-President, and they shall make distinct lists of all persons voted for as President, and of all persons voted for as Vice-President, and of the number of votes for each, which lists they shall sign and certify, and transmit sealed to the seat of the government of the United States, directed to the President of the Senate;—The President of the Senate shall, in the presence of the Senate and House of Representatives, open all the certificates and the votes shall then be counted;—The person having the greatest number of votes for President, shall be the President, if such number be a majority of the whole number of Electors appointed; and if no person have such majority, then from the persons having the highest numbers not exceeding three on the list of those voted for as President, the House of Representatives shall choose immediately, by ballot, the President. But in choosing the President, the votes shall be taken by states, the representation from each state having one vote; a quorum for this purpose shall consist of a member or members from two-thirds of the states, and a majority of all the states shall be necessary to a choice. And if the House of Representatives shall not choose a President whenever the right of choice shall devolve upon them, before the fourth day of March next following, then the Vice-President shall act as President, as

*The twelfth amendment, proposed in lieu of the original third paragraph of section 1 of Article II, was declared in a proclamation of the Secretary of State, dated September 25, 1804, to have been ratified by three-fourths of the States.

in the case of the death or other constitutional disability of the President.—The person having the greatest number of votes as Vice-President, shall be the Vice-President, if such number be a majority of the whole number of Electors appointed, and if no person have a majority, then from the two highest numbers on the list, the Senate shall choose the Vice-President; a quorum for the purpose shall consist of two-thirds of the whole number of Senators, and a majority of the whole number shall be necessary to a choice. But no person constitutionally ineligible to the office of President shall be eligible to that of Vice-President of the United States.

## AMENDMENT 13.*

*Section 1.* Neither slavery nor involuntary servitude, except as a punishment for crime whereof the party shall have been duly convicted, shall exist within the United States, or any place subject to their jurisdiction. Section 2. Congress shall have power to enforce this article by appropriate legislation.

## AMENDMENT 14.†

*Section 1.* All persons born or naturalized in the United States, and subject to the jurisdiction thereof, are citizens of the United States and of the State wherein they reside. No State shall make or enforce any law which shall abridge the privileges or immunities of citizens of the United States; nor shall any State deprive any person of life, liberty, or property, without due process of

*The thirteenth amendment was declared in a proclamation of the Secretary of State, dated December 18, 1865, to have been ratified by twenty-seven of the thirty-six States.

†The fourteenth amendment being declared by a concurrent resolution of Congress, adopted July 21, 1868, to have been ratified by "three-fourths and more of the several States of the Union," the Secretary of State was required duly to promulgate the text. He accordingly issued a proclamation, dated July 28, 1868, declaring the proposed amendment to have been ratified by thirty of the thirty-six States.

law, nor deny to any person within its jurisdiction the equal protection of the laws.

*Section 2.* Representatives shall be apportioned among the several States according to their respective numbers, counting the whole number of persons in each State, excluding Indians not taxed. But when the right to vote at any election for the choice of electors for President and Vice President of the United States, Representatives in Congress, the Executive and Judicial officers of a State, or the members of the Legislature thereof, is denied to any of the male inhabitants of such State, being twenty-one years of age, and citizens of the United States, or in any way abridged, except for participation in rebellion, or other crime, the basis of representation therein shall be reduced in the proportion which the number of such male citizens shall bear to the whole number of male citizens twenty-one years of age in such State.

*Section 3.* No person shall be a Senator or Representative in Congress, or elector of President and Vice President, or hold any office, civil or military, under the United States, or under any State, who, having previously taken an oath, as a member of Congress, or as an officer of the United States, or as a member of any State legislature, or as an executive or judicial officer of any State, to support the Constitution of the United States, shall have engaged in insurrection or rebellion against the same, or given aid or comfort to the enemies thereof. But Congress may by a vote of two-thirds of each House, remove such disability.

*Section 4.* The validity of the public debt of the United States, authorized by law, including debts incurred for payment of pensions and bounties for services in suppressing insurrection or rebellion, shall not be questioned. But neither the United States nor any State shall assume or pay any debt or obligation incurred in aid of insurrection or rebellion against the United States, or any claim for the loss or emancipation of any slave; but all such debts, obligations and claims shall be held illegal and void.

*Section 5.* The Congress shall have power to enforce, by appropriate legislation, the provisions of this article.

## AMENDMENT 15.*

*Section 1.* The right of citizens of the United States to vote shall not be denied or abridged by the United States or by any State on account of race, color, or previous condition of servitude.

*Section 2.* The Congress shall have power to enforce this article by appropriate legislation.

## AMENDMENT 16.†

The Congress shall have power to lay and collect taxes on incomes, from whatever source derived, without apportionment among the several States, and without regard to any census or enumeration.

## AMENDMENT 17.‡

The Senate of the United States shall be composed of two Senators from each State, elected by the people thereof, for six years; and each Senator shall have one vote. The electors in each State shall have the qualifications requisite for electors of the most numerous branch of the State legislatures.

When vacancies happen in the representation of any State in the Senate, the executive authority of such State shall issue writs of election to fill such vacancies: *Provided,* That the legislature

*The fifteenth amendment was declared in a proclamation of the Secretary of State, dated March 30, 1870, to have been ratified by twenty-nine of the thirty-seven States.

†The sixteenth amendment was declared in a proclamation of the Secretary of State dated February 25, 1913, to have been ratified by thirty-eight of the forty-eight States.

‡The seventeenth amendment was declared in a proclamation of the Secretary of State, dated May 31, 1913, to have been ratified by thirty-six of the forty-eight States.

of any State, may empower the executive thereof to make temporary appointments until the people fill the vacancies by election as the legislature may direct.

This amendment shall not be so construed as to affect the election or term of any Senator chosen before it becomes valid as part of the Constitution.

## AMENDMENT 18.*

*Section 1.* After one year from the ratification of this article the manufacture, sale, or transportation of intoxicating liquors within, the importation thereof into, or the exportation thereof from the United States and all territory subject to the jurisdiction thereof for beverage purposes is hereby prohibited.

*Section 2.* The Congress and the several States shall have concurrent power to enforce this article by appropriate legislation.

*Section 3.* This article shall be inoperative unless it shall have been ratified as an amendment to the Constitution by the legislatures of the several States, as provided in the Constitution, within seven years from the date of the submission hereof to the States by the Congress.

## AMENDMENT 19.†

The right of citizens of the United States to vote shall not be denied or abridged by the United States or by any State on account of sex.

Congress shall have power to enforce this article by appropriate legislation.

*The eighteenth amendment was declared in a proclamation of the Acting Secretary of State, dated January 29, 1919, to have been ratified by thirty-six of the forty-eight States.

†The nineteenth amendment was declared in a proclamation of the Secretary of State, dated August 26, 1920, to have been ratified by three-fourths of the whole number of States in the United States.

## *Appendix*

*Section 1.* The terms of the President and Vice President shall end at noon on the 20th day of January, and the terms of Senators and Representatives at noon on the 3rd day of January, of the years in which such terms would have ended if this article had not been ratified, and the terms of their successors shall then begin.

*Section 2.* The Congress shall assemble at least once in every year, and such meeting shall begin at noon on the 3rd day of January, unless they shall by law appoint a different day.

*Section 3.* If, at the time fixed for the beginning of the term of the President, the President elect shall have died, the Vice President elect shall become President. If a President shall not have been chosen before the time fixed for the beginning of his term, or if the President elect shall have failed to qualify, then the Vice President elect shall act as President until a President shall have qualified; and the Congress may by law provide for the case wherein neither a President elect nor a Vice President elect shall have qualified, declaring who shall then act as President, or the manner in which one who is to act shall be selected, and such person shall act accordingly until a President or Vice President shall have qualified.

*Section 4.* The Congress may by law provide for the case of the death of any of the persons from whom the House of Representatives may choose a President whenever the right of choice shall have devolved upon them, and for the case of death of any of the persons from whom the Senate may choose a Vice President whenever the right of choice shall have devolved upon them.

*Section 5.* Sections 1 and 2 shall take effect on the 15th day of October following the ratification of this article.

*Section 8.* This article shall be inoperative unless it shall have

*The twentieth amendment was declared in effect by proclamation of the Secretary of State, dated February 6, 1933.

been ratified as an amendment to the Constitution by the legislatures of three-fourths of the several States within seven years from the date of its submission.

## AMENDMENT 21.*

*Section 1.* The eighteenth article of amendment to the Constitution of the United States is hereby repealed.

*Section 2.* The transportation or importation into any State, Territory, or possession of the United States for delivery or use therein of intoxicating liquors, in violation of the laws thereof, is hereby prohibited.

*Section 3.* This article shall be inoperative unless it shall have been ratified as an amendment to the Constitution by conventions in the several States, as provided in the Constitution, within seven years from the date of the submission hereof to the States by the Congress.

*The twenty-first amendment was ratified by the 36th State, Utah, on December 5, 1933, and was declared immediately in effect by proclamation of the Acting Secretary of State.

# Table of Cases

DISCUSSED OR CITED IN THIS VOLUME

---

[ 290 ]